# THE HOME BOOK OF
# FRENCH COOKERY

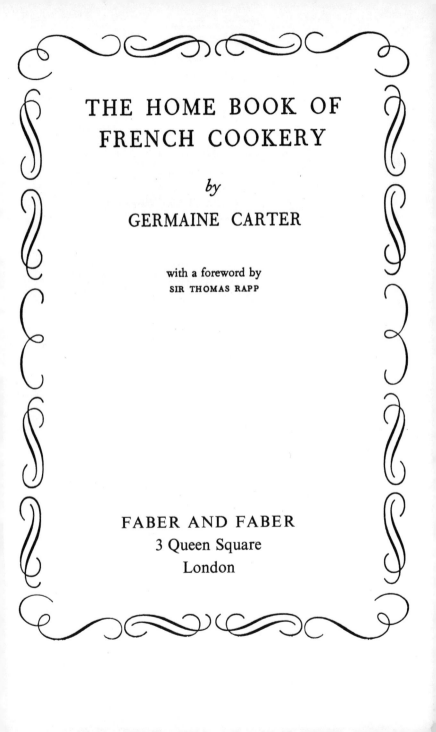

# THE HOME BOOK OF
# FRENCH COOKERY

*by*

## GERMAINE CARTER

with a foreword by
SIR THOMAS RAPP

## FABER AND FABER
3 Queen Square
London

*First published in 1952*
*by Faber and Faber Limited*
*3 Queen Square London W.C.1*
*First published in this edition 1973*
*Reprinted 1974*
*Printed in Great Britain*
*by Whitstable Litho Straker Brothers Ltd*
*All rights reserved*

*ISBN 0 571 10415 0 (Faber Paper Covered Editions)*

# FOREWORD

The circumstances under which this cookery book was written are probably unique and only less remarkable than the personality of the authoress, who found in its compilation one of the many activities with which she managed successfully to combat the infinite weariness of a five-year internment in Germany from 1940–5.

Germaine Carter comes of a North of France family which for generations has practised the art of cooking as only the French still understand it. For many years she not only collected recipes, including many handed down in her own family, but proved them in practice with a success to which her supremely happy and healthy husband bore eloquent witness.

Twice in her lifetime Germaine Carter suffered the German invasion of her country. In World War I, when still a young woman, she spent four unhappy years behind the German lines at Cambrai, where her father was mayor. She helped him in his efforts to alleviate the lot of its citizens, only to see him increasingly persecuted by the Germans, broken in health, sent into exile with her mother, and finally, when victory seemed to make an early reunion imminent, to learn that he had died from his privations in Brussels at the very moment when the liberating forces of the Allies were entering the city.

Between the two wars Germaine Carter, like so many Frenchwomen, helped to rebuild the shattered fortunes of her family, which had regained its former comparative affluence by the time of the outbreak of World War II. She was then living in Boulogne, where her husband was British consul. In May 1940, during the German drive toward the Channel ports, both had many opportunities to leave safely by sea for England, but they stayed behind evacuating refugees—British, American, Dutch, and other nationalities—until the last boat had left and the town was under intense German bombardment. Ten days of horror ended by their being taken captive by the Germans and thrown into prison at Lille.

Then began her five long years of internment in Brandenburg, the Rhineland, Silesia, and Bavaria, the grimness increasing as the war moved toward its final climax, with its accompaniment of virtual starvation for Germans and prisoners alike.

I first met Germaine Carter in Brandenburg in May 1941, having had the misfortune, a month previously in Yugoslavia, to be captured by a German armoured division; and we were destined to be fellow captives for the next two years. Volumes might be written on the psychology of prisoners of war and internees, but they fall roughly into two categories: those who accept their fate with resignation and become victims of increasing apathy, and those whose natural energy leads them to seek outlets in intense application to such occupations as they can invent, or to concentration on escape. This division is not definite: both tendencies may be observed at work in the same individual, and the result is often in doubt. But Germaine Carter's eager spirits never flagged: there was never an idle moment. The room she occupied with her husband shone with both cleanliness and Gallic wit; unbelievably succulent food was produced from the contents of Red Cross parcels (and how sought-after were the occasional American and Canadian parcels with their tin of real butter!) and, until the final decline set in, few prisoners can have lived so well on so little. A Swiss diplomat who, as representative of the protecting power, used to visit us occasionally was wont to declare that nowhere else in Germany could he find such deliciously cooked, if simple, food as Germaine Carter managed to produce for him. Nor was this mere flattery. He was always a welcome guest—our only contact with the outside world —for whom we carefully hoarded the best we could procure. I have often wondered whether he can have divined the devious means by which some of the fare was acquired, or how it was that we always managed to produce a bottle of good Rhine wine at a time when even our Gestapo guards were deprived of such luxuries.

The amount of time that an internee devotes to thoughts of food —how he can make the best of the little he has and the meals he hopes to have when he is again free—is not hard to understand. We were certainly no exception to this rule. One of the most popular members of our community was an engineer by profession who turned his knowledge and ingenuity to the manufacture of electrical gadgets, using odd scraps of junk, that enabled us to cook our food. Finally nearly everyone possessed a cooker and an immersion heater which we knew as a 'Dainty Dipper', though their use was jeopardized by frequent current failures and protests from our guards.

I often used to plan with Germaine Carter and her husband the meals we would enjoy together when I saw them in France after the war, and we would refer for ideas to the four recipe notebooks she had managed to save, containing her accumulated and well-tried experience. There came a time, during the hard winter of 1941-2, when for five months we had neither heat nor baths, and our spirits were at a low ebb; the activities we had invented began to pall; the frustrations of internment became unbearable; new occupations alone could give relief. It was then that I had the idea of this cookery book, and Germaine Carter embraced it with her wonted enthusiasm. For over a year, right up to the time of my own repatriation, we worked on it nearly every evening, to the merriment and good-natured chaffing of our fellow internees.

I must confess feeling at a great disadvantage in not having at my disposal any books of reference or a supply of cookery terms such as render so impressive the ordinary book of this nature, so that inadequate justice has been done to the French original. But the intrinsic merits of the recipes will, I hope, compensate for this deficiency. The defects of the book are in any case mine; the qualities are those of my good friend 'Auntie Froggie', as she was always affectionately known to her fellow prisoners.

The cup referred to throughout this book is the English measuring cup which holds half an Imperial pint or ten fluid ounces.

# CONTENTS

| | | |
|---|---|---|
| Foreword | *page* | 7 |
| HORS-D'OEUVRE | | 13 |
| Egg | | 14 |
| Meat and Fish | | 15 |
| Vegetable | | 16 |
| SOUPS | | 20 |
| Meat and Fish | | 21 |
| Vegetable | | 25 |
| ENTRÉES | | 31 |
| Cereal and Cheese Dishes: Gnocchi, Macaroni, Noodles, Rice, Semolina | | 31 |
| Croquettes | | 38 |
| Egg | | 41 |
| Meat and Poultry | | 48 |
| Vegetable | | 55 |
| FISH | | 63 |
| Fish | | 63 |
| GAME AND POULTRY | | 76 |
| Game | | 76 |
| Poultry | | 82 |
| MEATS | | 96 |
| Beef | | 96 |
| Mutton | | 102 |
| Pork | | 109 |
| Veal | | 112 |

# Contents

SAUCES        *page* 119
     White Sauces     119
     Other Sauces: Hollandaise, Mayonnaise, etc.     122

PÂTÉS     127

VEGETABLES     133

SALADS     150

DESSERTS     153
     Creams     153
     Cakes     167
     Small Cakes     177
     Fritters and Doughnuts     185
     Fruit     188
     Ice Creams     195
     Omelettes and Pancakes     197
     Soufflés     199

PASTRY, PIES AND TARTS     202
     Pastry     202
     Pies and Tarts     205

SAVOURIES AND SAVOURY BISCUITS     212

SANDWICHES     217

CONSERVES, JAMS AND JELLIES     219

SWEETMEATS AND CANDY     224

BEVERAGES     231

MENUS FOR ALL SEASONS     233

DINNERS FOR MORE IMPORTANT OCCASIONS     245

ENGLISH INDEX     249

FRENCH INDEX     264

# *HORS-D'OEUVRE*

Hors-d'oeuvre have never quite achieved their rightful place on the English table, and if and when English cookery books devote any space at all to their preparation or to their service, it is done grudgingly and not always correctly. They are confused with appetizers, first-course salads, and the hot or cold canapés which may be served with soup or a vegetable-juice cocktail. Any self-respecting Frenchman would rightly object to a 'peanut butter and bacon' sandwich, or a 'tomato-liver-paste cup' being included in the ranks of hors-d'oeuvre. We do serve oysters or clams as a first course, shrimps, crab meat, lobster, and other shellfish, and these are hors-d'oeuvre in the French sense.

Hors-d'oeuvre are oriental in origin. They were known to the ancient Chinese and the Turks. In Russia they are called *zakouski* with their inevitable and traditional accompaniment of vodka. In Italy the antipasto is an important first course, and other countries are rapidly becoming more familiar with the smörgåsbord of Scandinavia. The Near Eastern countries also serve first courses which resemble the French and Italian hors-d'oeuvre.

The French are not always *d'accord* as to when hors-d'oeuvre should or should not be served. Marie Antoine Carême, the nineteenth-century French culinary authority, is supposed to have disliked them so much he would not dignify them by serving them as a separate course. Some French authorities would not have them served at all if soup were part of the menu; Escoffier belonged to this school and he declared that the rule of serving them at luncheons only should be looked upon as being 'absolute'.

These '*délices de la bouche*', the hors-d'oeuvre, make an appetizing and economical addition to the home menu and are often a convenient means of utilizing fish, meat, and vegetables left over from the previous day. The choice of ingredients is very wide, and there is much scope for ingenuity in their preparation. The following suggestions include many of the more usual varieties found in French home and restaurant menus.

# *Egg Hors-d'oeuvre*

## EGGS MAYONNAISE OEUFS MIMOSA

Cut cold, hard-boiled eggs in halves lengthwise and remove the yolks. Fill the whites with thick mayonnaise. Grate the yolks and sprinkle over the eggs. Serve 1 or 2 halves to each person.

## EGG AND TOMATO TARTELETTES ROSES

Bake small Puff Pastry tart shells. Let them cool. Fill each with a mixture of mashed hard-boiled egg and Tomato Sauce. Garnish with chopped parsley. Serve 1 tartlet to each person.

## EGGS WITH ANCHOVIES OEUFS DURS AUX ANCHOIS

Cut hard-boiled eggs in halves lengthwise. Place an anchovy fillet on each half. Arrange on crisp lettuce leaves. Serve 1 or 2 halves to each person.

## EGGS WITH ANCHOVIES AND BUTTER OEUFS DURS AU BEURRE D'ANCHOIS

Cut hard-boiled eggs in halves, remove yolks, and replace with a mixture of finely mashed anchovy fillets well blended with equal amount of butter. After filling the whites, sprinkle with the finely chopped yolks. Serve 1 or 2 halves to each person.

# Meat and Fish Hors-d'oeuvre

## ANCHOVIES ANCHOIS

Use boneless anchovy fillets. Roll each, sprinkle with finely chopped hard-boiled egg. Arrange in a chilled flat dish, with or without lettuce. 2 to 4 make one serving when a generous number of other delicacies are served.

## BOILED BEEF WITH HERBS BOEUF EN PERSILLADE

Cut cold boiled beef into thin slices. Arrange in a shallow dish and sprinkle with finely chopped parsley, chives, onions, and hard-boiled egg. Pour over this a little salad oil and vinegar in the proportion of 2 parts oil to 1 of vinegar. Add salt and pepper to the vinegar and a little mixed or dry mustard; add only enough dressing to moisten the meat.

## FISH WITH MAYONNAISE POISSON À LA MAYONNAISE

Remove the skin and bones of boiled fish while still hot. Chill. Cut in small pieces and mix with mayonnaise to which chopped parsley and chives have been added. Allow 2 or 3 tablespoons of the mixture as a serving.

## SMOKED HERRINGS HARENGS FUMÉS

Rinse a kippered herring; drain. Cover with cold water and let stand overnight. Drain. At least 2 hours before serving, cut meat away from bones in long thin strips. Cover with olive oil and sprinkle with finely chopped hard-boiled egg.

## MUSSELS MOULES

Cook mussels, remove from shells, drain, and chill. Place on a dish and cover with mayonnaise.

*To cook mussels:* Scrub the shells with a brush, rinse under running water, drain. Melt a tablespoonful of butter in a large frying pan, add the mussels and cook until they are all open, the necessary water being supplied by the mussels.

## SAUSAGES AND COLD CUTS CHARCUTERIE

Smoked sausage, boiled or baked ham, boiled or baked smoked tongue, and other cold cuts are served sliced on the hors-d'oeuvre tray.

## TUNA FISH THON

Canned tuna fish is served in its own oil, or drained and covered with mayonnaise.

## VEAL MAYONNAISE VEAU À LA MAYONNAISE

Slice cold boiled or roast veal thin. Cover with mayonnaise to which prepared mustard, chopped parsley and chives have been added. Allow 1 or 2 slices per serving.

# *Vegetable Hors-d'oeuvre*

## ARTICHOKES ARTICHAUTS

Wash French, green, or globe artichokes. Pull off hard outer leaves and cut stem close to leaves. Cut off top ¾ inch down; stand them upside down in cold water for half an hour. Drain, cover with boiling salted water (1 teaspoon salt to 1 quart water), and cook until tender, about 25 to 40 minutes. Drain and chill. Either serve the heart or bottom alone with mayonnaise; or leave the artichoke whole, remove the choke from the centre, and fill with mayonnaise sprinkled with a little chopped hard-boiled egg yolk. If the heart is served separately, the leaves can be served with oil, vinegar, pepper, and salt. If served whole, halved, or otherwise, remove the choke or centre and discard it. Allow 1 artichoke per serving.

## JERUSALEM ARTICHOKES TOPINAMBOURS

Wash and scrub Jerusalem artichokes, cover with salted boiling water, and cook until tender. Peel, cube, or slice and serve cold with mayonnaise. One pound makes 4 hors-d'oeuvre servings.

## FRENCH BEANS WITH OIL HARICOTS VERTS EN SALADE

Cook tender young string beans as usual. Drain and chill. Season with salt, pepper, oil, and vinegar. Sprinkle with chopped parsley and chives.

Wax beans may be prepared the same way.

## BEETS BETTERAVES

Wash young beets, cover with salted boiling water, and boil 30 to 45 minutes. Drain; plunge into cold water. Drain and peel off the skin. Chill. Cut into thin slices, place in a shallow dish, and pour olive oil and vinegar in the proportion of 2 tablespoons of oil to 1 of vinegar over them. Add a little salt and pepper to the vinegar. Sprinkle with finely chopped onions. (Old beets must be boiled 2 to 4 hours; very old beets cannot be cooked tender.) Allow 1 or 2 very small beets as an hors-d'oeuvre serving.

## PICKLED CABBAGE CHOU MARINÉ

Wash a white or red cabbage, drain and slice it into a bowl. Sprinkle it with salt and leave 24 hours. Turn the cabbage occasionally. Drain and place it in a glass jar with 8 peppercorns, 10 cloves, 12 very small onions, 1 chili pepper, and ½ vinegar and ½ water to cover. Let stand for a minimum of 24 hours. Drain, arrange in a bowl or flat dish. One head makes 10 or more hors-d'oeuvre servings.

## CAULIFLOWER CHOUFLEUR

Cut up cold boiled cauliflower into flowerets. Chill. Cover with mayonnaise and sprinkle with chopped parsley. Arrange in a shallow dish for best effect.

## CUCUMBERS CONCOMBRES

Peel young, green cucumbers. Slice thin, sprinkle with salt, and allow to stand overnight. Pour off the water and add 2 parts oil to 1 of vinegar, enough to cover. Sprinkle with chopped parsley or chives. Arrange in a shallow dish. One cucumber makes 2 or more hors-d'oeuvre servings.

## AROMATIC CUCUMBERS CONCOMBRES AUX AROMATES

Place 1 teaspoon chopped fresh thyme, 4 peppercorns, 2 or 3 black currant leaves, and $\frac{1}{4}$ chopped clove of garlic in a bowl. Moisten with salt water, cover with sliced cucumbers. Repeat layers of aromatic mixture and cucumbers. Let stand covered 10 days. Remove the cucumbers from the aromatic mixture before serving. Place in serving dish.

## CUCUMBERS WITH CREAM CONCOMBRES À LA CRÈME

Cut peeled cucumbers into thin slices, sprinkle with salt, and let stand overnight. Drain, mix with thick cream and a little lemon juice. Sprinkle with chopped parsley. Arrange in shallow serving dish.

## GREEN OLIVES OLIVES VERTES AU FOIE GRAS

Drain the olives; remove stones with a sharp-pointed knife. Fill the centres with pâté de foie gras. Serve 2 or more to each person.

## POTATOES MAYONNAISE POMMES DE TERRE À LA MAYONNAISE

Slice cold boiled potatoes and cover with mayonnaise mixed with finely cut fresh herbs. The herbs may be parsley, chives, thyme, or any favourites.

## TOMATOES MAYONNAISE TOMATES À LA MAYONNAISE

Slice tomatoes thinly. Cover with mayonnaise to which chopped parsley and chives have been added. Allow 1 or 2 slices as an hors-d'oeuvre serving.

## TOMATOES WITH OLIVES TOMATES AUX OLIVES

Remove the centres from small ripe tomatoes. Chop some stuffed or stoned olives and mix with pepper, a little oil and vinegar. Fill the tomatoes with this mixture. Immediately before serving, pour a little cold tomato juice over the olives and replace the slice removed from the top of the tomato. Serve 1 to each person.

## TOMATOES WITH SALMON TOMATES AU SAUMON

Cut out the centres of small plump red tomatoes. Fill with cold cooked or canned salmon mixed with mayonnaise, chopped chives, and parsley. Cooked or canned shrimps may be substituted for the salmon. Serve 1 tomato to a person.

## VEGETABLES WITH MAYONNAISE LÉGUMES À LA MAYONNAISE

Cold cooked and drained vegetables may be served mixed with mayonnaise and sprinkled with chopped parsley and chives. Favourites are peas, broad beans, mushrooms, Jerusalem artichokes, asparagus, kidney beans, celery root. leeks. Allow 1 or 2 tablespoons per serving.

# SOUPS

It was Alexandre Dumas who said, '*Les Français aiment les soupes et la France est une nation soupière*', and how right he was! Not only does the Frenchman have soup for his luncheon, but for his dinner as well. It is served at the midnight supper, *réveillon*; at ten in the morning the boulevardier sips his cup of bouillon, just as the early workman or the late reveller will have visited his favourite bistro in Les Halles, hours earlier, for a bowl of onion soup.

In one of his letters Vincent Voiture exclaims, 'Balzac has invented a sort of potage that I esteem more than Pliny's "Panegyricus" or the longest harangue by Isocrates.' And it was Voltaire who said, 'I think more of a ray of sunshine and soup than I do of all the Courts in the world.' The very distinction between *potage* and *soupe* has occupied Frenchmen for centuries.

In the eighteenth century the *Dictionnaire de Trévoux* pointed out that the word *soupe* was indeed French, but 'extremely bourgeois', and that those who spoke French well said, 'Serve the potage', and not 'Serve the soup'. It was another French writer who remarked that there was a whole world of difference between 'It is the hour for soup' and 'Will you have a little more potage?' He goes on to say that the difference is not merely one that illustrates the richness of a language. Soup must have robust qualities. It is served in bowls or in thick substantial plates. 'It smokes, it smells good, but strong. Its aim is to nourish.' But potage is something else again. 'Of course potage nourishes as well, but with more tact than zeal; it, too, has its aim; it must be the preface to the rest of the food.'

Carême described more than five hundred soups in his writings and 'executed' some 196 kinds of French soup, and 103 foreign soups personally. Escoffier gives recipes for almost two hundred.

Other early and nineteenth-century French culinarians are equally devoted to this important dish.

The base of many French soups consists of potatoes cut in ¼-inch slices. These and any other vegetables used in the particular soup are placed in a saucepan, covered generously with cold water, and brought to a boil. The mixture is then allowed to simmer gently 2 hours, after which the whole soup is passed through a strainer and then reheated before serving.

To change the flavour of the soup add a beef, mutton, or veal bone; the scum formed in boiling should be carefully skimmed from the top of the soup.

## NURSERY SOUP PANADE
Recommended for children.

| | |
|---|---|
| 8 ½-in. slices dry bread | ⅛ tsp. pepper (optional) |
| 2 qts. hot water | 2 eggs |
| ½ tsp. salt | ½ cup heavy cream |

In a 2½-quart saucepan boil gently the bread, water, salt, and pepper, about 1 hour. Beat the eggs lightly with the cream; pour into a warm tureen and stir the hot soup into it. Serve at once. Serves 6 to 8. Omit pepper and use fresh milk instead of cream when made for children.

# Meat and Fish Soups

## BEEF BOUILLON BOUILLON DE BOEUF

| | |
|---|---|
| 2 lb. beef (not too lean) | 1 pinch pepper |
| 2 carrots | 2 qts. water |
| 2 turnips | thyme |
| 2 leeks | bay leaf |
| salt | 1 stalk celery |

Wipe the meat with a clean damp cloth. Scrape the carrots, peel and quarter the turnips, cut leeks in halves. Place in a 3-quart or 1-gallon saucepan. Season with salt and pepper. Add the water (according to taste), herbs, and celery. Cover the saucepan and let simmer 3 hours. Strain the soup. Serve the meat separately with mashed potatoes. This is served as a clear hot bouillon or used in other soups and sauces. Serves 4 or more.

## BISQUE POTAGE BISQUE

This is a fish soup for special occasions.

1 *tbs. butter*
1 *onion, sliced*
1 *leek, chopped*
1 *carrot, sliced*
1 *stalk celery, chopped*
*sprig thyme*
*bay leaf*
2 *tsp. salt*
⅛ *tsp. cayenne*
*meat of 6 soft-shell cooked crabs or*

2 *cups cleaned cooked shrimps or*
*meat of* 1 *small boiled lobster*
½ *cup cognac*
2 *tumblerfuls white wine, the same*
*volume of hot water*
1 *cup cooked rice*
2 *tbs. butter*
2 *tbs. cream*
2 *egg yolks, beaten*

In a 2-quart enamel saucepan melt the butter. Add the onion, leek, carrot, and celery and brown lightly, about 3 minutes. Add the herbs, seasoning, and the crab, shrimps or lobster. Shake the pan over moderate heat about 5 minutes, till all is well mixed. Add ¼ cup cognac, the wine and water. Cover the saucepan and let simmer 15 minutes. Then lift out the fish and put it through the mincer using the finest knife. Return the fish to the saucepan. Add the rice. Cook 5 minutes, then put all through a strainer. Return it to the saucepan and cook slowly for 1 hour, till thickened like cream. If too thick, add a little bouillon. If too thin, thicken with 1 tablespoon rice flour or cornflour first mixed with 2 tablespoons cold water.

Remove the saucepan from the heat. Add the butter, cream, egg yolks, and the remaining ¼ cup cognac. Reheat 2 minutes. Serve at once in warmed soup plates. Serves 4 to 6.

NOTE: One or 2 drops red food colouring may be added with the final ingredients.

# Soups : Meat and Fish

## CHICKEN BROTH BOUILLON DE POULE

| | |
|---|---|
| 1 *boiling fowl, cleaned* | *bay leaf* |
| 2 *carrots* | *stalk of celery* |
| 2 *turnips* | 2 *qts. water (or more if fowl is* |
| 2 *leeks* | *large)* |
| *salt* | 2 *tbs. tapioca or vermicelli* |
| *pepper* | *(optional) or* |
| *sprig of thyme* | 1 *egg, beaten* |

Clean the chicken, and place in a 3-quart or larger saucepan. Scrape
and slice the carrots. Peel the turnips, slice and cut the leeks. Place
vegetables in saucepan. Add seasonings, herbs, celery and water to
cover. Cover the saucepan and simmer gently until the fowl is tender,
1½ to 3 hours. Remove the chicken when done. Strain the soup. Reheat and serve. If preferred, thicken with tapioca or vermicelli (cook
¼ hour) or stir in the beaten egg, then serve at once. Serves 4.

NOTE: If the broth cooks down too much, as is the case when
the fowl requires long cooking, add 1 or more cups of hot water
for the last hour of cooking.

## CRAB SOUP BISQUE DE CRABES

Choose several small crabs and wash thoroughly in several changes
of cold water. Immerse in two quarts of boiling water, add salt and
a good pinch of pepper and boil for 5 minutes. Remove the crabs,
mince in a mincing machine and replace in water they were boiled
in, with a sprig of thyme, a bay leaf and a cupful of rice or some
potatoes. Boil for 1 hour, strain through a sieve and add, before
serving, a cup of thick cream, and if desired some spices and saffron.
Serve with small pieces of fried bread.

## CREAM CONSOMMÉ CONSOMMÉ VELOUTÉ

| | |
|---|---|
| 3 tbs. rice flour or | 2 qts. hot well-seasoned bouillon |
| 2 tbs. cornflour | or consommé |
| 1 cup water | 4 egg yolks, slightly beaten |
| | 1 cup cold bouillon |

Add the water a little at a time to the rice or cornflour. When smoothly mixed, stir into the 2 quarts boiling bouillon. Stir well, reduce heat, and boil gently 15 minutes. Mix the egg yolks with the 1 cup of cold bouillon; stir slowly into the bouillon. Reheat gently a few minutes. Do not let it come to a boil. Serve at once. Serves 4 to 6.

## CREAM SOUP SOUPE ONCTUEUSE

| | |
|---|---|
| 1 ham bone | 2 tbs. butter |
| 2 qts. water | ½ cup chopped raw or cooked |
| 8 medium-sized potatoes, peeled | sorrel |
| and quartered | ½ cup heavy cream |
| ¼ tsp. pepper | salt |

Have the butcher saw the ham bone almost in two. Place in a 3-quart saucepan and cover with water. Add the potatoes and pepper. Simmer 2 hours. Remove the bone. Pass the remainder through a sieve. Return it to the saucepan. Melt the butter in a small saucepan and stir the sorrel into it for 3 minutes. Mix this into the soup. Reheat 2 minutes, add the cream, season with salt, and serve at once. Serves 4 to 6.

## MADEIRA SOUP BOUILLON AU MADÈRE

| | |
|---|---|
| 3 pts. bouillon | 1 egg white |
| ¼ lb. chopped fresh beef | salt |
| 2 raw chicken wings | pepper |
| 3 tomatoes, peeled and sliced | ¼ cup Madeira |

In a 2½-quart enamel saucepan heat the bouillon with the meat, chicken wings, tomatoes, egg white, salt, and pepper. Cover and let simmer 2 hours. Strain through a sieve. Chill and serve in cups containing about 1 teaspoon Madeira each. Serves 4 to 6.

## SHRIMP SOUP POTAGE AUX BOUQUETS

| | |
|---|---|
| 2 *cups cooked, cleaned shrimps* | *bay leaf* |
| 8 *additional cooked, cleaned shrimps* | 4 *cloves* |
| 2 *tbs. oil* | ⅛ *tsp. saffron* |
| 2 *carrots, sliced* | 1 *tsp. salt* |
| 4 *onions, sliced* | ¼ *tsp. pepper* |
| 6 *cups water* | ¼ *cup grated dry cheese* |
| ½ *tsp. fresh thyme* | ¼ *cup small croûtons* |

Heat the oil in a 2-quart saucepan and sauté the shrimps, carrots, and onions until lightly cooked. Add the water, thyme, bay leaf, spices, and seasonings. Cover and let boil gently 1 hour. Add a little extra hot water if needed. Press through a sieve. Reheat about 2 minutes. Add a little grated cheese and a few croûtons to each serving and garnish with 2 whole shrimps. Serves 4.

Prawns may also be used for this soup.

# Vegetable Soups

## ALSATIAN SOUP POTAGE ALSACIEN

| | |
|---|---|
| ½ *lb. string beans* | 2 *qts. water* |
| 1 *small cabbage* | 4 *to 6 small smoked link sausages* |
| 3 *small carrots* | *or* |
| 2 *or 3 turnips* | 6 *slices larger smoked sausage* |
| 1 *cup broad beans* | 6 *medium-sized potatoes, peeled* |
| 1½ *tsp. salt* | *and sliced* |
| ¾ *tsp. pepper* | |

Prepare the vegetables, cutting up cabbage, carrots, and turnips. If dried broad beans are used, leave them to soak overnight.

Place the vegetables in a 1-gallon saucepan. Season with salt and pepper. Add the water. Bring slowly to boiling and let simmer 1½ hours, covered. Add the little sausages or the sausage slices and the potatoes. Boil 30 minutes longer. Do not strain this soup. Serves 4 to 6.

## CABBAGE SOUP SOUPE AU CHOU

1 head white cabbage
6 medium-sized potatoes
2 qts. water
2 tsp. salt
¼ tsp. pepper

2 tbs. butter or suet
1 tsp. meat extract or
1 bouillon cube plus ¼ cup hot
   water

Chop the cabbage finely. Peel the potatoes and cut in quarters. Place vegetables in a 3-quart saucepan. Add the water. Cover and boil slowly for 1 hour, or until the cabbage is very soft. Pass all through a strainer, mashing the cabbage and potatoes through. Reheat in the soup saucepan, adding the salt, pepper, butter or suet, and the meat extract or bouillon cube softened in water. When boiling, remove and serve. Serves 4 to 6.

*Variation.* Use endive or chicory in place of the cabbage, and with these vegetables use butter in place of suet.

## CARROT SOUP POTAGE JULIENNE

6 medium-sized potatoes
6 to 8 carrots
2 tbs. butter
2 tsp. salt

¼ tsp. pepper
2 qts. water
3 tbs. chopped parsley

Pare the potatoes and slice about ¼ inch thick. Scrape the carrots and slice like the potatoes. Place vegetables, butter, seasonings, and water in a 3-quart or larger saucepan. Bring to boil, then cover and let simmer 2 hours. Strain, pressing the potatoes and carrots to a purée. Reheat to boiling. Remove from the heat, stir in the parsley, and serve at once. Serves 4 to 6.

# Soups : Vegetable

## CELERY SOUP soupe au céleri

Make like Carrot Soup. Use 8 potatoes, 1 head of celery chopped fine, and the other ingredients as listed.

## CRESS SOUP soupe au cresson

Make like Carrot Soup. Use 8 potatoes, 1 large bunch water cress (3 cups chopped leaves only), and the other ingredients except parsley.

## LEEK SOUP soupe aux poireaux

| | |
|---|---|
| 6 *leeks* | 2 *tsp. salt* |
| 8 *medium-sized potatoes* | ½ *tsp. pepper* |
| 2 *qts. water* | 2 *tbs. tapioca or* |
| 2 *tbs. butter* | 3 *tbs. cooked rice or vermicelli* |

Cut off green tops and a thin slice at the root end of the leeks. Cut in small pieces. Pare potatoes and slice thin. Place in a 3-quart saucepan with the water, butter and seasonings. Cover the saucepan and boil slowly 2 hours. Add the tapioca, rice or vermicelli, and continue cooking 10 minutes. Do not strain. Serves 4 to 6.

## LETTUCE SOUP soupe à la laitue

| | |
|---|---|
| 1 *large head green lettuce* | 2 *tsp. salt* |
| 10 *medium-sized potatoes* | ½ *tsp. pepper* |
| 2 *qts. water* | ½ *cup heavy cream* |
| 2 *tbs. butter* | |

Wash the lettuce; pull leaves apart and break or cut fine. Wash, pare, and slice or chop the potatoes. Place in a 3-quart or larger saucepan; add the water and heat to boiling. Then add the butter, salt, and pepper. Cover the saucepan; boil slowly 2 hours. Strain through a sieve and reheat a few minutes.

Pour the cream in warmed tureen or soup bowls and stir soup in gradually. Serves 4 to 6.

## ONION SOUP I SOUPE AUX OIGNONS

| | |
|---|---|
| 10 *large onions, sliced* | *bay leaf* |
| 2 *qts. water* | 1 *tbs. melted suet* |
| 12 *medium-sized potatoes, sliced* | ½ *tsp. cayenne* |
| 1½ *tsp. salt* | 2 *tbs. grated Parmesan or other* |
| ½ *tsp. pepper* | *dry cheese* |
| 1 *tsp. fresh thyme or* | *extra cheese for 6 servings* |
| ½ *tsp. dried thyme* | |

Place the onions in a 3-quart saucepan with the water, potatoes, salt, pepper, thyme, bay leaf, and suet. Cover and let boil gently 2 hours. Strain through a sieve, pressing the vegetables through. Reheat, adding the cayenne; stir and continue cooking ½ hour. If a creamier texture is desired, thicken with a little flour (1 tablespoon flour blended with 1 tablespoon cold water, then stirred slowly into the soup).

Before serving stir the grated cheese into the soup. Pass more cheese to each person. Serves 4 to 6.

## ONION SOUP II SOUPE À L'OIGNON

| | |
|---|---|
| 2 *tbs. butter* | ½ *tsp. pepper* |
| 10 *large onions, sliced* | 6 *slices French bread, cut in* |
| 2 *qts. hot water* | *halves* |
| 1 *bouillon cube* | *butter* |
| 1½ *tsp. salt* | ¼ *cup grated dry cheese* |
| | *extra cheese for serving* |

In a fireproof 3-quart soup casserole melt the butter and sauté the onions lightly. Add the water, bouillon cube, salt, and pepper. Cover and let simmer 1 hour.

Toast the bread, butter it, and sprinkle thickly with grated cheese. Uncover the soup and stir well. Arrange the toast over the top of the soup and place the casserole in the oven (375° F.) until the cheese browns slightly. Serve at once from the casserole. Serves 4 to 6.

# Soups : Vegetable

## PEA SOUP SOUPE AUX POIS CASSÉS

| | |
|---|---|
| 2 cups dried peas | 2 tsp. salt |
| 2 qts. water | ¼ tsp. pepper |
| 1 onion, sliced | 6 tbs. croûtons |
| 2 tbs. butter | |

Wash the peas, drain, cover with cold water, and let them soak overnight. Drain, place in a 3-quart saucepan with the 2 quarts of water, onion, butter, salt, and pepper. Cover and boil slowly 3 to 4 hours, or till soft. Add more hot water if the liquid boils away quickly. Put through sieve; reheat. Serve with a sprinkling of croûtons on each. Serves 4 to 6.

## PUMPKIN SOUP SOUPE AU POTIRON

| | |
|---|---|
| 1½ lbs. raw pumpkin | 1 tbs. sugar |
| boiling water | ½ cup cooked rice |
| 2 qts. hot milk | ½ tsp. grated nutmeg |
| 1½ tsp. salt | ¼ cup croutons |
| ½ tsp. pepper | castor sugar (optional) |

Cut pumpkin in chunks, using heavy knife. Pare; discard seeds and fibres. Cover with boiling water in a 3-quart saucepan and boil 30 to 40 minutes. Drain; crush the pulp. Add the milk, salt, pepper, and sugar. Mix well and boil gently 5 minutes. Add the rice; stir and boil 5 minutes longer. Taste, and add more salt if needed. Season with nutmeg just before serving. Garnish each plate with croûtons. Sugar to taste may also be added if preferred. Serves 4 to 6.

## SORREL SOUP SOUPE À L'OSEILLE

| | |
|---|---|
| 1 tbs. butter | 1½ tbs. salt |
| 2 cups chopped sorrel | ½ tsp. pepper |
| 2 qts. hot water | 1 egg |
| 10 medium-sized potatoes, sliced | |

Heat the butter in a 3-quart saucepan. Stir the sorrel into it and cook 5 minutes. Add the water, potatoes, salt, and pepper. Cover and cook slowly 2 hours. Pass through a sieve, mashing the vegetables through. Reheat. Beat the egg in the tureen and slowly stir the hot soup into it. Serve at once. Serves 4 to 6.


## TOMATO SOUP SOUPE AUX TOMATES

3 or 4 tomatoes
2 tbs. butter
2 qts. hot water
6 potatoes, sliced
2 tsp. salt

$\frac{1}{2}$ tsp. pepper
2 tbs. tapioca
$\frac{1}{4}$ cup heavy cream
2 tbs. butter

Slice the tomatoes. Heat the butter in a 3-quart enamel saucepan. Add the tomatoes and cook 10 minutes. Add the water, potatoes, salt, and pepper. Cover and boil gently 1 hour. Press through a sieve, crushing tomatoes and potatoes to purée with the aid of a pestle. Reheat; gradually stir in the tapioca and continue boiling 10 minutes. Before serving, blend the cream and softened butter with a few spoonfuls of soup, then stir into soup saucepan. Serve at once. Serves 4 to 6.


## VEGETABLE SOUP POTAGE PRINTANIER

6 leeks
6 medium-sized potatoes
6 small carrots
1 bunch celery
2$\frac{1}{2}$ qts. water
veal or mutton shinbone

2 tbs. butter
2 tsp. salt
2 tbs. chopped parsley
pepper
celery salt

Cut off green tops of leeks; pare and slice potatoes; scrape carrots; chop celery. Add all with about 1 tablespoon chopped celery leaves to the saucepan. Add water, bone, butter, and salt. Bring to boil; reduce heat and cover. Let simmer gently 2 hours. Skim off scum from the bone as it rises to the surface. When the vegetables are tender, remove the bone and serve; or pass the soup through a sieve, reheat, and serve sprinkled with the parsley, pepper, and a little celery salt. Serves 4 to 6.

# ENTRÉES

In early cookery books the word entrée covered everything that came before the roast, including hors-d'oeuvre, soups, and *relevés* with which the entrées were frequently confused. A *relevé* followed the soup and literally 'relieved' it.

In the average French home an entrée is usually served in addition to a roast. The possibilities of this item of the menu are countless; one great French chef has enumerated more than fifteen hundred. The entrée in to-day's menus may be poultry, cheese, vegetables, or combinations of two or more of these.

Croquettes are favourite entrées in elaborate menus. A dish of noodles or an omelette is a typical entrée.

Gnocchi, macaroni in some form, creamed leftover fish, chicken, or a meat dish with salad and bread and butter, may serve for luncheon or supper.

Many of these entrées are perfect casserole or chafing-dish recipes for buffet suppers, bridge luncheons, and other party occasions.

## Cereal and Cheese Entrées

### ITALIAN CHEESE GNOCCHI GNOCCHI À LA ROMAINE

| | |
|---|---|
| 3 oz. semolina | flour |
| 3 cups boiling milk | ½ cup bouillon |
| 1 tsp. salt | 1 tbs. butter |
| ¼ tsp. pepper | ¼ cup bread crumbs |
| 3 oz. grated cheese | 1 oz. grated cheese |

Slowly stir the semolina (or corn meal, farina, or Cream of Wheat) and the salt and pepper into the boiling milk in a 2-quart saucepan.

Do not let the boiling stop; use wooden spoon and boil until thick. Do not cover the pan. Remove from the heat; add the 3 oz. of cheese.

Butter a large plate. Sprinkle well with flour. Pour the mixture on so that it is about 1 inch thick. When cool, cut in small squares or rounds with a biscuit cutter. Place in a buttered baking dish; add enough bouillon to moisten the bottom of the dish. Add dabs of butter; sprinkle with crumbs and cheese. Brown in a hot oven (425° F.) 15 minutes or a little longer. Serves 6.

## GNOCCHI PARISIENNE GNOCCHI À LA PARISIENNE

| | |
|---|---|
| 1 *cup boiling water* | 4 *eggs* |
| 3 *oz. butter* | 2 *oz. grated cheese* |
| ¼ *tsp. salt* | *boiling salted water* |
| ⅛ *tsp. pepper* | 1 *cup thin White Sauce* |
| 4 *oz. sifted flour* | ½ *tsp. nutmeg* |

Into the cup of boiling water stir the butter, salt, and pepper. Slowly add the flour, stirring until thickened. Remove from heat. Beat the eggs in one at a time, then half of the cheese. Form into small balls. Have about 1 quart of water boiling rapidly (1 teaspoon salt in the water). Drop a few balls at a time into the water and boil 10 minutes. Remove, drain, and place in a greased baking dish. Pour the White Sauce over; sprinkle with nutmeg and the remaining cheese. Brown in a moderate oven (325° F.). Serves 6.

## MACARONI CHEESE MACARONI AU GRATIN

| | |
|---|---|
| 2 *cups* (½ *lb.*) *broken macaroni* | ½ *cup heavy cream* |
| 1 *gal. boiling salted water* | ½ *cup cooled, boiled milk* |
| 3 *tbs. butter* | 3 *egg yolks, beaten* |
| 1 *cup grated cheese* | |

Drop the macaroni slowly into the boiling water (1 teaspoon salt to 1 quart water). Do not let the water stop boiling. When all the macaroni is added, boil 15 minutes, until the macaroni is tender.

Drain in a colander. Spread a layer in a buttered 2-quart baking dish; sprinkle generously with dabs of butter and cheese. Repeat layers. Pour over all the mixed cream, milk, and yolks. Sprinkle the top with cheese. Bake in a moderate oven (350° F.) until browned and bubbly. Serve hot. Serves 6.

## MACARONI TIMBALE TIMBALE DE MACARONI

| | |
|---|---|
| 2 *cups* (½ *lb.*) *broken macaroni* | 4 *egg yolks* |
| *boiling salted water* | ¼ *tsp. grated nutmeg* |
| 4 *oz. minced cooked ham* | 4 *egg whites* |
| 4 *oz. grated cheese* | *Cream Sauce or Tomato Sauce* |
| 1 *knob butter* | |

Drop the macaroni slowly into the boiling water (1 teaspoon salt to 1 quart). Do not let boiling stop. Boil 15 to 20 minutes, until the macaroni is tender. Drain. Mix with ham, cheese, dabs of butter, and the beaten yolks and nutmeg. Whip the four whites until stiff and mix in gently. Pour into a buttered mould. Bake in a hot (425° F.) oven 45 minutes. Serve at once with sauce. Serves 6.

NOTE: If the ham is not salty, add ½ to 1 teaspoon salt and ¼ teaspoon pepper to the mixture before adding the egg whites.

## HOW TO MAKE NOODLES

| 4 *eggs* | 1 *pound flour* | 1 *pinch salt* |
|---|---|---|

Put the flour in a mixing bowl, make a hole in the centre, then mix in one egg at a time and a little water, repeating the process until all eggs are mixed in. Knead well, sprinkle with flour, and roll on a pastry board for 10 minutes, finally rolling out thin sheets, which should be left for 24 hours. Then roll them in the form of cylinders and slice thin from the end with a sharp knife. They are now ready for use.

*To boil Noodles:* Use 3 quarts rapidly boiling water (with 2 teaspoons salt) for each cup of raw noodles. Drop them into the water gradually so as not to stop the boiling. Do not cover. Keep boiling rapidly 10 minutes, then cover and set the pan over hot water. Cook until tender, 20 minutes or longer. Drain in colander. Pour melted butter over, or add grated cheese, seasonings, or use as suggested in recipes. Allow 2 cups noodles for 6 servings.

## NOODLES MILANAISE GÂTEAU MILANAIS

| | |
|---|---|
| ½ *lb. broken noodles or spaghetti* | ¼ *tsp. nutmeg* |
| 3 *qts. boiling salted water* | 3 *eggs, beaten* |
| ½ *tsp. salt* | ¼ *cup cream* |
| ¼ *tsp. pepper* | 1 *cup minced ham* |

Drop the noodles or spaghetti slowly into the boiling water (1 teaspoon salt to 1 quart water). Do not let the boiling stop. Boil 15 minutes, or until the noodles or spaghetti are tender. Drain. Season; mix with the eggs, cream, and ham. Turn into a buttered ring mould. Set mould in a shallow pan half filled with water. Bake in a moderate over (350° F.) about 30 minutes. Turn out on to a dish and serve with a green salad. Serves 6.

## NOODLES WITH GRATED CHEESE NOUILLES AU GRATIN

| | |
|---|---|
| ½ *lb. broken noodles* | 2 *eggs, beaten* |
| 3 *qts. boiling salted water* | ½ *cup grated Gruyère cheese* |
| 1½ *cups thin White Sauce* | 1 *tbs. butter* |

Drop the noodles slowly into the boiling water (1 teaspoon salt to 1 quart water). Cook until tender, 20 minutes. Drain. Combine the White Sauce, eggs, and half the cheese. Pour over the noodles and mix. Put into a buttered 2-quart baking dish. Sprinkle with the remaining cheese; add dabs of butter. Bake in a moderate oven (350° F.) until browned and bubbly, about 15 minutes. Serves 6.

## NOODLES WITH HAM NOUILLES AU JAMBON

½ lb. broken noodles

2 onions, sliced

1 tbs. olive oil

4 ripe tomatoes, sliced

1 small clove garlic

1 tsp. salt

¼ tsp. pepper

4 tbs. grated Gruyère cheese

½ cup minced cooked ham

Boil the noodles and drain. (See preceding recipe.) Keep them hot in a colander over hot water. Cook the onions in the oil in a large saucepan; add the tomatoes, garlic, and seasonings and stir. Cook 15 minutes, or until the tomatoes are very soft. Press through strainer and reheat. Add the cheese and ham; mix and pour over the noodles. Serve hot. Serves 6.

## NOODLES WITH MINCED BEEF NOUILLES À LA BOLOGNAISE

Substitute minced boiled beef for the ham in the preceding recipe.

## NOODLES WITH TOMATOES NOUILLES À L'ITALIENNE

Omit the meat from the Noodles with Ham recipe.

## RICE ITALIENNE RIZ À L'ITALIENNE

½ cup rice

1 tbs. butter

1 onion, chopped fine

½ tsp. salt

¼ tsp. pepper

2 cups hot water or bouillon

1 tbs. tomato purée or paste

3 tbs. minced cooked or canned

    mushrooms

½ cup minced cooked ham

Wash and drain rice. Brown in the butter in a 1-quart saucepan. Add the onion, salt, and pepper. Stir and cook 2 minutes. Add the hot water or bouillon and cook until the rice is tender and the liquid absorbed, about 20 minutes. Mix with the other ingredients. Reheat, adding a very little bouillon if necessary. Serve hot. Serves 4.

## RICE WITH CALF'S LIVER RIZ AU FOIE DE VEAU

Follow the recipe for Rice Italienne; add 1 cup calf's liver, cut in small squares, to the pan when browning the rice. This replaces the ham.

## SEMOLINA CHEESE FINGERS QUENELLES DE SEMOULE

| | |
|---|---|
| 4 tbs. butter | 3 eggs, beaten |
| 2 cups hot milk | flour |
| 1 cup farina, semolina, or Cream of Wheat | boiling water |
| | hot Cream Sauce |
| ½ tsp. salt | 1 cup small cooked or canned |
| 3 oz. grated cheese | mushrooms |

Stir the butter into the hot milk in a 1-quart saucepan; stir in the cereal and salt. Let boil 15 minutes, stirring well. Remove from heat; stir in the cheese and the eggs, one at a time. Mix, pour onto a plate, and let stand overnight.

Cut in finger lengths; roll each in flour. Poach in rapidly boiling water 2 or 3 minutes. Drain and place on a warmed ovenware dish. Cover with the hot sauce and garnish with the mushrooms. Brown in a hot oven (450° F.) 10 minutes. Serves 4 to 8.

## CHEESE ENTRÉE COQUILLES AU PARMESAN

| | |
|---|---|
| 1 tbs. butter | 1 cup milk |
| 2 tbs. flour | ¾ to 1 cup grated Parmesan |
| ½ tsp. salt | cheese |
| ¼ tsp. pepper | 3 egg yolks |
| ¼ tsp. grated nutmeg | 4 egg whites, stiffly beaten |

Melt the butter in a saucepan. Stir the flour smoothly in; add seasonings and slowly add milk, stirring with a wooden spoon. When smooth and thickened, add the cheese and stir until smooth. Remove from the heat and let cool. Beat the yolks in smoothly, then the stiffly beaten whites. Pile into 8 or more large buttered scallop shells.

Brown in a moderate oven (350° F.). Serve hot. Serves 8 or more.

*Variation.* Add 2 or 3 tablespoons minced cooked ham or smoked tongue before adding the egg whites.


## CHEESE PUDDING PÂTÉS AU FROMAGE

2 cups hot milk
3 eggs, well beaten
1 cup grated Gruyère cheese
½ tsp. salt

¼ tsp. pepper
1 cup Cream Sauce or Tomato
   Sauce

Slowly mix the milk with the eggs, cheese, and seasonings. Pour into a buttered 1-quart baking dish or in 6 individual baking dishes. Bake in a moderate to low oven (300° F.) 15 minutes or until the pudding is set and browning on top. Serve with a spoonful of Cream Sauce or Tomato Sauce. Serves 6.


## CHEESE TART LORRAINE QUICHE LORRAINE

rich pie pastry for 1-crust pie
½ lb. Gruyère cheese, sliced thin
2 eggs
1 cup heavy cream

¼ cup cooked ham (cut in thin
   slices) or bacon
½ tsp. salt
¼ tsp. pepper

Line an 8-inch round or square pan with pie pastry; trim the edge and crimp it into a ridge. Cover the bottom and sides with thin slices of cheese. Cover with meat and seasonings. Beat the eggs with the cream and pour into the pan. Bake in a moderate oven (325° F.) 30 minutes. Serves 4 to 6.


## CHEESE RAVIOLI RAVIOLI AU FROMAGE

3 tbs. flour
½ cup cream or milk
1 tbs. butter
1 cup grated Gruyère
3 eggs

1 extra egg white
¼ tsp. salt
½ cup bread crumbs
oil or fat for deep frying

Put the flour in a 1-quart double boiler; place over hot water and slowly stir the milk or cream and butter into it. Add the cheese and stir in the slightly beaten yolks and the 3 stiffly beaten whites. Add seasoning; mix. Heat but do not boil. Stir. When thick enough to adhere to the spoon, turn out on a flat dish to cool.

Roll out on a floured pastry board. Cut with a round or fancy cutter; brush with egg white and sprinkle with bread crumbs. Fry in deep hot oil or fat. When ravioli are done, they rise to the surface. Drain on several thicknesses of paper towelling. Serve hot with Tomato Sauce. Serves 8.

# *Croquettes*

*How to Fry Croquettes.* Put three pints of good cooking oil, or the equivalent quantity of beef or pork fat, in a deep frying pan. Place on the fire, and before the liquid begins to smoke, introduce the croquettes, a few at a time. Reduce the fire; when the croquettes are well browned, remove and leave in a warm place. Proceed similarly with the remainder. Take great care not to burn the oil.

This generous use of oil brings visions of a great old country-house kitchen, huge iron kettles, and the shining copper pots and pans handy for other kinds of cookery. The use of good oil (which in France is olive oil) or beef or pork fat makes for delicious flavour.

## BEEF CROQUETTES CROQUETTES DE BOEUF

| | |
|---|---|
| 2 *cups minced or chopped boiled beef* | ½ *cup or more bouillon or hot water* |
| 1 *onion, chopped* | 1 *or 2 eggs* |
| 4 *tbs. minced cooked or canned mushrooms* | 1 *tsp. salt* |
| 1 *tbs. butter* | ¼ *tsp. pepper* |
| 1 *tbs. flour* | ½ *cup bread crumbs or flour* |
| | *oil or fat for deep frying* |

To mince the beef remove fat and tendons and mince or chop it fine. Heat the onion and mushrooms with the butter in a 1-quart saucepan. Stir, and when cooked, add the flour and cook 2 minutes longer, stirring with a wooden spoon. Slowly add enough hot water or bouillon to the consistency of a thick sauce. Remove from heat, stir 1 or 2 eggs into the mixture, then add the beef. Mix well. Season and spread on a plate to cool.

Shape into croquettes; roll each in crumbs or flour. Fry in hot oil or fat until browned, about 2 to 3 minutes. Drain on several thicknesses of paper towelling on a pan in a warm oven. Makes 12 to 16 small coquettes, 6 or more servings.

## LENTIL CROQUETTES CROQUETTES DE LENTILLES

Put lentils in cold water and boil gently until cooked and there is little liquid left. Press through a sieve. Mix with 1 or 2 beaten eggs, a knob of butter, salt and pepper; and make into croquettes. Roll in bread crumbs. Fry in deep hot oil or fat until golden. Drain on thick paper towelling and serve. Serves 8 to 12.

## MACARONI CROQUETTES CROQUETTES DE MACARONI

| | |
|---|---|
| *leftover Macaroni Cheese* | ½ *cup bread crumbs* |
| 1 *or 2 egg yolks* | *oil or fat for deep frying* |

Chop leftover Macaroni Cheese fine. Mix with 1 or 2 egg yolks as needed for a good consistency to shape. Roll in ball or cylinder shapes, dip in crumbs, and fry in deep hot oil or fat until lightly browned. Drain on several thicknesses of paper towelling. Allow 2 small croquettes per serving with Cream Sauce or Tomato Sauce.

## MACARONI AND VEAL CROQUETTES CROQUETTES DE VEAU ET MACARONI

| | |
|---|---|
| *leftover Macaroni Cheese* | *salt and pepper* |
| *leftover cooked veal* | 1 *or 2 egg yolks* |
| *thick White Sauce* | *oil or fat for deep frying* |

Use equal amounts of leftover Macaroni Cheese and cooked veal from which fat and gristle have been removed. Mince well together; moisten with thick White Sauce. Season with salt and pepper. Add the beaten yolk of 1 or 2 eggs. The mixture must be thick enough to hold shape. Let it stand an hour or two. Spread on a plate until firm. Then shape and fry as for other croquettes. Allow 1 or 2 croquettes per serving.

## MACARONI CROQUETTES NAPOLITAINE CRO-QUETTES NAPOLITAINES

| | |
|---|---|
| 3 oz. broken macaroni | 2 tbs. cream |
| boiling salted water | 1 egg |
| 3 oz. grated cheese | 1 cup bread crumbs |
| 8 oz. minced cooked ham | oil or fat for deep frying |

Drop the macaroni slowly into the boiling water (1 teaspoon salt to 1 quart water). Do not let the boiling stop. Boil 15 minutes or longer, until the macaroni is tender. Drain and cut it fine. Mix with the cheese, ham, and cream. Spread on a plate to cool. Let stand overnight in the refrigerator.

Shape into croquettes; dip in beaten egg, then in crumbs. Fry in deep hot oil or fat until lightly browned. Drain on several thicknesses of paper towelling. Serve hot with Cream Sauce, Tomato Sauce, or leftover gravy. Makes 24 small croquettes, 10 or more servings.

## SEMOLINA CROQUETTES CROQUETTES DE SEMOULE

| | |
|---|---|
| 1 tbs. butter | $\frac{1}{4}$ tsp. pepper |
| 2 cups hot milk | 1 egg, beaten |
| 1 cup farina, semolina, or Cream of Wheat | 1 cup bread crumbs |
| | oil or fat for deep frying |
| $\frac{1}{2}$ tsp. salt | 8 to 10 sprigs parsley, fried |

Stir the butter into the hot milk; stir in the cereal and seasonings; stir and boil 10 minues. Let cool. Spoon out pieces about the size of an egg. Roll each in egg, then in the crumbs. Fry in the hot oil or fat. Garnish with fried parsley. Serve with a savory sauce such as a meat gravy, Cheese Sauce, or Tomato Sauce. Serves 4 to 8.

## Entrées : Egg

## POTATO CROQUETTES CROQUETTES DE POMMES DE TERRE

2 cups mashed steamed potatoes
1 tbs. butter
2 eggs
1 tsp. salt
½ tsp. pepper
½ cup bread crumbs
oil or fat for deep frying

Mix the potatoes with the butter and 1 egg. Add the seasonings. Shape into croquettes; dip each in beaten egg. Then dip in bread crumbs. Fry in deep hot oil or fat until browned. Drain on thick paper towelling. Serve hot. Serves 4 to 6.

## POTATO AND HAM CROQUETTES CROQUETTES MILANAISES

4 oz. minced cooked ham
2 cups mashed potatoes
2 oz. grated Gruyère cheese
2 egg yolks
1 cup very thick White Sauce
1 extra egg yolk
½ cup bread crumbs
oil or fat for deep frying

Mix the ham, potatoes, cheese, and 2 egg yolks; add enough White Sauce to make a mixture just thick enough to hold its shape. Spread on a plate to cool. Shape into croquettes. Dip in beaten egg yolk, then in crumbs. Fry in deep hot oil or fat until browned. Serves 6 to 8.

# Egg Entrées

## EGGS BÛCHERONNE OEUFS BÛCHERONNE

4 round slices bread, toasted or
  fried in butter
4 round slices boiled or baked ham
4 eggs
½ tsp. salt
¼ tsp. pepper

Place the bread in a greased shallow baking dish. Lay a slice of ham on each. Beat the eggs with the seasonings and pour over the slices. Put in a moderate oven (350° F.) to cook the eggs, 5 to 7 minutes. Serves 4.

# Entrées : Egg

## CREAMED EGGS OEUFS À LA CRÈME

| | |
|---|---|
| 1 tbs. butter | 1½ tbs. grated cheese |
| 1 tbs. minced chives | ½ tsp. black pepper |
| 4 eggs | ¼ cup heavy cream |
| ½ tsp. salt | 4 slices toast |

Set a fireproof glass or pottery ramekin (with handle) over the lower part of a double boiler containing boiling water. Melt the butter in the dish. Sprinkle the chives over the butter. Break the eggs into dish, evenly placed. Sprinkle the whites with a little salt and the grated cheese. Sprinkle the yolks with pepper. Cover. When the eggs are cooked, pour a tablespoon of cream on each. Serve from the cooking dish on to the toast. Serves 4.

NOTE: Use small ramekins to cook 1 or 2 eggs for individual serving.

## EGGS JUSTINE OEUFS JUSTINE

| | |
|---|---|
| 6 hard-boiled eggs | 1 cup bread crumbs |
| 6 tbs. minced cooked or canned mushrooms | ¼ cup butter |
| | ½ lemon, juice only |
| ½ cup thick Cream Sauce | salt |
| 1 raw egg | |

Shell the hard-boiled eggs and cut in halves lengthwise. Remove the yolks. Mix mushrooms with the Cream Sauce and fill the whites. Dip these in beaten egg. Then dip in crumbs. Sauté in 1 tablespoon hot butter. Melt the remaining butter; mix with lemon juice and mashed yolks. Serve with the sautéed eggs. Serves 6.

## EGGS WITH CHEESE OEUFS EN SURPRISE

| | |
|---|---|
| 6 eggs | ½ cup thick White Sauce |
| 6 tbs. grated cheese | 2 whites, stiffly beaten |
| 2 egg yolks | |

Poach the eggs, drain, and place in a buttered baking dish. Sprinkle with cheese. Beat the 2 yolks lightly and add to cooled White Sauce. Mix the whites in. Pour over the eggs. Bake in a moderate oven (350° F.) until the sauce is bubbly and browning. Serves 6.

# Entrées : Egg

## EGGS IN JELLY OEUFS À LA GELÉE

½ lb. veal bones
½ calf's foot
piece of crackling
1 qt. water

½ tsp. salt
¼ tsp. pepper
1 tsp. meat extract
4 eggs, poached

Cover the bones, calf's foot, and crackling with the water in a sauce pan. Add the seasonings and meat extract. Boil until 1 cup of liquid remains. Pour over the poached eggs in 4 ramekins or a larger dish. Serves 4.

NOTE: For the modern small kitchen where bones and cracklings are not available, prepare plain gelatine. Soak 2 tablespoons gelatine in ¼ cup cold water, then dissolve in 1 cup hot bouillon. When beginning to jell, pour over the eggs as described.

## EGGS WITH PIQUANT SAUCE OEUFS À LA MARTINIQUAISE

4 eggs
2 tsp. dry mustard
1 cup olive oil
½ tsp. vinegar
½ tsp. salt

¼ tsp. pepper
1 hard-boiled egg, minced
1 onion, chopped
1 tbs. capers

Poach the eggs and place in 4 individual serving dishes. When cold, cover with the sauce and serve very cold. Serves 4.

*To make the sauce:* Place the mustard in a bowl; add the oil a drop at a time, always stirring in the same direction. When well mixed, add the vinegar a drop at a time, stirring carefully; add the salt, pepper, hard-boiled egg, onion, and capers. Blend well and pour over the eggs.

## EGGS ROSSINI OEUFS À LA ROSSINI

6 eggs
1 tbs. butter
1 tsp. salt

½ tsp. pepper
¼ cup grated cheese
½ cup heavy cream

Separate yolks and whites. Whip the whites until stiff. Melt the butter in a 1-quart baking dish. Pile the whites in; season with half the salt, pepper, and cheese. Carefully place the yolks on the whites; sprinkle with the rest of the salt, pepper, and cheese. Bake in a moderate oven (325° F.) until the yolks are cooked and the meringue delicately golden. Heat the cream but do not boil it. Pour the warm, heavy cream between the yolks and serve. Serves 6.

## EGGS WITH TOMATOES OEUFS SUR LE PLAT AUX TOMATES

| | |
|---|---|
| 2 *tbs. butter* | 4 *eggs* |
| 3 *tomatoes, cut in halves* | *salt and pepper* |
| ½ *tsp. salt* | |

Melt 1 tablespoon of the butter in a frying pan and cook the tomato halves about 5 minutes on each side; season lightly with salt. Place the tomatoes around the sides of a buttered baking dish and melt 1 tablespoon of butter in the centre. Remove from heat. Add the eggs carefully so as not to break the yolks. Bake in a moderate oven (350° F.) until the eggs are cooked. Season with salt and pepper. Serves 4.

## EGGS WITH WHITE SAUCE OEUFS À LA TRIPE

| | |
|---|---|
| 8 *hard-boiled eggs* | ½ *tsp. salt* |
| 2 *cups hot White Sauce* | ¼ *tsp. pepper* |
| 1 *tbs. minced onion* | |

Cut the eggs in quarters. Place in a warmed serving dish. Season the White Sauce with the onion, salt, and pepper. Pour over the eggs and serve. Serves 4.

## SWEDISH EGGS OEUFS FARCIS À LA SUÉDOISE

| | |
|---|---|
| 6 *hard-boiled eggs* | ½ *tsp. salt* |
| 3 or 4 *tbs. butter* | *Herb Sauce* |

Cut the eggs in halves, lengthwise. Mash the yolks; mix with an equal amount of butter. Season lightly with salt. Stuff into the whites. Serve with Herb Sauce. Serves 6.

# POACHED EGGS WITH ARTICHOKES OEUFS POCHÉS AUX FONDS D'ARTICHAUTS

| | |
|---|---|
| 6 artichokes | 1 cup Cheese Sauce |
| boiling water | ¼ cup grated cheese |
| 6 eggs | 1 tbs. butter |

Trim tips off leaves of artichokes. Cook in boiling salted water (1 teaspoon to 1 quart water) until tender, about 25 to 40 minutes. Drain; pull leaves out. Cut out choke and discard it. Place the hearts in a buttered baking dish.

Poach the eggs and place them on the artichoke hearts. Pour the sauce over them. Sprinkle with grated cheese and add dabs of butter. Bake in a moderate oven (325° F.) until the sauce is bubbly and browning on top. Serve hot. Serves 6.

## HOW TO MAKE AN OMELETTE

| | |
|---|---|
| 6 eggs | ¼ tsp. pepper |
| ½ tsp. salt | 3 tbs. butter |

Beat the eggs vigorously with a fork or egg whisk. Add a knob of butter, salt and pepper. Melt butter in a frying pan, tilting the pan to coat it well. Add the eggs. Use low heat and do not overcook. Use a fork to lift the omelette and prevent its buring. When cooked, fold the omelette in three and slide it on to a warmed dish. Serves 4.

## OMELETTE BRETONNE OMELETTE BRETONNE

This was a favourite omelette of the Restaurant du Mont St. Michel.

Follow directions for plain omelette, but whip the white of 1 egg. Cook as described. Serves 4.

## CHEESE OMELETTE OMELETTE AU FROMAGE

Add to the plain omelette recipe 2 tablespoons grated Gruyère, Parmesan, or Cheddar cheese when beating the eggs.

## MILK OMELETTE OMELETTE AU LAIT

Use 5 eggs in place of 6 in the plain omelette. Add 2 tablespoons of milk when beating the eggs.

## PEASANT OMELETTE OMELETTE AU LARD

Add 2 slices lean pork or bacon, cooked and chopped, to the plain omelette when folding it to serve.

## OMELETTE WITH FRIED BREAD OMELETTE AUX CROÛTONS

Add ½ cup cubes of bread fried in butter to the plain omelette when folding to serve.

## OMELETTE WITH HAM OMELETTE AU JAMBON

Add ½ cup minced cooked ham or bacon to the plain omelette before folding.

## OMELETTE WITH MUSHROOMS OMELETTE AUX CHAMPIGNONS

Add ½ cup chopped cooked or canned mushrooms to the plain omelette before folding. Sauté the mushrooms in butter.

## HOW TO MAKE A SOUFFLÉ

Points to remember in making a soufflé are:

1. Use a round or oval soufflé dish, previously warmed and buttered.
2. The whites of the eggs should be well beaten.
3. After the beaten whites have been added, very little stirring is necessary.
4. The dish should be only threequarters filled.
5. The dish should be placed on a hot brick in the oven.
6. The oven should remain closed while the soufflé is baking.

7. You must await the soufflé; the soufflé will not wait for you. Unless the soufflé is served immediately it leaves the oven, it will collapse.

## SOUFFLÉ NANTUA BOUCHÉES NANTUA

| | |
|---|---|
| 6 *tbs. butter* | 2 *tbs. cream* |
| 5 *eggs, separated* | $\frac{1}{4}$ *tsp. salt* |
| 5 *tbs. flour* | 2 *doz. cleaned cooked shrimps* |
| 5 *tbs. milk* | |

Heat the butter until melted. Add 1 yolk and beat smooth, 1 tablespoon of flour and beat smooth, 1 tablespoon of milk and beat smooth. Repeat until all yolks, flour, and milk have been used. Stir 10 minutes, then add the cream and salt and mix until smooth. Fold in the stiffly whipped egg whites. Butter 8 or 6 ramekins; place 3 or 4 shrimps in each. Half fill with the egg mixture. Bake in a moderate oven (325° F.) until the soufflé is set and golden. Serves 6.

NOTE: If tall ramekins are used, set them in a shallow pan containing very little water.

## CHEESE SOUFFLÉ SOUFFLÉ AU FROMAGE

| | |
|---|---|
| 1 *tbs. butter* | $\frac{1}{2}$ *tsp. salt* |
| 3 *tbs. flour* | $\frac{1}{4}$ *tsp. pepper* |
| 2 *cups milk* | 3 *eggs, separated* |
| $\frac{3}{4}$ *cup grated cheese* | 1 *tsp. baking powder* |

Heat the butter in a 1-quart saucepan. Stir the flour smoothly into it. Slowly add the milk, stirring until smooth. Add the cheese and seasonings and stir until very thick. Place the yolks in a buttered baking dish, add the mixture and the baking powder; stirring well. Fold in the stiffly beaten egg whites. Bake in a moderate oven (350° F.) 20 minutes. Makes 4 to 6 servings.

## HAM SOUFFLÉ SOUFFLÉ AU JAMBON

Add $\frac{1}{2}$ cup ground or finely minced ham to the Cheese Soufflé recipe before pouring on to egg yolks, and reduce the cheese to $\frac{1}{4}$ cup.

*Entrées : Meat and Poultry*

## SOUFFLÉ AUVERGNAT PONTIS AUVERGNAT

| | |
|---|---|
| ½ *lb. bacon or pork belly* | ½ *tsp. salt* |
| 1 *medium-sized onion* | *hot water* |
| 1 *cup mixed green herbs or* | 2 *cups sifted flour* |
| 1 *tbs. mixed dried herbs* | 2 *cups milk* |
| ½ *tsp. pepper* | 6 *eggs* |

Mince or chop the bacon as smooth and fine as possible with the onion, herbs, pepper, and salt. Stir to a smooth paste in a 2-quart saucepan, adding a little hot water. Blend the flour and milk until smooth and gradually add to the bacon paste. Mix and stir over heat. Add the eggs one at a time, stirring and cooking to the consistency of thick cream. Pour into a buttered baking dish. Bake in a moderate oven (350° F.) 45 minutes, or 'until a knitting needle comes out dry.' Serves 6.

# Meat and Poultry Entrées

## CALF'S BRAINS CERVELLES DE VEAU

| | |
|---|---|
| 1 *pair calf's brains* | 1 *small carrot, minced* |
| 1 *tsp. salt* | ½ *green pepper, sliced* |
| ½ *tbs. vinegar* | *bay leaf* |
| 2 *peppercorns* | 2 *tbs. butter* |
| 1 *sprig parsley* | 1 *tsp. minced parsley or chives* |
| 1 *small onion, sliced* | |

Prepare the brains by removing arteries and membranes. Cover with cold water and let soak 1 hour. Drain. Cover with water; add the salt, vinegar, peppercorns, parsley, onion, carrot, green pepper and bay leaf. Boil gently about 15 to 20 minutes. Drain. Break or cut into serving-size sections on a warmed serving dish. Melt the butter, pour over the brains, and sprinkle with the parsley or chives. Serves 8 or more.

NOTE: A mushroom sauce, or tomato, is sometimes served on boiled calf's brains.

## CALF'S BRAINS WITH CREAM SAUCE CERVELLES DE VEAU À LA SAUCE BLANCHE

Serve the calf's brains, cooked as described above, with well-seasoned Cream Sauce.

## HAM AND EGGS ENTRÉE AU JAMBON

1 *tbs. butter*
4 *thin slices boiled ham*
8 *eggs*
1 *tsp. salt*

½ *tsp. pepper*
8 *small sausages*
1 *cup hot Tomato Sauce*

Heat the butter in a large frying pan and sauté ham slices 2 or 3 minutes. Place 2 eggs on each slice of ham and cook until set or more thoroughly cooked. Season. Carefully lift a serving of ham and 2 eggs to each of 4 warmed plates. Garnish with 2 small cooked sausages and spoon some Tomato Sauce over the eggs. Serves 4.

## HAM PUDDING POUDING AU JAMBON

1 *cup thick White Sauce*
3 *eggs*
½ *cup grated Gruyère or other cheese*

½ *cup minced cooked ham*
*Cheese Sauce or Tomato Sauce*

Let the White Sauce cool slightly, then pour it slowly over the beaten eggs. Mix the cheese and ham into it. Pour into a buttered 1-quart baking dish. Set in a shallow pan half filled with water and bake in a moderate oven (325° F.) 35 to 45 minutes. Serve covered with Cheese or Tomato Sauce. Serves 4 to 6.

## HAM PANCAKES CRÊPES AU JAMBON

8 *thin pancakes*
8 *thin slices boiled ham*

1 *cup grated cheese*
2 *tbs. butter*

On each freshly made pancake place a matching slice of ham. Roll and place in buttered fireproof serving dish. Sprinkle with cheese; add dabs of butter. Brown under grill and heat until the cheese is golden. Serves 4.

## FRIED HAM AND CHEESE SANDWICHES CROQUE-MONSIEUR

4 slices boiled or baked ham or
   crisp bacon
8 slices bread

$\frac{3}{4}$ cup very thick cheese sauce
2 tbs. butter

Place the ham or bacon on 4 slices of bread. Spoon the cheese sauce over the meat. Cover with a slice of bread. Fry in the hot butter until browned on both sides. Cut diagonally in half and serve. Serves 4.

## HAM TARTLETS MOUSSELINES AU JAMBON

$\frac{1}{2}$ cup minced cooked ham
1 cup thick cream sauce

4 to 6 small baked tart shells
1 tbs. minced parsley

Mix the meat into the sauce; fill small tart shells. Place on baking sheet in a hot oven (425° F.) and heat 10 minutes. Sprinkle with parsley and serve. Serves 4 to 6.

## CHICKEN SCALLOPS COQUILLES DE VOLAILLE

1 cup water
$\frac{1}{2}$ lemon, juice only
$\frac{1}{2}$ cup chopped cleaned mushrooms or canned mushrooms

2 cups minced cooked chicken
$1\frac{1}{2}$ cups thick cream sauce
$\frac{1}{2}$ cup bread crumbs

Heat the water with the lemon juice. When boiling add the mushrooms and cook 10 minutes. Add the chicken, stir, and cook until smooth and hot.

Place a generous tablespoon of chicken mixture in each of 6 large scallop shells, then fill with cream sauce. Sprinkle with crumbs. Bake in a hot oven (400° F.) until bubbly and browned. Serves 6.

NOTE: When this scallop is prepared in 1 large dish, use a shallow baking dish. Fill half full with cream sauce. Spread the chicken mixture in the dish; pour the remaining sauce over and sprinkle with crumbs.

# Entrées : Meat and Poultry

## SNAILS BOURGOGNE ESCARGOTS DE BOURGOGNE

| | |
|---|---|
| 2 doz. live snails | 1 tsp. minced chervil |
| boiling water | ½ tsp. salt |
| 2 garlic buds, minced fine | ¼ tsp. pepper |
| ½ cup butter | ½ cup minced parsley or mixed |
| ¼ cup minced chives | herbs |

Most home cooks buy snails prepared, or stuffed, at the fish market. These are heated in the oven or on top of the range with a little butter or sauce and eaten hot.

To prepare live snails soak them in salt water 30 minutes; wash in 2 or 3 waters, scrubbing the shells clean. Crack the shells and drop them into rapidly boiling water (1 teaspoon salt to 1 quart water). Boil 15 minutes; drain. Pick the flesh out of the shells with a prong or a fork. Wash the snails in warm water. Remove head and intestines and discard them. Boil the meat twice again for 2 minutes each time, changing the water. Clean whole shells carefully and replace the meat. Mix the garlic, butter, chives, chervil, and seasonings. Stuff the shells with this mixture. Warm in the oven or in a frying pan. Serve sprinkled with minced parsley or a mixture of green herbs. Serves 4.

NOTE: Cleaned snail shells are sold in packages at speciality grocery stores or at the fish dealers'.

## FROGS' LEGS IN BUTTER GRENOUILLES SAUTÉES

| | |
|---|---|
| 4 frogs' legs | ¼ tsp. pepper |
| 1 onion, minced | ¼ tsp. powdered cloves |
| 1 shallot, minced | 2 tbs. butter |
| 1 small clove garlic, minced | 1 tbs. minced parsley |
| 1 lemon, juice only | 1 lemon, sliced thin |
| ½ tsp. salt | |

Wash the legs in cold water. Skin them, rinse, and let stand 1 hour in the refrigerator in a mixture of the onion, shallot, garlic, lemon juice, salt, pepper, and cloves. Turn them frequently so they are coated with the seasonings. Drain and sauté in the butter 5 to 8 minutes, or until cooked and browned. Sprinkle with parsley and serve with sliced lemon. Serves 4 or more.


## QUENELLES QUENELLES

1¼ *cups minced cooked veal*
2 *slices bread soaked in*
2 *or 3 tbs. milk*
2 *tbs. butter*

1 *egg*
½ *tsp. salt*
*boiling water*

To prepare veal, remove tendons and fat and chop fine or put through the mincer several times. Squeeze the excess milk out of the bread. Mix meat, bread, butter, and beaten egg together. Season and press through a sieve. Let stand a few hours in the refrigerator. Roll, cut into finger lengths, and poach in boiling water.

Use as garnish on soups and around creamed dishes. Serves 8 or more.

*Variation.* Use cooked fish or poultry in place of veal.

This same mixture of smooth meat, fish, or chicken, combined with a thick White Sauce, with a few sautéed mushrooms added, may be steamed or baked in a ring mould, then served with a sauce.

In place of mushrooms add minced cooked macaroni and use thick cream in place of White Sauce.


## TRIPE À LA MODE DE CAEN TRIPE À LA MODE DE CAEN

2 *lb. boiled or pickled tripe*
*boiling water*
1 *calf's foot*
2 *sheep's trotters*
1 *cup kidney fat or suet, chopped*
4 *tbs. minced onions*
4 *tbs. minced carrots*
2 *leeks*
1 *tsp. fresh thyme or*
½ *tsp. dried thyme*

2 *bay leaves*
2 *sprigs parsley*
½ *tsp. minced chervil*
1 *sliver garlic*
1 *tsp. salt*
½ *tsp. pepper*
2 *cups cider or white wine*
2 *cups bouillon or hot water*
⅓ *cup cognac (optional)*

Select clean-looking tripe; that from old beef is tough. Wash it in cold water. Remove any loose skin. Plunge in boiling water, then in several changes of cold water. Cut into 2-inch squares.

Wash the calf's foot and sheep's trotters; cut or break in 2 or 3 parts. Arrange the tripe and the feet in a large earthenware fireproof dish. Leave space in the middle and add the fat, vegetables, and herbs. Sprinkle with salt and pepper and top with a layer of tripe. Add the cider or wine, bouillon or hot water, and the cognac. Stew slowly with the lid on for about 5 hours, adding boiling water or bouillon if necessary. Remove from the heat; let cool. Skim the top. The next day reheat and stew slowly again 4 hours. Before serving, remove the bones and any herbs remaining. Serves 6.

## SAUSAGES WITH STEWED APPLES CHIPOLATAS À LA COMPOTE DE POMMES

Serve small sausages, cooked as in the following recipe, with hot apple sauce or slices of apple sautéed in butter.

## SAUSAGES WITH POTATO PURÉE CHIPOLATAS À LA PURÉE DE POMMES DE TERRE

| | |
|---|---|
| 8 *small link sausages* | 2 *or* 3 *cups hot mashed potatoes* |
| 1 *tbs. butter* | |

Prick the sausages. Heat the butter in a frying pan until browned. Add the sausages and cook 10 minutes, or until cooked thoroughly and browned. Serve on a warmed plate garnished with mashed potatoes, and spoon the pan gravy over them. Serves 4.

## VEAL MEDALLIONS MÉDAILLONS DE VEAU

| | |
|---|---|
| 4 *cups minced cooked veal* | 1 *egg yolk* |
| 3 *slices bread soaked in milk* | ¾ *cup flour* |
| 1 *tsp. salt* | 2 *tbs. butter* |
| ½ *tsp. pepper* | *hot water* |
| 1 *tbs. heavy cream* | 1 *lemon, juice only* |

Mix the meat with the softened bread (from which the milk has been squeezed), seasonings, cream, and beaten egg yolk. Divide into 12 parts and shape into patties. Sprinkle with flour and sauté in butter. When lightly browned on both sides, remove to a hot dish. Add a little boiling water and the lemon juice to the pan, stir, and boil 5 minutes. Pour a little over the medallions. Serve with steamed or boiled potatoes. Serves 6.

## VEAL AND PORK PIE TOURTE LORRAINE

| | |
|---|---|
| 4 oz. chopped cooked pork | rich pastry for 2-crust pie |
| 4 oz. chopped cooked veal | 1 egg |
| 2 onions, sliced | ½ cup heavy cream |
| 1½ tsp. salt | 1 tbs. flour |
| ½ tsp. pepper | |

Mix the meat and onions; season with salt and pepper. Cover and let stand in the refrigerator overnight.

Line a shallow casserole with pastry, crimping the edge into a rim. Fill with the meat. Beat the egg slightly, mix with the cream and flour, and pour over the meat. Cover with pastry, crimping the edge to the lower pastry. Pierce the top in several places with a fork, or cut in a fancy pattern, or make a hole in the centre. Place in a hot oven (450° F.) 15 minutes to bake and brown the crust. Then lower heat to 350° and bake 30 minutes longer. Serves 6.

## VOL-AU-VENT WITH SWEETBREADS VOL-AU-VENT
### AU RIZ DE VEAU

| | |
|---|---|
| 1 pair sweetbreads | 1 tbs. butter |
| 1 tbs. butter | 2 tbs. flour |
| 1 onion, sliced | 2 tbs. cream |
| 1 tsp. salt | 1 large vol-au-vent, or |
| ½ tsp. pepper | 8 or 10 croûtons and |
| 1 cup sliced cooked or canned | 1 lemon, sliced thin |
| mushrooms | |

Clean and skin a good-sized veal sweetbread without putting in water. Place it whole in a saucepan, where a tablespoonful of butter has already been browned. Add a sliced onion and brown the sweetbread. Then add salt, pepper, and a little water to prevent burning and boil gently for half an hour with the lid on the saucepan. When cooked remove the sweetbread and cut into slices of about an inch thick.

Clean half a pound of mushrooms and boil in water for a quarter of an hour.

Prepare a sauce by heating in a saucepan one tablespoonful of butter mixed with two tablespoonfuls of flour. Add slowly the gravy from the sweetbread and the water in which the mushrooms have been cooked. The sauce must be thick. Heat up the sweetbread and the mushrooms in the sauce, adding two tablespoonfuls of cream. Do not allow to boil. Then pour into a vol-au-vent of short flaky pastry, or into a dish, which can be garnished with small squares of bread fried in butter and thin slices of lemon.

# *Vegetable Entrées*

## STUFFED ARTICHOKE HEARTS ARTICHAUTS FARCIS AU MAIGRE

| | |
|---|---|
| 4 *artichokes* | 1 *tbs. minced parsley* |
| *boiling salted water* | 2 *hard-boiled egg yolks, mashed* |
| 1 *slice dry bread* | 1 *tsp. salt* |
| ¼ *cup milk* | ¼ *tsp. pepper* |
| 3 *or 4 small cooked or canned mushrooms* | 1 *tbs. bouillon or meat juice* |
| | 3 *tbs. butter* |

Trim tips off leaves of artichokes. Place in saucepan, cover with boiling salted water (1 teaspoon salt to 1 quart water), and boil until the leaves are tender and easily removed. Drain. Pull off leaves; cut out choke and discard it. Place the hearts in a buttered baking dish.

Mix a stuffing of the bread soaked in the milk, the mushrooms, parsley, yolks, seasonings, and bouillon or juice. Cook 5 minutes in half the butter. Heap it on the artichoke hearts; dot with the remaining butter. Bake in a moderate oven (350° F.) until the stuffing is browned. Serves 2 to 4.

# ARTICHOKES STUFFED WITH MEAT ARTICHAUTS
### FARCIS AU GRAS

4 *boiled artichokes*
*hot water*
¼ *cup sausage or minced meat*
2 *tbs. chopped cooked or canned*
   *mushrooms*
1 *slice bread soaked in*

2 *tbs. bouillon*
¼ *tsp. salt*
⅛ *tsp. pepper*
3 *tbs. butter*
1 *lemon, juice only*

Trim off tips of leaves; cut out choke and discard it. Press the leaves outward to make a good space in the centre. Boil the artichokes in salt water.

Mix the meat, mushrooms, bread, and seasonings. Cook 10 minutes in 1 tablespoon butter. Mix and stir. Fill the artichokes. Pour a little melted butter on top of each.

Place in a buttered baking dish; bake in a moderate oven (350° F.) 10 minutes. Squeeze lemon juice over before serving. Serves 4.


## RUSSIAN CABBAGE CHOU À LA RUSSE

18 *cabbage leaves*
*boiling water*
1½ *cups chopped cooked meat and*
   *bacon*
1 *tbs. butter*
1 *onion, chopped fine*

*salt*
¼ *tsp. pepper*
2 *tbs. cooked rice*
1 *egg yolk*
4 *slices bacon*
1 *cup water or bouillon*

Cover washed cabbage leaves with boiling salt water.

Brown the meat in the butter; add the onion, seasonings, and rice. Cook and stir 2 minutes. Let cool and add the egg yolk.

Drain the cabbage leaves. Place a spoonful of the meat mixture in the centre of each, roll the leaf, and fold the ends under. Lay the bacon in the bottom of a saucepan. Arrange the rolls on it; add a little bouillon or water to cover. Cover the pan and boil gently 1½ hours. Serve with the sauce. Serves 6 or more.

## STUFFED CABBAGE CHOU FARCI

| | |
|---|---|
| 1 *head cabbage* | ½ *tsp. salt* |
| *boiling salted water* | ¼ *tsp. pepper* |
| ¾ *cup sausage meat or other* | 3 *slices bacon* |
| *chopped meat* | 1 *slice fat pork* |
| 1 *onion, minced* | 1 *cup hot water* |

Remove any damaged leaves and cut off stem close to cabbage. Boil in salted water until tender, 25 to 30 minutes for young cabbage, 1 hour for older heads. Drain. Cut a hole in the top and scoop out cavity. Mix the meat, onion, salt and pepper and stuff into the cabbage. Lay the top leaves in place and tie the head with string to hold its shape.

Place the bacon slices on the bottom of a saucepan; set the cabbage head on them. Lay the fat pork on top and add the hot water to the saucepan. Cover and boil gently about 1 hour. Remove strings before serving. Serves 4 to 8.

## STUFFED RED CABBAGE CHOU ROUGE FARCI

| | |
|---|---|
| 1 *head red cabbage* | 1 *cup bouillon* |
| *boiling salted water* | 1 *slice carrot* |
| 6 *or* 8 *thin strips (lardings) pork fat* | 1 *slice onion* |
| ¾ *cup sausage meat* | 1 *clove* |
| 1 *or* 2 *tbs. chopped cooked mush-* | 1 *sprig thyme* |
| *rooms or canned mushrooms* | 2 *bay leaves* |
| 1 *tbs. butter* | ½ *tsp. salt* |
| 1 *tbs. flour* | ¼ *tsp. pepper* |

Cook cabbage in boiling salted water until tender, 25 to 30 minutes, or longer. Drain. Cut a hole in the top and scoop out a cavity. Fill it with the mixed meat and mushrooms. Cover with cabbage leaves; tie the head with string to hold its shape.

Melt the butter in a large saucepan; stir the flour in; add the bouillon and other ingredients. Stir and let come to boil. Put the stuffed cabbage in this mixture. Cover the pan and boil gently 1½ hours. Remove string before serving. Serves 4 to 8.


## STUFFED EGGPLANT AUBERGINES FARCIES

| | |
|---|---|
| 3 *medium-sized eggplants* | 2 *shallots, minced* |
| *boiling water* | 1 *tsp. salt* |
| 1 *cup cooked rice* | ¼ *tsp. pepper* |
| ½ *cup minced cooked calf's liver* | 1 *tbs. butter* |
| ¼ *cup minced cooked ham* | 1 *egg yolk* |
| 2 *slices bacon, cooked and minced* | ½ *cup grated cheese* |

Cut stalks off eggplants, cover with boiling water, and boil 10 minutes. Drain, run cold water over them, and drain again. Cut in halves, lengthwise, and scrape out the centres. Chop or mash centres and mix with the rice, liver, ham, bacon, shallots, and seasonings. Melt 1 tablespoon butter in a saucepan; heat the mixture, stirring until hot and lightly browned, about 10 minutes. Let cool; mix with egg yolk. Stuff the eggplant halves. Place in a buttered baking dish. Sprinkle with cheese and dabs of butter. Bake in a moderate oven (325° F.) about 15 minutes, or until browned. Serves 6 or more.

*Variation.* Vegetable marrows may be used instead of eggplants.


## EGGPLANT WITH CHEESE AUBERGINES AU ·FROMAGE

| | |
|---|---|
| 2 *medium-sized eggplants* | 2 *cups thick White Sauce* |
| 2 *tbs. oil* | 2 *tbs. tomato purée or paste* |
| 1 *tsp. salt* | ¼ *cup grated cheese* |

Cut eggplants into thick slices. Sauté on both sides in the oil. Season with salt. Flavour the White Sauce with the tomato purée or paste and cheese.

Cover the bottom of a large buttered baking dish with a layer of eggplant; pour some of the sauce over it. Repeat layers and sauce. Bake in a moderate oven (325° F.) about 45 minutes. Serves 4.

## LETTUCE WITH BACON LAITUE À L'ÉTOUFFÉE

| | |
|---|---|
| 4 *heads lettuce* | 6 *to* 8 *slices bacon* |
| *boiling salted water* | 1 *cup bouillon* |

Select medium-sized cabbage lettuces, remove the outer leaves. Cover with boiling water (1 teaspoon salt to 1 quart water) and boil 5 minutes. Drain. Place the bacon in the bottom of a saucepan. Put the lettuce on top and add the bouillon. Cover and cook gently 30 minutes, or until the bacon is thoroughly cooked. Serves 3 to 4.

## STUFFED MUSHROOMS I CHAMPIGNONS FARCIS

| | |
|---|---|
| 6 *large mushrooms* | 1 *tumblerful milk* |
| 3 *eggs* | *pepper* |
| *a pinch chopped parsley* | *salt* |
| 2 *tbs. semolina* | 3 *tbs. cream* |

Remove the stalks from the mushrooms and chop them up with two hard-boiled eggs and a pinch of parsley.

Boil two tablespoonfuls of semolina in a tumblerful of milk with a little pepper and salt. Add, when off the boil, a beaten egg and the chopped stalks and hard-boiled eggs. Fill the concave part of the mushrooms with this mixture in the shape of a pyramid and on top of each place a teaspoonful of fresh cream. Bake in the oven until the mushrooms are cooked.

## STUFFED MUSHROOMS II CHAMPIGNONS FARCIS

| | |
|---|---|
| 1 6 *large mushrooms* | ½ *tsp. salt* |
| 2 *tbs. olive oil* | ¼ *tsp. pepper* |
| 1 *slice crustless bread* | 1 *tbs. meat juice or bouillon* |
| 2 *tbs. milk* | 1 *tbs. butter* |
| 1 *tsp. parsley* | ½ *cup bread crumbs* |
| 2 *hard-boiled egg yolks* | 4 *to* 8 *toast slices* |

Cut off the mushroom stems and chop fine. Sauté the caps in olive oil until browned. Soften the bread in the milk and mix with chopped stems, parsley, chopped yolks, seasonings, and meat juice. Cook 3 minutes in the butter. Stuff into the caps. Place in a buttered baking dish. Sprinkle the top with crumbs. Bake in a hot oven (425° F.) 10 to 20 minutes, or until browned. Serves 8.

## ONION PASTRY TARTE AUX OIGNONS

| | |
|---|---|
| *rich pastry for large open tart* | ¼ *tsp. pepper* |
| *4 large onions* | *20 very small onions* |
| *2 tbs. butter* | *1½ cups thick White Sauce* |
| ½ *tsp. salt* | *1 tbs. sugar* |

Line a deep round baking pan with rich pie pastry and prick in several places with a fork. Chill several hours, then bake in a hot oven (500° F.) until golden, about 20 minutes.

Peel and chop the 4 onions. Cook in 1 tablespoon of butter and the seasonings until tender. Strain and mix with an equal amount of thick White Sauce. Pour into the baked pastry shell.

Skin and wash the little onions; brown in 1 tablespoon of butter. Add the sugar and, if necessary, a few drops or 1 tablespoon of hot water. When browned, arrange them over the pie. Bake in a hot oven (375° F.) until the top is browned, about 10 to 15 minutes. Serves 6.

## STUFFED TOMATOES TOMATES FARCIES AU MAIGRE

| | |
|---|---|
| *6 medium-sized tomatoes* | *3 hard-boiled eggs, chopped* |
| *2 slices bread soaked in* | *salt and pepper* |
| *3 tbs. milk* | *2 tbs. butter* |
| *1 tsp. chopped parsley* | *1 tbs. water* |
| *2 shallots, chopped* | |

Cut a slice from the tops of the tomatoes and scoop out the centres. Season each with salt. Squeeze the milk out of the bread and mix bread with the tomato pulp, parsley, shallots, and eggs. Season lightly with salt and pepper. Cook this mixture in 1 tablespoon butter a few minutes, then fill the tomatoes. Replace top slices and set tomatoes in a buttered baking dish to which has been added 1 tablespoon of water. Add dabs of butter to tops of tomatoes. Bake in a moderate oven (350° F.) 20 to 30 minutes. Lift the tomatoes to a hot serving dish or serve from the casserole. Serves 6.

## TOMATOES STUFFED WITH PEAS TOMATES FARCIES AUX PETITS POIS

| | |
|---|---|
| 6 tomatoes | 1 tbs. water |
| 1½ tsp. salt | 1 cup hot green peas cooked in |
| butter for baking dish | butter |

Cut a slice from the top of each tomato. Scoop out centres and season the tomatoes with salt. Place in a buttered baking dish, adding 1 tablespoon water to dish. Bake in a moderate oven (350° F.) 20 minutes. Fill tomatoes with the hot peas and serve. Serves 6.

## TOMATOES STUFFED WITH MEAT TOMATES FARCIES AU GRAS

| | |
|---|---|
| 6 medium-sized tomatoes | ¼ tsp. pepper |
| 1 cup ground cooked veal | ½ tsp. salt |
| ½ cup ground cooked sausage meat | 2 tbs. bouillon |
| 1 slice bread soaked in bouillon | 1 tbs. butter |
| 1 hard-boiled egg, chopped | 1 tbs. flour |
| | 1 sliver garlic, chopped (optional) |

Cut a slice off the tops of the tomatoes, and scoop out the centres. Save this pulp for the sauce. Mix the meat. Squeeze the bouillon out of the bread and add the bread, egg, pepper, and salt to the meat. Cook in the bouillon 5 minutes. Fill the tomatoes and set in a buttered baking dish to which 1 tablespoon of water has been added. Bake in a moderate oven (350° F.) 20 minutes. Make a sauce of the butter, the flour, and tomato pulp, stirring smoothly until slightly thickened. Add the garlic if liked. Pour over the tomatoes and serve. Serves 6.

## TOMATOES STUFFED WITH SHRIMPS TOMATES FAR-CIES AUX CREVETTES

*6 medium-sized tomatoes*
*⅛ tsp. salt*

*18 to 24 cooked, shelled, and cleaned shrimps*
*½ to 1 cup thick mayonnaise*

Have all ingredients very cold. Cut slice off tops of the tomatoes, and scoop out centres. Season the interiors with salt. Chop or mince all of the shrimps but 6. Mix with mayonnaise, using enough to coat the shrimps. Stuff the tomatoes; decorate the top of each with a whole shrimp. Serve cold. Serves 6.

## VEGETABLE MARROWS COURGETTES FARCIES

Follow the recipe for Stuffed Eggplant. Peel the marrows, cut in halves, and steam or boil 15 to 20 minutes. Stuff and continue as described.

# FISH

There are some three hundred and fifty species of edible fish. The reason for this plenitude may well be that given by Saint Augustine, who pointed out that fish were not included in the malediction pronounced by God upon the creatures of the earth in punishment for their faults. The reason for this exception was twofold: first, because the waters had not contributed to man's original sin, and second, because water was destined to help him atone for his sins through the Deluge and through baptism. Be that as it may, wherever there is water on the face of the earth, there is usually fish 'for man to catch and woman to cook,' as André Simon, the great wine and food authority of the twentieth century, so aptly puts it.

There is much to be learned from the French, who excel in the particular gastronomic field of sea-food cookery. Is there a cookery book of note that does not contain a recipe for *Sole à la Marguery?* Or *Homard à l'Américaine*, or is it *Amoricaine?*—the French discuss that bit of spelling as much as the English do 'rarebit' or 'rabbit'.

## *Fish*

### HOW TO BOIL FISH COURT BOUILLON

Put a large sliced onion, a sliced carrot, salt, pepper, a sprig of thyme, a bay leaf, and a tablespoon of vinegar in about 2 quarts of water; the actual quantity may be varied in accordance with the size of the fish to be cooked. Boil gently for 30 minutes. Let cool, then add the fish and boil gently until tender, about 5 minutes per pound for thick fish; 2 minutes per pound for small fish.

# Fish

The French serve boiled fish on a dish covered with a napkin. This absorbs surplus moisture.

## FISH PIE MORUE EN TURBAN

| | |
|---|---|
| 2 *lb. cod* | ½ *tsp. thyme* |
| 1 *qt. Court Bouillon* | ½ *tsp. orégano* |
| 8 *small potatoes* | 1 *tsp. salt* |
| ¼ *lb.* (½ *cup*) *butter* | ¼ *tsp. pepper* |
| 1 *tsp. chopped parsley* | 1 *cup Cheese Sauce* |

Cut fish in chunks, and boil gently 3 minutes in the bouillon. Remove skin and bones.

Cover potatoes with salted water, and cook until done, about 30 minutes. Drain, skin, and mash half of them. Mix with the fish and beat and mash smoothly with the butter. Add the herbs and salt and pepper.

In a buttered baking dish arrange the fish mixture in the form of a turban. Slice the rest of the potatoes in the centre. Pour the Cheese Sauce over them. Brown in a moderate oven (350° F.) until golden, about 20 minutes. Serves 4 to 6.

## FRIED FISH FRITURE DE POISSON

| | |
|---|---|
| 8 *to* 12 *sprats, whitebait or other small fish* | 1 *tbs. oil* |
| | 1 *tsp. salt* |
| 2 *eggs, beaten* | ¼ *tsp. pepper* |
| 4 *tbs. flour* | *oil or fat for deep frying* |
| 1 *tsp. cognac* | |

Slit the fish down the underside; remove contents. Remove head and tail.

Mix eggs and flour smoothly; add brandy, 1 tablespoon oil, and seasonings. Dip the fish in this batter and fry in deep hot fat until browned, about 5 to 7 minutes. Drain on several thicknesses of paper towelling. Serves 4 to 6. An alternative batter can be made of flour moistened with beer.

# Fish

## GRILLED HERRINGS HARENGS GRILLÉS

| | |
|---|---|
| 4 to 8 fresh herrings | ½ tsp. salt |
| 2 to 4 tbs. butter | ¼ tsp. pepper |
| 1 tsp. prepared mustard | |

Open fish flat; place under the grill or in a heavy frying pan with a little fat. Broil on the flesh side first, then turn and broil the other side until the skin is brown and crisp; 5 to 8 minutes. Melt the butter; let it brown a little. Stir mustard, salt, and pepper into it. Mix. Pour over the herrings and serve. Allow 1 or 2 herrings per serving.

## SOUSED HERRINGS HARENGS MARINÉS

| | |
|---|---|
| 4 to 8 fresh herrings | 6 or 8 shallots, sliced |
| 1 tsp. fresh thyme | ½ tsp. salt |
| 2 or 3 bay leaves | ¼ tsp. pepper |
| 2 or 3 onions, chopped | 1 cup white wine |
| 1 garlic bud, chopped | 1 cup vinegar |

Select small- to medium-sized fresh herrings. Mix herbs, onions, garlic, shallots, salt, and pepper. Arrange half of the fish in a baking dish and sprinkle with half of the seasoning. Place the rest of the fish in the dish and sprinkle with the remaining seasoning. Pour the wine and vinegar over. Cover. Cook 30 minutes in a moderate oven (350° F.). Let cool and then place in the refrigerator in the baking dish for several hours. Serve cold. Serves 4 or more.

## HERRINGS IN WHITE WINE HARENGS AU VIN BLANC

| | |
|---|---|
| 4 to 8 small fresh herrings | 2 bay leaves |
| 1 cup white wine | ½ tsp. salt |
| 1 cup water | ¼ tsp. pepper |
| 1 tsp. fresh thyme | |

Select small- to medium-sized fresh herrings. Place in a lightly buttered baking dish. Mix the rest of the ingredients and pour over the fish. Place in a moderate oven (350° F.) and cook covered 20 to 30 minutes. Baste frequently with the sauce in the dish. Uncover for last few minutes of baking. Serves 4 or more.

NOTE: Use only enough wine and water to cover the fish. The amount depends on the size of the fish.

## LING À L'AMÉRICAINE LOTTE À L'AMÉRICAINE

| | |
|---|---|
| 2 *lb. ling, cod or eel* | ⅛ *tsp. cayenne* |
| 2 *tbs. oil* | 1 *tsp. curry powder* |
| 1 *onion, sliced* | ¼ *tsp. saffron* |
| 1 *cup hot water* | *sprig of thyme* |
| 2 *tbs. tomato purèe or paste* | *bay leaf* |
| 1 *tsp. salt* | *Rice Italienne* |
| ½ *tsp. pepper* | |

Cut the cleaned fish in serving-size pieces. Sauté in the oil in a 2-quart saucepan; add the onion, water, purée and seasonings. Cover and boil gently 20 minutes. Add more liquid if necessary. Remove the bay leaf and as many bones as possible. Serve with Rice Italienne or boiled rice. Serves 4 to 6.

## SALMON STEAKS TRANCHES DE SAUMON GRILLÉES

| | |
|---|---|
| 2 *or* 3 1-*in. slices salmon* | 1 *tsp. salt* |
| *oil* | ¼ *tsp. pepper* |

Brush the salmon with oil; season with salt and pepper. Rub the grill pan grid with fat. Broil slowly. Turn the steaks, using a spatula or pancake turner. When both sides are browned and tender (15 minutes), serve with boiled potatoes with butter and lemon juice. If steaks are very large, they will make 4 to 6 servings.

# Fish

## MACKEREL IN BROWN SAUCE MAQUEREAUX

2 lb. fresh mackerel
1 cup white wine
1 tsp. salt
½ tsp. pepper
1 tbs. minced parsley

1 tbs. chopped shallots
1 tbs. oil
3 onions, chopped
1 tbs. flour
1 cup hot water

Cut the cleaned fish in serving-size pieces and place in a bowl. Pour over it the wine and add the salt, pepper, parsley, and shallots. Cover and let stand in the refrigerator 3 hours.

Heat the oil in a 2-quart saucepan with the onions. Sprinkle with flour, stir, and brown. Add the water, mix, and bring to boil. Add the fish, cover, and boil slowly 20 minutes, or until the fish is done. Remove the fish. Boil the sauce until the quantity is reduced to half. Pour over the mackerel and serve cold. Serves 4.

## BAKED FILLETS OF SOLE SOLE AU GRATIN

4 to 8 fillets of sole
butter for baking dish
1 tsp. salt
¼ tsp. pepper

½ cup white wine
½ cup water
¼ cup bread crumbs
1 tbs. butter

Place the fillets in a greased baking dish. Sprinkle with salt and pepper. Pour the wine and water over all; sprinkle with crumbs and dot with butter. Bake in a moderate oven (350° F.) 25 minutes, or until fish is cooked and top browned. Serves 4 to 8.

## SOLE MARGUERY SOLE À LA MARGUERY

4 to 8 fillets of sole
2 cups Court Bouillon
cooked mussels
cooked or canned mushrooms
1 tbs. butter
2 tbs. flour

1 cup liquid from mussels or
   bouillon
2 tbs. heavy cream
2 egg yolks
1 cup small cooked cleaned
   shrimps

Cook the fillets in Court Bouillon 2 minutes.

Melt the butter, stir the flour in smoothly, and gradually add 1 cup of the bouillon and liquid from mussels. Stir and cook until thickened. Add the cream and egg yolks. Stir and remove from the heat.

Arrange the drained fish, mussels, and mushrooms in a buttered baking dish. Pour the sauce over; arrange shrimps around the edges and over the top in the sauce. (If fillets are large, double the sauce.) Brown in a moderate oven (350° F.) until bubbly, about 15 minutes. Serves 4 to 8.


## SOLE MEUNIÈRE SOLE MEUNIÈRE
*See* Variation under Trout Meunière, below.


## SKATE WITH BLACK BUTTER RAIE AU BEURRE NOIR

*cleaned and dressed skate*  
*Court Bouillon*  
*1 tbs. vinegar*  
*capers or chopped parsley*  
*3 tbs. butter*  
*1 tsp. prepared mustard*  
*salt and pepper*

Skate is usually sold cleaned and ready for cooking. If bought whole, it should be scrubbed and washed in plenty of clean water to remove the stickiness; detach the 'wings' (they are the only edible parts). Cook in Court Bouillon to cover containing 1 tablespoon vinegar. After 2 minutes of slow boiling, drain, skin the pieces by scraping each side. Drain; place in a warmed serving dish. Sprinkle thickly with capers or chopped parsley. Melt the butter in a saucepan. When it begins to brown, stir the mustard in and add a little salt and pepper. Mix and quickly pour over the hot fish. Serve at once. One pound cleaned skate serves 3 or 4.


## TROUT MEUNIÈRE TRUITES MEUNIÈRE

*4 or 6 fresh trout*  
*1 tsp. salt*  
*½ tsp. pepper*  
*Flour*  
*4 tbs. butter*  
*1 lemon, juice only*

Season the fish, then roll in flour. Melt 2 tablespoons of butter in a frying pan. When sizzling hot, brown the fish, cooking over moderate heat until cooked through and browned on both sides,

4 to 5 minutes per side. Sprinkle with lemon juice and top with a dab of butter. Serves 4 or more.

*Variation.* Use small sole or other fish in this recipe. Leave the cleaned fish whole with head and tail, or cut off head and tail.

## TROUT WITH CREAM TRUITES À LA CRÈME

| | |
|---|---|
| 4 *cleaned fresh trout* | 2 *tbs. butter* |
| 1 *tsp. salt* | 1 *cup heavy cream* |
| ½ *tsp. pepper* | |

Place the cleaned fish in a buttered baking dish. Season, add dabs of butter, and pour the cream over. Bake uncovered in a moderate oven (350° F.) about 20 minutes, or until the cream sauce is bubbling and the fish cooked. Serve in the dish in which baked. Serves 4.

## TURBOT WITH WHITE SAUCE TURBOT À LA SAUCE BLANCHE

| | |
|---|---|
| 2- *to* 3-*lb. halibut or turbot* | *Cream Sauce or* |
| 1 *qt. Court Bouillon* | *Green Sauce* |

Place the cleaned fish in a pan. Add the bouillon and boil gently until the fish is tender, about 2 minutes per pound. 'When a knitting needle enters the fish easily the fish is ready.'

Use some of the bouillon from the pan as the liquid in making the sauce. Serves 4 or more.

## EEL WITH TARTARE SAUCE ANGUILLE À LA TARTARE

| | |
|---|---|
| 2 *lb. eel* | 1 *sprig thyme* |
| 2 *qts. Court Bouillon* | *bay leaf* |
| 1 *tbs. butter* | 1 *tsp. salt* |
| 2 *tbs. flour* | ½ *tsp. pepper* |
| ½ *cup red wine* | 1 *cup water* |
| 1 *onion, sliced* | |

Ask the fishmonger for 2 pounds of eel cut from a large eel so the bones are less numerous. Add to the bouillon in a 3-quart or larger saucepan. Boil 12 minutes, or until tender. Remove from the bouillon and let cool slightly, then remove skin and bones carefully without breaking the flesh.

Melt the butter in a 1-quart saucepan and stir the flour smoothly into it. Add the wine, onion, herbs, and seasonings. Stir smoothly, gradually adding the water. When boiling and smooth, add the fish. Boil until completely cooked. Heat through and serve. Serves 4 or 5.

## CRAB MAYONNAISE TOURTEAU À LA MAYONNAISE

| | |
|---|---|
| 3 *large live hard-shell crabs* | 1 *tbs. vinegar* |
| 2 *qts. boiling water* | *mayonnaise* |
| 2 *tsp. salt* | 1 *tsp. prepared mustard* |
| ½ *tsp. pepper* | 2 *tbs. chopped parsley* |
| 1 *sprig thyme* | 1 *tbs. chopped hard-boiled egg* |
| *bay leaf* | |

Plunge the cleaned crabs into a pan of boiling salted water (1 teaspoon salt to 1 quart water) with seasonings, herbs, and vinegar added. Boil 10 minutes. Drain; cover with cold water to cool. Pull off the claws and remove the 'apron'. Separate the shells, keeping the upper one whole. Remove the gills, intestines, and sand bag (the latter at left under the head). Break the body in half and remove the meat. Crack larger claws and pull out meat with a lobster pick. Scrape the soft white meat from the shell and add to the rest. The fat is dark green or black and looks inedible but is good and should be kept.

Mix the mayonnaise and mustard; combine with crab meat and chill. To serve, scrub 2 of the shells, rinse and dry them. Heap with the crab mixture. Sprinkle thickly with parsley and egg. Serves 2.

# Fish

## CRAB THERMIDOR TOURTEAU THERMIDOR

1 tbs. butter
1 tbs. chopped shallots
½ cup dry white wine
¾ cup White Sauce
½ cup heavy cream

½ tsp. dried parsley
crab meat from 5 or 6 crabs
4 tbs. grated cheese
4 crab shells

In a 1½-quart saucepan heat the butter and sauté the shallots. When lightly cooked, add the wine and let it boil down to half its measure. Stir this into the White Sauce; add the cream, parsley, and crab meat. Add half the cheese; mix. Fill the scrubbed and dry crab shells. Sprinkle the rest of the cheese on top. Brown in a moderate oven (350° F.) 20 minutes. Serves 4.

## LOBSTER À L'AMÉRICAINE HOMARD À L'AMÉRICAINE

1 medium-sized live lobster
boiling salted water
2 tbs. oil
1 onion, sliced
½ cup hot water
2 tbs. tomato purèe or paste
1 tsp. salt
¼ tsp. pepper

⅛ tsp. cayenne
1 tsp. curry powder
¼ tsp. saffron
sprig of thyme
bay leaf
1 lemon, sliced
4 to 8 toast triangles or bread
    fried in butter

Plunge the live lobster into briskly boiling salted water (1 teaspoon salt to 1 quart water). Boil until the shell is bright red; Drain. Cut in sections without removing shell. Brown the sections, except the head, in the oil, along with the onion, in a 1-quart saucepan. Add the water, tomato purée or paste, seasonings, and herbs. Mince the inside of the lobster head and add to the sauce in the pan. Cover and cook 20 minutes. Serve on the hot fried bread or toast with a garnish of thin lemon slices. Serves 2 to 4.

# GRILLED LOBSTER, SAUCE AMÉRICAINE HOMARDS
## GRILLÉS À LA SAUCE AMÉRICAINE

| | |
|---|---|
| 2 to 4 *small lobsters* | 1 or 2 *shallots, chopped* |
| 1 *cup bread crumbs* | ½ *tsp. salt* |
| ¼ *cup cooked rice* | ¼ *tsp. pepper* |
| ¼ *cup minced parsley* | 2 *tbs. butter* |

Choose small lobsters. Plunge into boiling water and boil for five minutes. Remove and cut into two parts longitudinally. Fill the empty spaces with a mixture made from bread crumbs, boiled rice cooked in bouillon, a little parsley and some chopped shallots, the whole having been passed through a sieve. Sprinkle with bread crumbs, salt and pepper and place pieces of butter on top. Grill.

## SAUCE AMÉRICAINE

| | |
|---|---|
| 5 or 6 *crabs* | 2 *tbs. tomato juice* |
| 2 *tbs. oil* | *salt, pepper, cayenne* |
| 1 *sliced onion* | 1 *tsp. curry* |
| 1 *cup water* | 1 *pinch saffron* |

Brown the crabs in the oil with a sliced onion. Add the water, tomato juice, salt, pepper, curry and saffron. Boil for 20 minutes.

Take out the crabs, pass through a mincer, return to the saucepan and heat.

# LOBSTER À LA MORLAISE HOMARD À LA MORLAISE

| | |
|---|---|
| 1 *small- or medium-sized live lobster* | 2 *shallots, chopped* |
| *boiling salted water* | 1 *tbs. chopped parsley* |
| 2 *tbs. oil* | 1 or 2 *tarragon leaves* |
| ¼ *cup cognac* | ⅛ *tsp. cayenne* |
| 1 *cup dry white wine* | ½ *tsp. salt* |
| 1 *tbs. tomato paste or purèe* | 1 *tbs. butter* |
| | 1 *tbs. heavy cream* |

Take a live lobster and kill by plunging into boiling water. Cut into sections without removing shell.

Put about two tablespoonfuls of olive oil in a saucepan and, when very hot, add the sections of lobster, excluding the head, a liqueur-glassful of brandy, a cupful of dry white wine, a tablespoonful or more of concentrated tomato purée to produce a thick sauce, two chopped shallots, a little parsley, some tarragon leaves, a little cayenne pepper and salt. Boil for 20 minutes.

Chop the inside of the lobster head and heat for some minutes with a little butter. Add to the first mixture, together with a tablespoonful of thick cream. Reheat without boiling. Serves 2 to 4.

## CRAYFISH BELLE-VUE LANGOUSTE EN BELLE-VUE

| | |
|---|---|
| 1 *large live crayfish or small lobster* | 4 *hard-boiled eggs* |
| 1 *qt. Court Bouillon* | *mayonnaise* |
| *crisp lettuce* | ½ *cup Vegetable Salad* |

Plunge cleaned lobster or crayfish into boiling bouillon and boil 10 to 15 minutes according to size. The shell must be bright red. Drain. Cut the bony menbrane on the inside of the tail shell with scissors, then spread the tail slightly and pull out the flesh in a single piece. Open this in the crease in the underside and very carefully remove and discard the intestinal vein which runs the entire length.

If the coral and green substances remain in the shell, shake them out and set aside for garnish. Pull off the woolly gills from the underside. Cut the lobster meat and heap back into the shell pieces. (The smaller crayfish is opened the same way.) Arrange the lobster or crayfish on lettuce. Garnish with any coral or green substance from the meat.

Cut the eggs in halves; grate the yolks over the lobster; fill the whites with Vegetable Salad mixed with mayonnaise. Spoon mayonnaise on the lobster and serve.

## MUSSELS MOULES

| | |
|---|---|
| *fresh mussels* | 2 *small onions, chopped* |
| 4 *tbs. butter* | 3 *tbs. flour* |

Wash and scrub the mussel shells, discarding any open ones. Wash again thoroughly in several cold waters. Melt the butter in a heavy frying pan; stir the onions in and add the mussels. Sprinkle with flour. Cover and shake the pan over the heat 5 minutes. Stir the mussels and continue to cook until all the shells open. Serve in a soup plate with the liquid from the pan poured over. Serves 4.

## MUSSELS IN SCALLOP SHELLS coquilles de moules

*fresh mussels prepared as in the
   preceding recipe*
*2 tbs. butter*
*2 tbs. flour*
*½ cup milk*

*½ cup mussel liquor*
*8 small cooked or canned shrimps*
*butter for shells*
*½ cup bread crumbs*
*2 tbs. butter*

Remove the cooked mussels from the shells. Melt the butter in a saucepan; stir the flour smoothly in and gradually add the milk and mussel liquor. When the sauce is smooth and thickened, add the mussels and shrimps.

Rub 6 scallop shells or dishes lightly with butter. Fill with mixture, sprinkle with bread crumbs, and dot with butter. Bake in a moderate oven (350° F.) until browned, about 20 minutes. Serves 6.

## PILAFF—MUSSELS WITH RICE moules au riz

*cooked mussels*
*1 onion, chopped*
*2 tbs. butter*
*1 cup rice*

*¼ tsp. pepper*
*2 tomatoes, peeled*
*mussel liquor*
*hot water*

Remove the cooked mussels from the shells. Sauté the onion in the butter in a 1-quart or larger saucepan. Stir the rice into the butter. Add the pepper, tomatoes, mussel liquor, and as much hot water as needed to cover the rice. Cover and boil 20 minutes, or until the rice is tender. Add the mussels. Serve hot with Curry Sauce. Serves 4 to 6.

## SCALLOPS WITH GRATED CHEESE coquilles saint
### jacques gratinées

*1 pt. shelled fresh scallops*
*water to cover*
*bay leaf*
*thyme*
*1 tsp. salt*
*¼ tsp. pepper*
*1 tbs. butter*

*2 tbs. flour*
*1 cup scallop liquor*
*2 tbs. grated Gruyère cheese*
*½ cup heavy cream*
*½ cup bread crumbs*
*2 oz. grated cheese*

Place the scallops in a 1-quart saucepan and cover with water. Add the herbs and seasonings and boil gently until the scallops begin to shrivel, about 8 minutes. Remove from liquid (save the liquid).

Melt the butter. Blend the flour smoothly into it and gradually add 1 cup of liquid in which the scallops cooked. Stir until thickened. Stir in the 2 tablespoons of cheese, stirring all smoothly. When the sauce becomes thick, add a cupful of thick cream. Mix with scallops and fill 4 to 8 buttered scallop shells. Sprinkle top with crumbs and cheese. Brown in a moderate oven (350° F.) 15 minutes, or until bubbly. Serves 4 to 8.

NOTE: Mashed potatoes may be used to make a border around the edge of any creamed dish browned in a scallop shell. This border keeps the sauce from bubbling out.

## SCALLOPS WITH PORT WINE COQUILLES SAINT JACQUES AU PORTO

Prepare scallops as in the preceding recipe. Make the thick sauce, adding ¾ cup port wine instead of cheese, then add the cream. Mix with the scallops. Pour into a baked patty shell or small patty shells. Serves 4 or more.

## SHRIMPS IN SCALLOP SHELLS COQUILLES DE CREVETTES

| | |
|---|---|
| 2 *cups cleaned boiled shrimps* | ½ *tsp. salt* |
| 1½ *tbs. butter* | ¼ *tsp. pepper* |
| 3 *tbs. flour* | *red food colouring* |
| 1 *cup dry white wine* | ½ *cup bread crumbs* |
| ½ *cup water* | |

Melt the butter in a 1-quart saucepan. Stir the flour smoothly into it, then slowly add the wine and water, stirring until thickened. Season with salt and pepper and add 1 or 2 drops of red food colouring. Mix with the shrimps. Pour into 6 or more scallop shells. Sprinkle with crumbs and brown in a moderate oven (350° F.) 15 minutes or longer. Serves 4 to 6.

# GAME AND POULTRY

Any French housewife could tell English cooks that game need not be strange or difficult to cook. Moreover, such dishes as the following make delicious and quite economical meals.

The marinade is important.

## Game

### PICKLING MIXTURE FOR GAME MARINADE

Before roasting furred game—i.e. deer, hare, or rabbit—place the dressed and cleaned animal for 4 days in the following mixture:

| | |
|---|---|
| 1 *cup red wine* | 1 *small carrot, sliced* |
| ¼ *cup cognac (optional)* | 1 *onion, sliced* |
| 3 *bay leaves* | ½ *tsp. salt* |
| 2 *small sprigs thyme* | ¼ *tsp. pepper* |

The quantities should be increased if the size of the game requires it. Mix and pour over the meat in a glass, enamel pan or an earthenware baking dish. Cover and place in the refrigerator. Turn the meat every day and make sure all parts are moistened. The liquid should be drained off and made into a sauce as directed below.

## MARINADE SAUCE

| | |
|---|---|
| 1 *tbs. butter* | 1 *cup juice from roasting pan* |
| 2 *tbs. flour* | ½ *cup vinegar* |
| 1 *cup Marinade* | 3 *shallots, sliced* |

Heat the butter and stir until browned. Slowly stir the flour in and cook until browned; add the Marinade and pan juice, stirring slowly. Cook until thickened.

Heat the vinegar and shallots in an enamel pan until the liquid is cooked down to 1 tablespoonful. Add to gravy. Mix and serve. Enough for 3 or 4 servings of game.

## STUFFED PHEASANT FAISAN FARCI

Follow directions for Roast Partridge, but before roasting, stuff the cleaned and drawn birds with this stuffing:

| | |
|---|---|
| 1 *cup sausage meat* | ½ *tsp. salt* |
| 1 *cup liver pâté or minced cooked calf's liver* | ¼ *tsp. pepper* |

Mix well; add additional seasoning. Stuff the birds and skewer or sew up. Each bird serves 4 or more.

## ROAST PHEASANT FAISAN RÔTI

Follow directions for Roast Partridge.

## ROAST PARTRIDGE PERDREAUX RÔTIS

| | |
|---|---|
| 1 *or 2 large partridges, dressed and cleaned* | ½ *tsp. pepper* |
| | *hot water* |
| 2 *to 4 thin slices fat pork* | 2 *slices bread sautéed in* |
| 1½ *tsp. salt* | 1 *tbs. butter* |
| | 1 *lemon, sliced* |

Wipe the dressed and cleaned bird with a clean cloth. Wrap with 1 or 2 slices of pork and skewer or tie the pork in place. Place in a roasting pan; season. Roast in a moderate oven (350° F.) 30 minutes.

When the birds begin to brown, add about 1 tablespoon hot water to the pan for each bird. Baste until completely roasted. A few minutes before the bird is done, place a slice of bread fried in butter under each bird. Remove skewers or string and serve on toast on a hot platter with thin slices of lemon. Potato chips and a salad are also served. A large partridge serves 2 persons.

## PARTRIDGE WITH CABBAGE PERDRIX AU CHOU

| | |
|---|---|
| 2 *partridges, dressed and cleaned* | 1 *tsp. salt* |
| 1 *tbs. butter* | ½ *tsp. pepper* |
| 1 *onion, sliced* | 1 *head cabbage* |
| 1 *or 2 slices bacon, chopped* | *boiling water* |
| | 4 *slices bread fried in butter* |

Older birds, not suitable for broiling or roasting, are prepared this way. Brown in the butter in a large saucepan. Add the onion and bacon, cooking until the birds are browned. Season with salt and pepper.

Wash the cabbage carefully. Cut in quarters or smaller pieces, cover with a little boiling water, and boil 5 minutes. Drain. Add to pan containing the birds; add 1 cup hot water and additional seasoning for the cabbage. Cover and simmer 1 hour. The liquid should be boiled down. Place the 4 slices of bread on a warmed platter with a half partridge on each; garnish with the cabbage and serve hot. Serves 4.

## QUAIL ON TOAST I CAILLES SUR CANAPÉ

| | |
|---|---|
| 4 *quail, plucked, singed, cleaned,* | 3 *tbs. butter* |
| *and drawn* | 2 *slices bacon, chopped* |
| 1½ *tsp. salt* | 4 *slices bread fried in butter* |
| ½ *tsp. pepper* | |

Season the quail. Brown gently in the hot butter and bacon. Cook slowly until tender and browned. Serve each on a slice of fried bread. Serves 4.

# Game

## QUAIL ON TOAST II CAILLES SUR CANAPÉ

4 quail baked or fried in butter
4 cups hot mashed potatoes
½ cup heavy cream
1 egg yolk
4 slices bread fried in butter

½ tbs. flour
½ cup hot water
¼ cup cognac
1 or 2 tbs. heavy cream

Cook the quail as described in preceding recipe, or roast. Beat mashed potatoes into the cream and beaten yolk. Pile on a warmed serving dish. Cut the bread slices in halves or quarters and arrange around potatoes. Place the hot quail on toast (whole or in halves).

Make a sauce in the pan where the quail were cooked by stirring in the flour. When it is smooth and brown, add the hot water, stir, and let boil until slightly thickened, stirring constantly. Add the cognac. Just before serving add a little heavy cream. Serves 4 or 8.


## ROAST HARE OR RABBIT RÂBLE DE LIÈVRE OU DE LAPIN

hindquarters of a hare
Marinade
1 slice fat pork

Marinade Sauce
Chestnut Purée

Cut the hindquarters of a dressed, cleaned, and drawn hare in serving pieces. Place in a crock with Marinade. Let stand, covered, in the refrigerator 2 days. Drain, saving the liquid.

Wrap meat with the fat pork and place in a roasting pan in a moderate oven (325° F.). Let brown and cook through, ¾ to 1 hour. Baste a few times with a little of the Marinade. Serve with Marinade Sauce and hot Chestnut Purée. Serves 2 to 4.

*Young rabbit* is prepared the same way. Use 2 hindquarters of rabbits cut in serving pieces. Lay strips of fat pork over them in the roasting pan. Serves 4.

# Game

## STEWED RABBIT RAGOÛT DE LAPIN

| | |
|---|---|
| 1 *young rabbit, dressed, cleaned,* | ½ *tsp. pepper* |
| *drawn, and cut in pieces* | 1 *tbs. flour* |
| 1 *tbs. butter* | 1 *cup hot water* |
| 1 *onion, sliced* | 4 to 8 *small peeled potatoes* |
| 1 *tsp. salt* | |

Brown rabbit in butter with onion and seasonings. Sprinkle with flour and cook a few minutes. Add the water and potatoes; cover and cook slowly 1½ hours. Serves 4 to 8.

## RABBIT WITH PRUNES LAPIN AUX PRUNEAUX

Add 15 to 20 softened prunes to Jugged Rabbit when the liquid in the saucepan begins to boil.

## JUGGED HARE OR RABBIT CIVET DE LIÈVRE OU DE LAPIN

| | |
|---|---|
| 1 *hare, dressed, cleaned, and cut at* | 1 *cup red wine* |
| *joints in serving pieces* | 1 *cup water* |
| 1 *onion, sliced* | *sprig thyme* |
| 1 *tbs. butter* | *bay leaf* |
| 2 *slices bacon, chopped* | 1 *tsp. salt* |
| 3 *tbs. flour* | ½ *tsp. pepper* |

Brown the meat with onion in the butter and bacon. When it is browned, sprinkle with flour and continue to cook until flour is browned. Add the wine, water, herbs, and seasonings. Cover and simmer about 2 hours, when the pan liquid should be as thick as cream. Serve at once, or for better flavour reheat just before serving. Steamed or boiled potatoes are served with it. Serves 8.

*Young rabbit* in this recipe is cooked with 2 or 3 potatoes per person added to the pan for the last hour of cooking.

# Game

## CREAMED RABBIT LAPIN À LA CRÈME

| | |
|---|---|
| 1 *young rabbit, skinned, cleaned, and cut in pieces* | 1 *tsp. salt* |
| | ½ *tsp. pepper* |
| 2 *tbs. butter* | 1 *cup heavy cream* |

Brown slowly in butter. Season with salt and pepper. Cover and cook slowly 1 hour. Add a very little hot water to the pan if necessary to prevent burning. Pour the cream in just before serving. Serves 4 or more.

## ROAST VENISON CHEVREUIL RÔTI

*leg, haunch, or saddle of venison*   *flour*
*Marinade*   *Marinade Sauce*
8 *slices fat pork or bacon*

Let stand in Marinade 2 days in an enamel saucepan. Keep in the refrigerator. Drain. Save the liquid.

Place the meat in a roasting pan; lay the pork or bacon over the roast. Put in a hot oven (450° F.) 20 minutes. Reduce heat to moderate (325° F.) and continue roasting; allow 10 to 15 minutes per pound. Venison should be served rare. Baste every 15 minutes with the juices in the pan and some of the Marinade. Turn the roast when it is half done and continue roasting. Serve with Marinade Sauce. A haunch or leg will yield 10 or more servings; a saddle, 8 or more.

## ROAST WOODCOCK OR SNIPE BÉCASSES, BÉCASSINES RÔTIES

Woodcock and snipe, according to French tradition, are eaten undrawn. The plucked, dressed birds have only the lower intestines removed; the taste is thereby improved and no misgivings need be felt as both birds are very clean feeders.

After plucking, singeing, and cleaning as described, roast like pheasant. Garnish with thin slices of lemon and serve on thin slices of toast with salad. One breast makes 2 servings, one breastline makes 1 serving.

## WOODCOCK SALMIS SALMIS DE BÉCASSE

2 *freshly roasted woodcock*  
1 *tbs. butter*  
2 *shallots, sliced*  
1 *bay leaf*  
½ *tsp. fresh thyme*  
1 *tbs. flour*  
½ *cup hot water*  
½ *cup red wine*

*salt and pepper*  
¼ *cup cognac*  
½ *lemon, juice only*  
1 *tsp. olive oil*  
8 *strips or triangles of bread fried in butter*  
1 *lemon, sliced thin*

Roast the woodcock on toast as described, basting well. When roasted, remove wings, legs, and breast meat. From the remaining carcass remove the breast bone, mincing or grinding together the rest of the bones, all giblets, and the toast.

Brown the butter in a saucepan with the shallots, bay leaf, and thyme; stir in the flour smoothly until browned. Add the gravy from the roasting pan, stirring slowly to mix smoothly. Add the hot water, mix, and stir. Add the wine, a little salt and pepper, and the minced bones and toast. Mix well. Add the cognac and the parts of the birds previously put aside. Cook gently 20 minutes.

Just before serving, add the lemon juice and olive oil and remove the shallots, bay leaf, and thyme. Serve garnished with thin slices of lemon and small pieces of bread fried in butter. This dish should be eaten with steamed potatoes and a green salad. Serves 4.

# *Poultry*

## CHICKEN WITH PORT WINE POULET AU PORTO

4 *oz. butter*  
1 *young chicken (about 2 lb.), dressed, cleaned, and cut in pieces*  
½ *tsp. pepper*  
1 *tsp. salt*

½ *cup port wine*  
1 *cup minced canned or cooked mushrooms*  
1 *tbs. flour*  
2 *tbs. heavy cream*

Melt the butter; brown the chicken, cut into suitable portions. Cover and cook slowly 30 minutes. Season and add the wine. Cover again and continue to cook slowly 30 minutes. Add the mushrooms and mix. Cook 15 minutes.

Remove the chicken and mushrooms to a warmed serving dish. Stir the flour into the pan juices. Mix and cook 2 minutes. Gradually add the cream, stirring until it boils. Pour over the chicken and serve. Serves 4.

## BOILED CHICKEN WITH RICE POULE AU RIZ

| | |
|---|---|
| 1 *boiling fowl, dressed and cleaned* | 1 *tsp. salt* |
| 2 *carrots sliced* | ½ *tsp. pepper* |
| 2 *turnips, sliced* | 6 *tsp. rice* |
| 2 *leeks, chopped* | 1 *egg yolk* |
| *boiling water to cover* | *Cream Sauce* |

Place the cleaned fowl breast up on a rack in a large saucepan. Add the vegetables and just barely enough water to cover. Add salt (1 teaspoon per quart of water) and a little pepper. Cover and boil slowly 20 to 30 minutes per pound. Skim off the scum. When tender, remove the bird from the liquid. Cover the bird and keep it warm.

Wash the rice. Cover with cold water, bring to boil, and boil 1 minute. Drain and replace in the saucepan. Cover with the liquid in which the chicken was cooked. Boil 20 minutes, adding more liquid as it is absorbed by the rice. When ready to serve, place the yolk of an egg in the serving dish and stir the rice slowly into it. Place the fowl on this; serve with Cream Sauce. Serves 6 to 8.

NOTE: Any remaining liquid may be used in soup or sauce.

## CHICKEN IN CASSEROLE POULET EN COCOTTE

| | |
|---|---|
| 1 *young chicken, cleaned, dressed,* | 12 *small onions* |
| *and drawn* | 1 *tsp. salt* |
| 1 *tbs. butter* | ½ *tsp. pepper* |

Brown the bird in the butter in a saucepan with the onions. Add the seasonings. When the chicken is golden colour all over, place in a deep earthenware casserole with the onions and pan juices. Cover and cook in a moderate oven (325° F.) 50 minutes to 1 hour. Serve in the dish in which it cooked. Boiled or steamed potatoes sliced and sautéed in butter should be eaten with the chicken. Serves 6 to 8.

## CHICKEN PIE COQ EN PÂTE

| | |
|---|---|
| 1 *young chicken, dressed, cleaned,* | 1 *tsp. salt* |
|    *cut in pieces* | ½ *tsp. pepper* |
| 3 *tbs. butter* | *rich pie pastry* |
| ¾ *cup chopped cooked ham* | 1 *egg, beaten* |
| 3 *tbs. water or bouillon* | |

Butter a deep pie dish or casserole and arrange the pieces in it. Add dabs of butter and scatter the ham throughout. Add the hot water or bouillon, season, and cover with pastry. Crimp the edge of the pastry to the baking dish. Gash the pastry in a few places or pierce with a fork. Brush with the beaten egg. Bake in a slow oven (300° F.) about 1½ hours. Serves 6 or more.

## ROAST CHICKEN POULET RÔTI

| | |
|---|---|
| 1 *roasting chicken* | ½ *tbs. butter, or* |
| 2 *tbs. salt* | 1 *slice fat pork* |
| ½ *tsp. pepper* | ¼ *cup water* |

Season with salt and pepper. Place in a roasting pan. Spread the butter on the breast or lay the pork over it. Pour a little water in the pan if necessary. Roast in a moderate oven (325° F.) 1½ hours (for 4- to 5-pound fowl). Baste every 15 or 20 minutes with the pan juices. A bird is roasted when, if tipped toward the tail end, the juices run out perfectly clear. Pierce the flesh in several places with a skewer to be sure the bird is perfectly cooked.

Serve hot or cold with potato chips or mashed potatoes or potato croquettes and a green salad. Serves 6 or more.

## STUFFED CHICKEN POULET FARCI

| | |
|---|---|
| 1 roasting chicken, dressed, cleaned, and drawn | 2 slices bread soaked in milk |
| | 6 slices bacon, cooked and chopped |
| 1 chicken liver, chopped | 2 egg yolks, beaten |
| 1 tbs. chopped parsley | 1 tsp. salt |
| 2 shallots, chopped | ½ tsp. pepper |
| 1 tbs. butter | 1 slice fat pork |

Mince the liver, parsley, shallots, butter, bread (milk squeezed out), and bacon. Add the yolks and mix well. Season and stuff into the bird. Sew up the opening or use skewers. Lay the slice of fat over the breast and tie it in place with string. (Remove string before serving.)

Place the chicken breast up in a roasting pan. Roast in a moderate oven (325° F.) 20 minutes per pound, or about 1 hour for a 4-pound chicken. Baste frequently, pour about 2 tablespoons of hot water if necessary. Serve hot or cold with mashed potatoes. Serves 6 or more.

*Variation.* Another good stuffing may be made with ½ cup *pâté de foie gras*, ½ cup sausage meat, 1 truffle, chopped, the bread, and seasonings.

## BRAISED CHICKEN POULET SAUTÉ

| | |
|---|---|
| 1 young fowl cut in pieces | ½ cup white wine |
| 1½ tsp. salt | 1 tomato, sliced |
| ½ tsp. pepper | 1 sliver garlic, chopped |
| 1½ tbs; butter | 1 tbs. chopped parsley |
| 2 onions, chopped | |

Sprinkle with salt and pepper. Brown in butter with onions. When the meat is golden, add the wine and tomato. Cover and cook slowly about 1 hour for young chicken, 2 hours for older fowl. Add a little hot water if necessary halfway through the cooking. Before serving sprinkle with garlic and parsley. Serves 6 or more.

# *Poultry*

## CHICKEN WITH WHITE SAUCE POULET AU BLANC

| | |
|---|---|
| 1 *young chicken dressed, cleaned* | ½ *tsp. pepper* |
| 2 *cups thin White Sauce* | 1 *egg yolk* |
| 1 *onion, quartered* | 1 *lemon, sliced thin* |
| 1 *sprig thyme* | 2 *or 3 slices bread fried in* |
| 1 *bay leaf* | *butter* |
| 1 *tsp. salt* | |

Tie the chicken wings and legs with thin string.

Prepare a thin white sauce with one tablespoonful of butter, 2 tablespoonfuls of flour and half a cup of warm water added gradually. When well mixed add a further cup of warm water. Now put in the onion, thyme, bay leaf, salt and pepper. Place the chicken in this sauce, simmer for ¾ of an hour to 1 hour, according to the size of the fowl.

Serve on a hot dish with the sauce in which cooked, enriched by adding the yolk of an egg after removal from fire. Garnish with thin slices of lemon and small squares of toast fried in butter. Serve with steamed potatoes.

## CHICKEN WITH WHITE WINE POULET CHASSEUR

| | |
|---|---|
| 1 *fowl, dressed, cleaned, and drawn* | ½ *cup white wine* |
| 1 *tbs. butter* | ½ *cup hot water* |
| 1 *onion, sliced* | 3 *or 4 medium tomatoes, sliced* |
| ½ *tsp. pepper* | 1 *cup chopped canned or cooked* |
| 1 *tsp. salt* | *mushrooms* |
| 2 *tbs. flour* | 3 *or 4 slices bread fried in butter* |

Brown in a large saucepan with the butter, onion, and seasonings. When the chicken is golden all over, sprinkle with flour and turn so the flour is absorbed in the gravy. Add the wine, hot water, tomatoes, and mushrooms. Cover and cook slowly 45 minutes to

2 hours, depending on the age of the fowl. When it is tender, serve with the pan gravy. Garnish with small squares of fried bread. Mashed potatoes should be served with it. Serves 6 or more.

## CHICKEN IN ASPIC POULET EN GELÉE

1 tbs. butter
1 pork rind
2 or 3 carrots, sliced
2 or 3 onions, sliced
1 young fowl, dressed, cleaned, and drawn
1 slice fat pork
½ calf's foot
1 tsp. salt
½ tsp. pepper
4 or 5 cups bouillon or

2 cups water and
2½ cups white wine }
2 tbs. butter
3 tbs. flour
¼ cup chopped canned or cooked mushrooms
1 cup heavy cream
2 tbs. plain gelatine
1 cup cold water
¾ cup hot water
sliced truffles

Rub the bottom of a 3-quart saucepan with butter, place the rind and sliced vegetables in it. Cover the breast of the chicken with the pork, tying it in place, and put in the saucepan. Add the calf's foot, seasoning, and bouillon or mixed wine and water to cover. Cover and boil gently 55 minutes Remove the chicken and let it cool. Save the liquid.

Melt the butter in a saucepan; stir the flour in and when browned add the mushrooms. Slowly stir in enough liquid from the saucepan to make a thick creamy sauce. Add the cream and dissolved gelatine; stir. Pour over the chicken in a deep serving dish. Let cool and chill. Garnish with sliced truffles. Serves 6 or more.

NOTE: To dissolve the gelatine, stir it into 1 cup cold water and let stand until softened. Then dissolve it in the hot water.

## DUCK SALMIS SALMIS DE CANARD

| | |
|---|---|
| 1 *roast duck* | ½ *tsp. pepper* |
| 3 *or 4 slices of toast on which duck roasted* | 1 *sprig thyme* |
| | 1 *bay leaf* |
| 1 *tbs. butter* | ¼ *cup cognac* |
| 2 *shallots, sliced* | ½ *lemon, juice only* |
| 1 *tbs. flour* | 1 *tsp. olive oil* |
| 1 *cup sauce from roasting pan* | 2 *slices bread* |
| ½ *cup hot water* | 1 *tbs. butter* |
| ½ *cup red wine* | 1 *lemon* |
| 1 *tsp. Salt* | |

Remove the wings, legs, and breast meat from the roasted bird. Remove the breast bone; mince and grind the rest of the bones with the giblets and the toast on which the duck was roasted. Cook 20 minutes and strain.

Brown the butter; add the shallots and flour, stirring well until all is browned. Gently stir in the gravy from the roasting pan, the hot water, red wine, seasonings, herbs, and strained bone mixture. Add the cognac, wings, legs, and breast meat. Cook gently about 20 minutes. Before serving, add the lemon juice and olive oil. Stir. Remove the shallots, thyme, and bay leaf.

Serve garnished with small fancy-shaped pieces of bread sautéed in butter, and slices of lemon. Serve with hot boiled potatoes and a green salad. Serves 4 to 6.

## DUCK WITH TURNIPS CANARD AUX NAVETS

Serve roast duck with a garnish of mashed turnips.

## DUCK WITH ONIONS CANARD AUX OIGNONS

Prepare like Duck with Olives, substituting 4 or 6 medium-sized onions for the olives. Or prepare the duck without olives or onions and serve garnished with mashed cooked onions.

## DUCK WITH OLIVES CANARD AUX OLIVES

1 *young duck*
1 *tbs. butter*
2 *onions, sliced*
1 *tsp. salt*

½ *tsp. pepper*
1 *cup hot water*
24 *olives, stones removed*

Brown the duck in a large casserole in the butter. Add the onions, seasonings, and water. Cover. Cook gently 1 hour. Add the olives, and continue to cook until the duck is tender, about 1½ hours in all, depending on the age of the bird. Serves 6 or more.

## DUCK WITH GREEN PEAS CANARD AUX PETITS POIS

1 *young duck*
1 *tbs. butter*
1 *tsp. salt*
½ *tsp. pepper*

2 *tbs. water, orange juice or hot*
*water and lemon juice*
2 *or 3 cups green peas*
4 *or 8 small new potatoes*

Place the prepared bird in a roasting pan with a piece of butter; season with salt and pepper. Add a little water to the pan. Roast in a moderate oven (325° F.) 12 to 15 minutes per pound. Baste every 20 minutes with hot water. When done and golden brown, serve with green peas and new potatoes cooked together. Serves 6 or more.

## DUCKLING ROUENNAIS CANETON ROUENNAIS

1 *duckling*
3 *tbs. butter*
1 *tsp. salt*
¼ *tsp. pepper*

2 *shallots, chopped*
½ *cup red wine*
½ *cup cognac*

Place the prepared bird in a roasting pan, spread the breast with 1 tablespoon butter, and roast in a hot oven (425° F.) 30 minutes. Remove the legs and grill them. Cut off all the meat from the carcass.

Spread 2 tablespoons butter in a baking dish. Add salt, pepper, and shallots. Place the duck legs and meat on this seasoning.

Grind the duck carcass to a powder (omit the breastbone). Mix with the wine and brandy. Ignite and pour over the dish while burning. Set dish in hot oven and bake 15 minutes. Serves 6.


## DUCK WITH ORANGE CANARD À L'ORANGE

| | |
|---|---|
| 1 *young duck* | $\frac{1}{4}$ *tsp. pepper* |
| 4 *to* 6 *oranges, peeled and sliced* | *butter* |
| 2 *oranges, juice and peel* | $\frac{1}{4}$ *cup Italian vermouth* |
| 1 *tsp. salt* | 2 *oranges, quartered* |

Remove seeds from the sliced oranges and fill the inside of the prepared duck as full as possible. Use small skewers or sew the vent. (Remove skewers or string before serving.) Place in a roasting pan or casserole with the juice and grated peel of 2 oranges. Season and butter the duck breast. Roast uncovered in a moderate oven (325 F.), 12 to 15 minutes per pound, or a little longer for older bird. About 5 minutes before serving add the vermouth to the pan gravy, stir, and heat. Remove the duck to a serving dish and garnish with orange sections. Serve the gravy separately. Serves 6 or more.


## GOOSE GIBLETS, STEWED RAGOÛT D'OIE

| | |
|---|---|
| *goose giblets* | 6 *medium-sized potatoes* |
| 1 *tbs. butter* | 4 *turnips* |
| 4 *small onions, sliced* | 1 *tsp. salt* |
| 2 *cups hot water* | $\frac{1}{2}$ *tsp. pepper* |

Brown the giblets a little in butter and onions in a 2-quart saucepan. Add hot water. Begin to cook slowly.

Wash and peel the potatoes and leave whole. Add to the saucepan. Wash, peel, and slice the turnips. Add with seasonings. Cover and simmer 1 to 2 hours. The liquid should cook down to the thickness of a ragoût. Serves 4.

## ROAST GOOSE RÔTI D'OIE

4- to 6- lb. young goose
salt and pepper
hot water
orange juice
2 cups stuffing (such as chopped
steamed or boiled chestnuts, sliced

orange; or orange and prunes
  mixed; or chopped onion)
pastry cases (optional)
mashed potatoes or turnips
jelly or apple sauce, etc.

Truss like duck, using a skewer through the lower part of the bird. Tie the legs in place, 1 inch apart; run the string lengthwise under the back, bring around, and tie on the skewers. A goose is usually stuffed with chestnuts. The opening can be sewn or fastened with small skewers or poultry pins. Allow 2 cups stuffing for a 4-pound goose.

Place the bird on a rack in the roasting pan in a moderate oven (350° F.) and roast 18 to 25 minutes per pound, according to the age of the bird. (An older bird should be washed in strong soda water, drained, covered with cold water, and boiled 1 hour before roasting.) Baste as the bird cooks, using hot water and orange juice every 20 minutes. As a rule, fat need not be rubbed on a goose, and other fats such as bacon strips need not be used because this bird's flesh is well larded with its own fat.

To serve, place the hot goose on a warmed dish. Garnish with pastry shells filled with mashed potatoes and decorated with slices of truffles and crisp lettuce. Or serve turnips or boiled or puréed chestnuts and a tart jelly, apple sauce, or apple in some form. Serves 6 to 8.

## GUINEA FOWL WITH GRAPES PINTADE AUX RAISINS

1 guinea fowl, dressed, cleaned,
  and drawn
1 slice fat pork
1 tbs. butter
1 tsp. salt
½ tsp. pepper
hot water

1 cup white wine
1 cup Madeira wine
1¼ cups cognac
4 or 6 slices bread fried in butter
cooked guinea fowl liver
2 cups seedless white grapes

Rinse the cleaned bird; wipe dry. Place the pork over the breast and tie it in place with clean string. (Remove string before serving.) Brown the fowl in the butter; season; turn several times until golden all over. Add a little hot water to the pan. Cover and let cook slowly until tender, 20 to 30 minutes per pound. The liquid should be cooked away. Add the wine and bring to boil; then pour ¼ cup cognac over the fowl, ignite, and cover the pan at once. Boil about 10 minutes.

To serve, carve the fowl and place on slices of bread fried in butter and spread with the mashed liver of the fowl. Pour the hot pan gravy over all and surround with mounds of drained grapes which have soaked in the remaining cup of cognac. Serves 6.

NOTE: Wash the grapes; pull off stems. Place in a bowl and cover with cognac for an hour or longer. The drained-off cognac should be used in a dessert sauce.

## BRAISED PIGEONS PIGEONS EN COCOTTE

| | |
|---|---|
| 4 *pigeons, dressed, cleaned, and* | 1 *tsp. salt* |
| *drawn* | ½ *tsp. pepper* |
| 2 *tbs. butter* | 1 *cup hot water* |
| 2 *onions, sliced* | |

Choose pigeons that are no longer young and tender. Brown them in the butter in a saucepan; add the onions and cook until the birds are golden. Add the seasonings and hot water. Cover and cook slowly 1 to 1½ hours, depending on the age of the birds. The pan liquid should be cooked down to a brown gravy. Serve with hot mashed potatoes. Serves 4.

## PIGEONS WITH CABBAGE PIGEONS AUX CHOUX

| | |
|---|---|
| 2 *pigeons* | *boiling water* |
| *pigeon livers* | 2 *slices bacon* |
| 2 *slices bread soaked in cognac* | 2 *tbs. flour* |
| 1 *cup sausage meat* | *salt and pepper* |
| ⅛ *tsp. cayenne* | 1 *cup hot water or bouillon* |
| ⅛ *tsp. mixed spices* | 1 *carrot, sliced* |
| 1 *tsp. salt* | 1 *onion, sliced* |
| 1 *small cabbage* | |

# Poultry

The day before you want to serve this dish prepare the pigeons. Mix the mashed pigeon livers with the soaked bread, 4 oz. sausage meat, the cayenne, spices, and salt. Stuff the birds; skewer or sew the opening. Place in the refrigerator until the next day.

Cook the cabbage in boiling salt water to cover (1 teaspoon salt to 1 quart water). Drain.

Cut the bacon in small pieces and heat in a saucepan. Brown the pigeons in this, then sprinkle with flour and a little pepper and salt. Let cook 5 minutes. Turn the pigeons and let cook 2 minutes. Add the hot water or bouillon and cook 10 minutes.

Place the cabbage, carrot, and onion in a baking dish. Put the pigeons on this base; add the rest of the sausage meat and the gravy from the pan. Cover. Bake in a moderate oven (350° F.) about 1 hour. Serves 4.

## ROAST PIGEONS OR SQUABS PIGEONS RÔTIS

4 squabs or young pigeons, dressed, cleaned, and drawn
4 slices fat pork
1½ tsp. salt
½ tsp. pepper
4 slices bread fried in butter

Cut the pork slices in halves and lay them on the birds' breasts; tie them in place. (Remove strings before serving.) Season well. Lay the birds in a baking pan and roast in a moderate oven (350° F.) 25 minutes or longer, until golden and tender. Serve on fried bread and pour the pan juices over them. Serves 4 or more.

## ROAST STUFFED TURKEY DINDE FARCIE

1 medium-sized roasting turkey, dressed, cleaned, and drawn
1½ tsp. salt
½ tsp. pepper
2 slices fat pork or bacon
stuffing
chestnut purée

Fasten the pork or bacon over the breast, salt and pepper, and secure with string. (Remove string before serving.) Stuff with one of the mixtures given below. Place in a roasting pan and roast uncovered in a moderate oven (325° F.) 18 to 25 minutes per pound. Baste frequently with the pan juices or with a little bouillon or hot water. Serve with Chestnut Purée. Serves 10 to 12.

STUFFING I. Estimate a generous cupful of stuffing for every pound of bird.

| | |
|---|---|
| 1 *lb. fat pork* | 2 *lb. chestnuts* |
| ½ *cup port wine* | *boiling water* |
| ½ *tsp. salt* | 4 *or more truffles, thinly sliced* |
| ¼ *tsp. pepper* | |

Mince the fat pork and mix with the wine and seasonings. Steam the chestnuts until the shells burst, then peel them. Boil 10 minutes and remove inner skins by rubbing them off. Stuff the turkey with alternate layers of the pork, chestnuts, and truffles. Makes 5 cups of stuffing.

STUFFING II

| | |
|---|---|
| ½ *lb. turkey livers or calf's liver* | ½ *lb. chestnuts, cooked and* |
| ½ *lb. fat pork* | *mashed* |
| *salt and pepper* | 2 *truffles, sliced* |
| ½ *cup heavy cream* | 4 *egg yolks* |
| | ½ *cup cognac* |

Mix the liver and pork. Season with about 1 teaspoon salt and a little pepper. Mix the mashed chestnuts and cream; combine with the meat. Add the truffles, egg yolks, and cognac. If too thin, add bread crumbs or sausage meat to make the right consistency for stuffing. Makes about 4 cups.

STUFFING III. Equal amounts of liver pâté and sausage meat with a few sliced truffles.

## TURKEY GIBLETS RAGOÛT DE DINDE

*turkey giblets*
*4 small onions, sliced*
*1 tbs. butter*
*1½ cups hot water or bouillon*

*4 small potatoes*
*½ tsp. salt*
*¼ tsp. pepper*

Brown the giblets and onions in butter in a saucepan. After the onions are tender add the hot water or bouillon. Wash and peel the potatoes. Add with the salt and pepper. Cook gently about 1 hour. Serves 2 to 4.

# MEATS

French cooks have their own ways with meat, as anyone well knows who has ever tasted *Boeuf Bourguignon* or that simplest of all dishes, yet never made as well elsewhere, *Boeuf bouilli*. If you examine a recipe for roast leg of lamb or veal you may well marvel at its simplicity; but follow it as closely as you will, add or subtract, change or improve, you will rarely if ever succeed in bringing to your table quite the same thing that the French cook makes of it. Favourite French meat dishes deserve your best consideration if you would capture their flavour and quality.

## Beef

### BEEF BOURGUIGNON BOEUF BOURGUIGNON

| | |
|---|---|
| 1½ *lb. round of beef* | ½ *cup water* |
| 1 *tbs. butter* | 1 *tsp. salt* |
| 2 *onions, sliced* | ½ *tsp. pepper* |
| 2 *tbs. flour* | ¼ *cup cognac* |
| 1 *cup red Burgundy* | |

Cut the meat in 12 pieces. Brown the butter in a 2-quart saucepan. Add the meat and onions. When the meat is browned, sprinkle it with flour; stir. Add the wine, water, salt, pepper. Cover and bring to boil, then simmer 3 hours. Just before serving, pour the cognac over the meat. Ignite and serve. Serves 6.

## BEEF MINCED WITH POTATOES BOEUF HACHÉ AUX POMMES DE TERRE

1 *lb. round of beef*
2 *qts. cold water*
2 *turnips, sliced*
2 *carrots, sliced*
2 *leeks, sliced*
1 *tsp. salt*
½ *tsp. pepper*

2 *cups sausage meat, cooked until brown*
1 *onion, minced*
1 *egg, beaten*
*butter for baking dish*
2 *cups mashed potatoes*
*salt and pepper*

Place the meat in a 3-quart saucepan. Add the water, turnips, carrots, and leeks. Season. Cover and bring to boil, then simmer 3 hours. Remove the meat and mince fine. Mix with the browned sausage meat. Add the onion and egg. Place in a buttered baking dish, cover with the mashed potatoes, and sprinkle lightly with salt and pepper. Add a few dabs of butter. Place in a moderate oven (375° F.) until browned, about 20 minutes. Serves 6 to 8.

## BRAISED BEEF WITH ONIONS BOEUF AUX OIGNONS

1½ *lb. round of beef*
1 *tbs. butter*
6 *large onions, sliced*

1 *tsp. salt*
½ *tsp. pepper*
1 *cup hot water*

Cut the meat in 12 pieces. Brown lightly in the butter in a heavy saucepan. Add the onions and brown lightly. Season. Add the water. Cover and cook gently 3 hours. Serves 6.

## BEEF IN PIQUANT SAUCE BOEUF AU FOUR

3 *tbs. butter*
2 *onions, chopped*
1 *egg, beaten*
½ *tsp. salt*
¼ *tsp. pepper*
1 *tbs. chopped chives*
1 *tbs. chopped parsley*

8 *thin slices boiled beef*
2 *tbs. flour*
*salt and pepper*
1 *tsp. prepared mustard*
*hot water*
2 *or 3 small pickles, chopped*

Melt 1 tablespoon butter in a saucepan; add the onions and cook until tender. Add slowly to the beaten egg. Season the mixture and add the chives and parsley. Dip the slices of beef into this mixture, then put in a shallow baking dish rubbed with 1 tablespoon butter. Bake in a moderate oven (375° F.) about 15 minutes, or until hot. Serve with the following sauce: brown 1 tablespoon of butter; stir the flour in smoothly; add about ¼ teaspoon salt and the same of pepper. Add the mustard and enough hot water to make a cream consistency. Stir continually until mixture bubbles and boils and is like thick cream. Add the chopped pickles; pour over the meat and serve. Serves 4 to 8.

## BOILED BEEF BOEUF BOUILLI

| | |
|---|---|
| 1½ lb. brisket of beef | 2 leeks, sliced |
| 2 qts. cold water | 2 tsp. salt |
| 2 turnips, sliced | ½ tsp. pepper |
| 2 carrots, sliced | Tomato Sauce |

Place meat in a 3-quart saucepan. Add the water, vegetables, salt, and pepper. Cover. Bring to boil, then simmer 3 hours. Remove the beef to a warmed serving plate. Serve with Tomato Sauce. Serves 6.

NOTE: The broth in which the meat cooked should be skimmed, put through a sieve, and reheated as beef soup or broth. There should be 4 to 6 servings.

## COLD BOILED BEEF BOEUF VINAIGRETTE

| | |
|---|---|
| 8 slices cold boiled beef | 1 tsp. dry mustard |
| 2 tbs. oil | 2 onions, chopped fine |
| 1 tbs. vinegar | 2 tbs. chopped parsley |
| ½ tsp. salt | 1 hard-boiled egg, chopped |
| ¼ tsp. pepper | |

Place the slices in a deep serving dish. In a separate bowl mix the oil, vinegar, and seasonings, beating well. Pour over the meat; sprinkle with the onions, parsley, and egg. Let stand in a cold place about 1 hour before serving. Serves 4 to 8.

### FRIED FILLETS OF BEEF TOURNEDOS

1½ lb. fillet of beef
6 slices pork fat
1 tbs. butter

1 tsp. salt
½ tsp. pepper
Béarnaise Sauce

Cut the meat in round slices about ½ inch thick and 4 inches across. Wrap a slice of pork fat around each; secure with small skewers (toothpicks) or tie with string. Brown the butter in a frying pan; place the meat in it and cook lightly on both sides. When the bacon is cooked sufficiently, the meat will be done. Remove skewers or string. Serve hot with Béarnaise Sauce. Serves 6.

### FILLET OF BEEF WITH OLIVES FILET DE BOEUF AUX OLIVES

3 slices fat pork
2 lb. fillet of beef
1 tbs. butter
1 tsp. salt
½ tsp. pepper

½ tbs. flour
½ cup Madeira wine
½ cup water
2 cups olives, stones removed

Cut 2 of the pork slices into thin larding strips and use a larding needle to draw them through the meat. Wrap the other slice around the meat and skewer or tie it in place. (Remove skewers or string before serving.)

Brown the butter in a heavy saucepan; add the meat and seasonings. Brown on all sides. Stir the flour into the pan; add the wine and water, stirring continually until smooth. Add the olives. Cover and simmer 45 minutes. When served, the beef should be red in the centre. Serves 6.

### OX TONGUE IN PIQUANT SAUCE LANGUE DE BOEUF

1 ox tongue
2 qts. water
2 turnips, sliced
2 carrots, sliced
2 leeks, sliced
salt and pepper

1 tbs. butter
2 tbs. flour
1 cup water
½ cup vinegar
3 shallots, sliced
½ small clove garlic

Rinse the tongue; drain. Place in a 3-quart saucepan with the water, turnips, carrots, leeks, about 1 teaspoon salt and ½ teaspoon pepper. Cover and bring to boil, then simmer 3 hours. Drain, slice, and serve with the sauce.

To make the sauce, brown the butter in a saucepan; stir the flour in smoothly and add the water, stirring steadily. In a second small saucepan heat the vinegar, shallots, garlic, and about a pinch each of salt and pepper. Boil until reduced to 1 tablespoon. Stir it into the first sauce; mix and heat. Pour over the sliced tongue. Sauce for 6 servings, or about ½ of the tongue.

## OXTAIL HOTPOT QUEUE DE BOEUF BOUILLI

According to French legend, this recipe was introduced into England by William the Conqueror.

| | |
|---|---|
| 2 *lb. oxtail cut in sections at the joints* | 3 *carrots, sliced* |
| 2½ *qts. water* | 3 *turnips, sliced* |
| 2 *pig's feet* | 3 *leeks, sliced* |
| 1 *pig's ear* | 1 *head cabbage, quartered* |
| 1 *cup haricot beans soaked overnight* | 2 *tsp. salt* |
| | ½ *tsp. pepper* |

Place in a 1-gallon saucepan the oxtail, water, cleaned pig's feet and ear. Drain the beans which have soaked overnight and add; then add the washed and sliced or quartered vegetables. Add seasoning. Cover, bring to boil, then simmer 3 hours. Skim top if scum appears. Serve hot. Serves 4 to 6.

## PORTERHOUSE STEAK CHÂTEAUBRIAND

| | |
|---|---|
| 2 *lb. boned porterhouse steak* 1½ *in. thick* | ½ *tsp. freshly ground pepper* |
| 3 *tbs. butter* | *fat or suet for broiler* |
| 1½ *tsp. salt* | 1 *tbs. minced parsley* |
| | *Béarnaise Sauce* |

Allow the fat around the edges to remain. Make incisions at intervals of about an inch with a pointed knife; this keeps the steak from curling. Rub with about 2 tablespoons butter and season well. Heat the grill. Lay the steak on the grids and broil under good heat. Turn the steak as soon as the top is seared; do not pierce the steak with a fork in turning it (use two large kitchen spoons or a spoon and a pancake turner). Leave the broiler door open. When the first bloody juice appears in the broiler pan, the steak is ready for those who like it rare.

Place 1 tablespoon butter on a warmed plate; lay the steak on it. Spread the top with butter and sprinkle with parsley. Serve at once with Béarnaise Sauce. Serves 4 to 6.

## ROLLED BEEF WITH SAUSAGE ROULÉS DE BOEUF

| | |
|---|---|
| 8 *thin slices raw beef* | 1 *onion, sliced* |
| 8 *small sausages or* ¾ *cup sausage* | 1 *tbs. flour* |
| *meat* | 1 *cup red wine* |
| 1 *tsp. salt* | ½ *cup hot water* |
| ½ *tsp. pepper* | *salt and pepper* |
| 1 *tbs. butter* | |

Cut the pieces of beef about 5 inches long and 3 inches wide. On each slice place a sausage or spoonful of sausage meat. Season with salt and pepper. Roll up and tie with string or skewer with toothpicks.

Brown the butter in a 2-quart saucepan; add the meat rolls and onion and let brown 3 or 4 minutes. Sprinkle with flour. Stir the pan juices; add the wine, water, and a little salt and pepper if needed. Cover; cook over moderate or low heat and let simmer 1 or 2 hours. Serves 4 to 8.

## STEWED BEEF WITH CARROTS BOEUF À LA MODE

| | |
|---|---|
| 1½ *lb. rump of beef* | 1 *tsp. salt* |
| 3 *slices fat pork* | ½ *tsp. pepper* |
| 1 *tbs. butter* | 1 *cup hot water* |
| 1 *onion, sliced* | 6 *carrots, sliced* |
| ½ *calf's foot* | |

Pierce the flesh in several places with a thin sharp knife. Into these slits poke bits of the fat pork. Place one large slice of the pork around the meat. Skewer or tie in place.

Brown the butter in a heavy saucepan. Place the beef in the hot fat and sear lightly on all sides. Add the onion. When the meat is browned and the onion tender, add the calf's foot, salt, and pepper. Cook 5 minutes, turning the calf's foot twice. Add the water and carrots. Cover the pan and cook slowly 3 hours. Serves 4 or more.

## ROAST BEEF RÔTI DE BOEUF

| | |
|---|---|
| *4 to 5 lb. sirloin of beef* | *hot water* |
| *salt and pepper* | *butter* |

Place the roast in a roasting pan. Put on top of the meat half a tablespoon butter, salt and pepper, and put in a hot oven. Roast 15 to 20 minutes per pound. Baste frequently; adding 3 tablespoons of water to the pan. Serve hot or cold. Serves 8 to 10 or more.

# *Mutton*

## CURRIED LEG OF MUTTON GIGOT D'AGNEAU AU CURRY

| | |
|---|---|
| 1 *tbs. lard* | *leg of mutton* |
| 1 *onion* | 1 *tbs. curry powder* |
| 1 *bay leaf* | 2 *cups cream* |
| 1 *sprig thyme* | 1 *lemon, juice only* |
| 1 *tsp. salt* | *hot rice* |

Heat the lard in a large iron pan. Slice the onion into it; add the herbs and salt. Brown the meat on all sides; cover and cook 10 minutes. Sprinkle with the curry. Pour the cream and lemon juice in the pan; cover and cook slowly 1½ hours, or until the mutton is cooked through and done; 20 minutes per pound.

Remove the meat, slice, cover with the sauce from the pan, and serve with hot rice prepared by the recipe below. Serves 6 to 12.

RICE

| | |
|---|---|
| 1 tbs. butter | ¼ tsp. pepper |
| 2 tbs. olive oil | ¼ tsp. cayenne |
| 1 cup unwashed rice | 3 cups bouillon |
| ½ tsp. salt | |

Heat the butter in a 1-quart saucepan; add the oil and rice and stir until the rice is golden. Season; cover with bouillon. Cover and boil 20 minutes, or until the rice is soft and the liquid absorbed. Serve hot with the mutton curry. Makes 4 to 6 servings.

## ROAST LEG OF MUTTON WITH HARICOT BEANS
### GIGOT DE MOUTON RÔTI AUX HARICOTS

| | |
|---|---|
| leg of mutton | 1 small garlic bud |
| 1 tbs. butter | 1 lb. haricot beans |
| salt and pepper | 1 tbs. cream |
| 1 bay leaf | 2 tbs. Tomato Sauce |
| 1 sprig thyme | |

Place the meat in a roasting pan. Spread with the butter and season with salt and pepper. Put the herbs in the roasting pan; insert the garlic in the joint of mutton near the knuckle. Place in a hot oven (500° F.) 15 minutes; reduce heat to moderate (325° F.) and add about 3 tablespoons water to the bottom of the roasting pan. Baste frequently; allow 15 to 20 minutes per pound roasting time. The meat should be well cooked through, not rare. Serves 8 or more.

Haricot beans should be served with this roast. Prepare as follows: soak the beans overnight or 24 hours in water to cover. Drain and put in a stewpot with enough water to cover. Add salt and pepper. Cook until tender; drain and serve very hot with 1 tablespoon of cream and 2 tablespoons Tomato Sauce stirred into them.

# BONED SHOULDER OF MUTTON WITH TURNIPS
## EPAULE DE MOUTON AUX NAVETS

| | |
|---|---|
| 1½ *lb. boned shoulder of mutton* | ½ *tsp. pepper* |
| 1 *tbs. butter* | 4 *turnips or salsify, sliced* |
| 1 *onion, sliced* | 8 *potatoes, quartered* |
| 1½ *tsp. salt* | 1½ *cups hot water* |

Roll and tie the meat. Brown the butter in a heavy pan. Place the meat and onion in the butter. Cook until the meat is browned on all sides. Season. Add the sliced turnips or salsify and the quartered potatoes. Add the hot water. Cover and stew 2 hours. Serves 4 or more.


# SHOULDER OF MUTTON WITH SORREL EPAULE
## DE MOUTON À L'OSEILLE

Prepare Stewed Mutton as described in the preceding recipe. Serve it with hot braised sorrel prepared as follows:

| | |
|---|---|
| 2 *lb. sorrel* | ½ *tsp. salt* |
| 1 *tbs. butter* | ½ *tsp. pepper* |

Wash the sorrel thoroughly through several changes of cold water. Lift from the water to a saucepan; add the butter. Cover and cook 20 minutes, depending on the age of the sorrel. Season and serve with Mutton. Serves 6.


# SHOULDER OF MUTTON WITH MIXED VEGETA-
## BLES RAGOÛT DE MOUTON AUX LÉGUMES

Prepare Stewed Mutton as described in the preceding recipe. Add 4 to 6 small carrots and turnips and 1 cup French beans to the stew. Cook with the stew. Such additions increase the number of servings to 8 or 10.

## LEG OF MUTTON MARINADE GIGOT DE MOUTON
### MARINÉ

| | |
|---|---|
| 1 *cup olive oil* | 4 *shallots, sliced* |
| 1 *carrot, sliced* | 2 *small cloves garlic, chopped* |
| 2 *onions, sliced* | *sprig thyme* |
| 2 *cups white wine* | 1 *peppercorn* |
| ½ *cup vinegar* | 1 *tsp. salt* |
| 4 *sprigs parsley* | *leg of mutton* |

Heat the oil in 1-quart saucepan; add the carrot, onions, wine, vinegar, parsley, shallots, garlic, thyme, and seasonings. Boil slowly 1 hour. Let cool. Place the leg of mutton in a large bowl or crock. Pour the marinade over it and let stand covered in the refrigerator 2 days. Turn the meat several times during the 48 hours.

To roast the mutton, drain, wipe, and place on a rack in a roasting pan. Roast in hot oven (475° F.) 15 minutes. Reduce heat to moderate (350° F.) and continue roasting 15 minutes per pound. Serves 8 or more. When done, serve with this sauce:

SAUCE

| | |
|---|---|
| 1 *tbs. butter* | 1 *cup marinade liquid* |
| 2 *tbs. flour* | |

Heat the butter; stir the flour smoothly in. Slowly add 1 cup of the marinade in which the meat soaked. Stir and cook until the gravy is smoothly thickened. Makes a little more than 1 cup. Double the recipe for a large roast.

Serve potatoes with the roast.

## MUTTON CUTLETS CÔTELETTES DE MOUTON

| | |
|---|---|
| 4 *thin cutlets or chops of lamb or* | 1 *egg, beaten* |
| *mutton* | 1 *cup bread crumbs* |
| 1½ *tsp. salt* | 2 *tbs. butter if necessary* |
| ¼ *tsp. pepper* | |

Wipe the cutlets with a clean damp cloth; season well. Mix the egg. Dip the cutlets in the egg, then in the crumbs. Place on greased grill rack and broil 8 to 10 minutes, or until browned on both sides and cooked through; or fry the chops in 2 tablespoons butter. Serves 4.

## PILAFF—MUTTON WITH RICE MOUTON AU RIZ

| | |
|---|---|
| 1½ *lb. shoulder of mutton* | 1 *tsp. salt* |
| 1 *tbs. butter* | ½ *tsp. pepper* |
| 2 *onions, sliced* | ½ *cup rice* |
| 3 *cups hot water* | |

Cut the meat in small pieces. Brown in the butter with the onions in a 2-quart saucepan. Cook 15 minutes. Pour the fat off and save; add 3 cups water and seasonings. Cook 1½ hours. Remove the meat and save the liquid.

Put the fat poured from the meat pan in a 1-quart saucepan. Add the rice, and stir and cook until the rice is browned. Add the water in which the meat boiled, and boil 20 minutes. There should be about 2 cups of liquid.

When the rice is done and the liquid absorbed, place it in a warmed serving dish. Place the meat on top, or mix the meat and rice and serve. Serves 4.

## MUTTON WITH BAKED BEANS CASSOULET

| | |
|---|---|
| 1 *lb. haricot beans, soaked overnight* | 2 *small cloves garlic* |
| | 1 *bay leaf* |
| 2 *pieces pork rind or fat pork* | 1 *sprig thyme* |
| 1 *lb. bacon* | 1 *carrot* |
| 1 *sausage* | 1½ *tsp. salt* |
| 1 *lb. mutton shoulder* | ¼ *tsp. pepper* |

Place the soaked and drained beans in a 3-quart saucepan. Cover with 2 quarts water. Add the other ingredients and boil slowly 1½ to 2 hours, until the beans are tender and the liquid cooked down. The consistency should be that of a very thick stew. Make the following sauce:

SAUCE

| | |
|---|---|
| 1 tbs. lard | 1 cup gravy from the bean pot |
| 2 large onions, chopped | 4 tomatoes, chopped |
| 1 small clove garlic, crushed | |

Heat the lard; brown the onions and garlic in it. Stir in the gravy and tomatoes. Boil and stir 10 minutes.

In a deep casserole pour half of the beans; add the meat from the stewpot cut in small pieces. Omit the rind. Add the rest of the beans. Pour the sauce in. Cover and bake in a moderate oven (300° F.) about 1 hour. Serves 10 or more.

## SHEEP'S TROTTERS PIEDS DE MOUTON POULETTE

| | |
|---|---|
| 6 sheep's trotters | ½ tsp. pepper |
| 2 qts. water | 1 cup White Sauce |
| 2 carrots, sliced | ¼ cup chopped canned or cooked |
| 2 turnips, sliced |     mushrooms |
| 2 onions, sliced | 2 egg yolks |
| 2 leeks, sliced | ½ cup heavy cream |
| 1 tsp. salt | 1 lemon, juice only |

Ask for the feet of young sheep and have them cleaned and scraped by the butcher. Wash them through several waters. Place in a 3-quart saucepan with the washed and sliced vegetables and salt and pepper. Bring to boil, then simmer 3 to 4 hours, or until the meat falls off the bones. Remove bones and discard. Drain any remaining liquid.

Add the mushrooms to the White Sauce; bring to boil and remove from heat. Beat the yolks with the cream and lemon juice just enough to mix; add to the White Sauce. Pour over the meat from the trotters and serve hot. Serves 6.

## SADDLE OF MUTTON FILET DE MOUTON À LA GELÉE DE GROSEILLE

Cover the meat with a marinade as in Leg of Mutton Marinade. When ready to roast the joint, heat the marinade and reduce it to half the original amount. Then assemble:

| | |
|---|---|
| 1 *tbs. butter* | 1 *tsp. salt* |
| 4 *slices bacon, chopped* | ½ *tsp. pepper* |

Place the drained meat in a roasting pan, with a pat of butter, add the chopped bacon and seasonings, and roast in a hot oven 20 minutes per pound. Baste every 10 minutes with the marinade liquid. Serves 8 to 10.

### GRAVY OR SAUCE

| | |
|---|---|
| 1 *tbs. butter* | ⅛ *tsp. cayenne* |
| 2 *tbs. flour* | 1 *cup Madeira wine* |
| 1 *cup liquid from the roasting pan* | 1 *tbs. red currant jelly* |

Heat the butter and stir the flour into it. When smooth, add the pan liquid, cayenne, and wine. Stir and boil until thickened. Stir the jelly in just before serving. Makes about 2 cups of gravy.

Garnish the platter with rich pastry tarts filled with red currant jelly.

## GRILLED SHEEP'S KIDNEYS ROGNONS DE MOUTON GRILLÉS

| | |
|---|---|
| 8 *sheep's kidneys* | 1 *tsp. salt* |
| *boiling water* | ½ *tsp. pepper* |
| 2 *tbs. butter, melted* | 1 *tbs. minced parsley* |

Select fresh kidneys free of any discolouration. Wipe them with a clean damp cloth, cut the fat away. Scald and drain. Split each open; run a skewer through to hold it flat. Brush with melted butter and grill under broiler heat 10 minutes. Remove skewers; add melted butter, seasonings, and parsley and serve. Serves 4.

## SHEEP'S KIDNEYS WITH FRENCH BEANS ROGNONS
### DE MOUTON HARICOTS VERTS

| | |
|---|---|
| 8 *sheep's kidneys* | *salt and pepper* |
| 2 *bacon slices, chopped* | *hot water* |
| 1 *lb. green or yellow string beans* | |

Wipe the kidneys as described in the preceding recipe. Heat the bacon in a frying pan; add the kidneys and cook until browned and tender, 10 minutes or longer. Remove from the heat.

In a 2-quart saucepan place the washed and cleaned beans. Season with salt and pepper. Pour the kidneys and pan fat over them; add hot water to cover. Cover the pan and cook slowly 1 hour, or until the beans are tender. Serves 6.

# *Pork*

## BOILED HAM JAMBON

If you buy a wrapped ham, follow the packer's instructions for boiling it. If you buy an old-fashioned country ham, wash and scrub it. Put it in cold water for 6 hours, changing the water every hour. Drain; wipe dry. Put in a large saucepan, cover with cold water, and bring to boil. Simmer 20 minutes per pound, a little less if the ham is to be served cold. When done, let cool in the cooking water. Drain and serve. Allow $\frac{1}{4}$ to $\frac{1}{3}$ pound per serving.

## BOILED HAM IN PIE CRUST JAMBON EN CROÛTE

| | |
|---|---|
| *freshly boiled ham* | 1 *or* 2 *eggs* |
| *rich pie pastry* | $\frac{1}{4}$ *cup water* |

Remove the rind from the freshly boiled ham. Cover with the pastry, fitting it neatly around the meat with the fingers. Brush the pastry with the egg. Place in a roasting pan. Bake in a hot oven (450° F.) 10 minutes. Lower the heat to moderate (350° F.) and bake 20 minutes longer.

## VEAL AND HAM FILLETS ESCALOPES AU JAMBON

4 *thin slices tender veal*  
4 *thin slices boiled ham*  
1 *tbs. butter*  
2 *tbs. flour*  
½ *cup Madeira wine*  

½ *cup water*  
½ *cup olives, seeds removed*  
1 *tsp. salt*  
½ *tsp. pepper*  

Pound the veal with the edge of a heavy plate until tender. Lay a slice of ham on each slice of veal. Roll and skewer with toothpicks or tie with string. (Remove skewers or string before serving.)

Brown the butter in a saucepan; add the meat rolls. Brown them, sprinkle with flour, and stir the pan juices up over the rolls. Add the wine, water, olives, and seasonings. Cover and bring to boil, then simmer 45 minutes. Serve hot with the pan sauce. Serves 4.

## BRAISED HAM JAMBON BRAISÉ

6-*lb. ham*  
2 *cups white wine*  
2 *cups fine bread crumbs*  
3 *shallots, chopped*  

¼ *cup chopped cooked or canned mushrooms*  
½ *cup heavy cream*  
1 *tsp. flour*  

Place ham in pan and boil gently in water for 1½ hours. Remove. Add the wine; steam 45 minutes. Lift out, remove the rind, and rub the ham all over with crumbs. Heat the juice in the pan with the remaining ingredients, stirring smoothly until thickened. Serve with the hot ham. This makes a little more than 2 cups of gravy; 12 to 18 servings of ham.

## FILLET OF PORK MARINADE FILET DE PORC MARINÉ

3 *lb. boned pork shoulder or loin*  
1 *cup wine*  
1 *cup vinegar*  
1 *tsp. salt*  
½ *tsp. pepper*  
2 *small cloves garlic, chopped*  
1 *bay leaf*  

1 *clove*  
2 *sprigs thyme*  
2 *sprigs mint*  
2 *sprigs parsley*  
1 *tbs. butter*  
*Chasseur Sauce*

Wipe the meat with a clean damp cloth. Mix the wine, vinegar, salt, pepper, garlic, and herbs. Place the meat in this mixture in a crock. Cover and place in the refrigerator. Let stand 2 days.

Remove the meat from the marinade; dry it. Place in a baking pan. Add butter on top. Roast in a moderate oven (350° F.) 30 minutes per pound. Serve hot with Chasseur Sauce. Serves 6 or more.

CHASSEUR SAUCE
*marinade liquid*                              2 *tbs. flour*
1 *tbs. butter*

Boil the marinade liquid drained from the ham until it is reduced to half its volume. Brown the butter, add flour smoothly into it. Stir in the liquid and boil until slightly thickened. Makes about 1 cup gravy.

## SHOULDER OF PORK WITH VEGETABLES JAMBETTE
### AUX LÉGUMES

| | |
|---|---|
| 3-*lb. shoulder of pork* | 3 *turnips, sliced* |
| 2½ *qts. water* | 3 *leeks, sliced* |
| ½ *lb.* (1 *cup*) *haricot beans* | 1 *head cabbage, quartered* |
| *soaked overnight* | 1½ *tsp. salt* |
| 3 *carrots, sliced* | ½ *tsp. pepper* |

Place the meat in a 3-quart saucepan with the water and beans. Add the vegetables. Season and bring to boil, then cook slowly 3 hours. Serve the meat surrounded with the vegetables. The remaining liquid may be strained and used as a soup base. Serves 6.

## PORK CUTLETS OR CHOPS CÔTELETTES DE PORC

Prepare like Mutton Cutlets. Serve with Chestnut Purée or Mashed Potatoes.

# *Veal*

## ROAST VEAL RÔTI DE VEAU

2 *lb. boned leg of veal*      1 *tsp. salt*
1 *slice fat pork*      ½ *tsp. pepper*

Cover the meat with 1 slice fat pork. Place in a roasting pan. Season.
Roast in a moderate oven (350° F.) 20 to 25 minutes per pound.
The veal is ready when the pan gravy is brown. Serve with spinach
and potatoes. Serves 5 or 6.

## STUFFED BREAST OF VEAL POITRINE DE VEAU FARCIE

2 *lb. boneless breast of veal*      1 *tsp. salt*
2 *slices bread soaked in milk*      ½ *tsp. pepper*
2 *onions, chopped*      1 *tbs. butter*
½ *cup cooked or canned mushrooms,*      2 *small onions, sliced*
   *chopped*      1 *cup hot water*
2 *chicken livers, chopped*      *salt and pepper*
1 *egg, beaten*

Pound the meat flat with the edge of a heavy plate. Squeeze the
excess milk out of the bread and mix bread with the onions, mushrooms, and chopped chicken livers. Add the egg, salt, and pepper,
and mix well. Spread this stuffing on the veal. Roll and tie meat
with clean string or use small skewers. (Remove string or skewers
before serving.)

Brown the butter in a 2-quart saucepan. Add the meat and small
onions. Brown the meat on all sides. Add the water and seasonings.
Cover and let simmer 2 hours, or until meat is very tender. Serves
4 to 6.

## STUFFED FILLETS OF VEAL LES OISEAUX SANS TÊTES

| | |
|---|---|
| 4 *thin slices tender veal* | ½ *tsp. pepper* |
| 1 *cup sausage meat, lightly sautéed* | 1 *tbs. butter* |
| 1 *cup minced veal* | 1 *onion, sliced* |
| 2 *shallots, minced* | ½ *tbs. flour* |
| 1 *tsp. salt* | 1 *cup hot water* |

Pound the meat with the edge of a heavy plate. Mix the sausage, minced veal, shallots, and seasoning. Spread this mixture on the 4 pieces of meat. Roll; tie or skewer. (Remove string or skewers before serving.)

Brown the butter in a saucepan; add the rolls and sliced onion. When lightly browned, sprinkle with flour. Continue to cook; add the water. Cover and cook 45 minutes to 1 hour. Serves 4.

## VEAL FILLETS WITH CREAM ESCALOPES DE VEAU À LA CRÈME

| | |
|---|---|
| 4 *thin slices tender veal* | ½ *tsp. pepper* |
| 1 *tbs. butter* | ½ *cup warm heavy cream* |
| 1 *tsp. salt* | |

Pound the veal a little with the edge of a heavy plate. Heat the butter in a frying pan. Cook the veal slowly until tender and golden. Season when half cooked. When ready to serve, add the cream. Heat but do not boil. Serves 4.

## FILLETS OF VEAL WITH BACON ROULÉS DE VEAU

| | |
|---|---|
| 4 *thin slices veal* | ½ *tbs. flour* |
| 4 *slices bacon* | 1 *cup water* |
| 1 *tbs. butter* | 1 *tsp. salt* |
| 1 *onion, sliced* | ½ *tsp. pepper* |

Pound the veal with the edge of a heavy plate. Place 1 slice of bacon on each slice of veal. Roll up; tie or skewer securely. (Remove string or skewers before serving.)

Brown the butter and onion in a frying pan or saucepan. Place the rolls in the hot fat and brown. Sprinkle with a tablespoonful of flour; add the water and seasonings. Cover; cook slowly 45 minutes. Remove the lid; let the sauce cook down if necessary. Serve hot. Serves 4.


## STEWED VEAL WITH WHITE SAUCE BLANQUETTE DE VEAU

2 *lb. breast of veal cut in*
   *serving pieces*
2 *cups thin White Sauce*
1 *onion, sliced*
1 *tsp. salt*
½ *tsp. pepper*

12 *small potatoes, peeled*
1 *egg yolk, beaten*
½ *lemon, juice only*
1 *cup cooked or canned mush-*
   *rooms (optional)*

Cut the meat in serving-size pieces. Place in a 2- or 3-quart saucepan with the White Sauce, onion, seasonings, and potatoes. Cover; let cook slowly 1 hour.

Put yolk in a warmed deep serving dish. Slowly add the sauce from the stew pan, stirring constantly. Add the lemon juice, potatoes, and meat. Serve hot. Serves 4 to 6.

NOTE: Add small whole or sliced mushrooms to the stew if liked.


## BRAISED OR STEWED VEAL RAGOÛT DE VEAU

2 *lb. loin or leg of veal*
2 *thin slices fat pork*
1 *tbs. butter*
1 *onion, sliced*
1 *tbs. flour*

½ *cup wine*
½ *cup water*
3 *tomatoes, sliced*
1 *tsp. salt*
½ *tsp. pepper*

Wrap the fat around the meat and skewer or tie it in place. Brown the butter and onion together in a pan. Add the meat; brown on all sides. Sprinkle with flour. Add the wine, water, tomatoes, salt, and pepper. Cover and cook 1½ hours. Serve with steamed potatoes. Serves 4 to 6.

# VIENNESE VEAL CUTLETS CÔTELETTES DE VEAU PANNÉES

4 *veal cutlets*
1 *egg, beaten*
½ *cup fine bread crumbs*

2 *tbs. butter*
1 *tsp. salt*
½ *tsp. pepper*

Pound each cutlet a little; dip in the egg, then in crumbs. Sauté in the hot butter until golden on both sides and cooked through. Season while cooking. Serve hot with fried potatoes. Serves 4.

# VEAL CUTLETS WITH WHITE WINE CÔTELETTES DE VEAU AU VIN BLANC

4 *cutlets of veal*
1 *tbs. butter*
1 *tsp. salt*
½ *tsp. pepper*
1 *tsp. mixed herbs*
2 *small onions, chopped*

1 *shallot, chopped*
1 *small clove garlic, chopped*
1 *cup white wine*
1 *tsp. prepared mustard*
2 or 3 *small gherkins, chopped*

Pound the meat with the edge of a heavy plate. Brown the butter in a frying pan. Cook the cutlets until lightly browned on both sides. Season; add the herbs, onions, shallot, garlic, and wine. Cover and cook slowly 30 minutes or longer, until the meat is well cooked. Remove the cutlets to a warmed serving platter. Stir the mustard and gherkins into the pan sauce; bring to boil. Pour over the meat and serve. Serves 4.

# GRILLED VEAL CUTLETS CÔTELETTES DE VEAU GRILLÉES

4 *veal cutlets*
1 *egg, beaten*
1 *tbs. water*
1 *tsp. salt*

½ *tsp. pepper*
½ *cup bread crumbs*
½ *cup hot water*
*Madeira Sauce*

Dip each piece in egg mixed with water. Season; dip in crumbs. Place on a greased gridiron and cook under moderate heat until browned on both sides, about 15 minutes. Serve with Madeira Sauce. Serves 4.

## VEAL KIDNEYS WITH WHITE WINE ROGNONS DE VEAU AU VIN BLANC

Prepare kidneys as described in the following recipe. Substitute ½ cup white wine and ½ cup water for the cream and cognac. Cover and cook slowly 20 minutes.

## VEAL KIDNEYS ROGNONS DE VEAU

| | |
|---|---|
| 2 *veal kidneys, sliced* | ½ *tsp. pepper* |
| 3 *tbs. butter* | 2 *tbs. thick cream* |
| 2 *shallots, chopped* | ¼ *cup cognac* |
| 1 *tsp. salt* | |

Scald the kidneys. Remove skin. Cut away excess fat. Slice thin and cook in the butter with the shallots and seasonings 5 to 10 minutes, or until the kidneys turn a light colour. Add the cream. Stir; heat but do not boil. Pour into a warmed serving dish. Pour the brandy over; ignite and serve. Serves 4.

## VEAL LOAF PAIN DE VEAU

| | |
|---|---|
| 1 *lb. lean veal* | ½ *tsp. salt* |
| ½ *lb. pork* | ½ *tsp. pepper* |
| 4 *slices bread soaked in milk* | 1 *slice of fat pork* |
| 1 *egg, beaten* | |

Mince together 1lb. of lean veal and ½ lb. pork. Mix with 4 oz. crustless bread soaked in milk, and drained, one egg, salt and pepper. Make into a roll, surround with a thin slice of uncooked pork fat, tie carefully with thin string and roast for 1 hour. May be eaten hot or cold.

## VEAL IN JELLY VEAU DE GELÉE

| | |
|---|---|
| 2 *lb. veal* | 1 *bay leaf* |
| 5 *small onions* | 1 *tbs. butter* |
| ½ *calf's foot* | 1 *tsp. salt* |
| *sprig thyme* | ½ *tsp. pepper* |

Wipe the veal with a clean damp cloth. Place it with all ingredients in a 2-quart saucepan. Add water to cover. Simmer covered 3 hours.

Remove the meat to a crock or bowl. Strain the liquid over it and chill in the refrigerator. Slice and serve. Serves 6 to 8.

## CALF'S LIVER SAUTÉ FOIE DE VEAU

4 *slices calf's liver*          *pepper*
1 *tbs. butter*                  ½ *lemon, juice only*
*salt*

Place one piece of liver per person in a frying pan in which a knob of butter has been melted. Add salt and pepper. Fry both sides for about ten minutes altogether. Before serving sprinkle with the juice of half a lemon. Serve with mashed potatoes.

## CALF'S LIVER WITH WINE SAUCE FOIE DE VEAU SAUCE
### BORDELAISE

1 *lb. calf's liver*             ½ *tsp. pepper*
2 *slices fat pork*              3 *shallots, sliced*
3 *tomatoes, chopped*           1 *cup red wine*
¼ *cup cognac*                   ½ *tbs. butter*
1 *tsp. salt*

Take 1 lb. calf's liver. Pierce it in several places with a thin sharp knife. Insert pieces of 1 slice of pork in these slits. Place in a dish; add the tomatoes and brandy. Let stand 1 hour in the refrigerator. Remove the meat; season with salt and pepper. Place in a baking dish; surround with a slice of pork. Bake in a moderate oven (325°F.) 1 hour.

Heat the remaining mixture of tomatoes and brandy with the shallots and wine. Boil until reduced to half its volume. Add the butter; stir. Pour over the liver or serve with it. Serves 4.

## CALF'S HEAD TÊTE DE VEAU

| | |
|---|---|
| ½ *calf's head* | 1 *tsp. salt* |
| 2 *qts. water* | 3 *tbs. vinegar* |
| 1 *lemon* | ½ *tsp. pepper* |
| 2 *carrots, sliced* | 1 *cup crumbs* |
| 2 *turnips, sliced* | 1 *tbs. butter, melted* |
| 2 *leeks, sliced* | *hot Tomato Sauce* |

Have the butcher clean and bone the calf's head. Cover with water and bring to boil. Drain; cover with cold water. Add the lemon, vegetables, seasonings, and vinegar. Cover and boil until tender, about 2 hours. Drain. Mix the crumbs and the melted butter. Spread over the calf's head. Serves 6. Serve with hot Tomato Sauce or make a sauce as follows:

SAUCE

| | |
|---|---|
| 2 *tbs. olive oil* | ¼ *tsp. pepper* |
| 1 *tbs. vinegar* | ½ *tsp. dry mustard* |
| ½ *tsp. salt* | 1 *tsp. mixed dried herbs* |

Mix the ingredients together. Serve with the meat.

# SAUCES

Dumas might well have been more accurate had he called his people '*une nation saucière*' rather than '*une nation soupière*', for no nation on the face of the earth is so occupied with its sauces and their preparation as the French. Any Frenchman, every Frenchman, can wax eloquent on topics culinary, but when it comes to sauces there is no adjective, no superlative, with which he can do justice to his subject.

The importance of sauces in French cookery is evidenced by the fact that Escoffier in his *Guide Culinaire*, which contains some three thousand recipes, devotes his first chapter to them.

There is much to learn from older cuisines, and since it is quite obvious that many people are not born sauce makers, perhaps with patience and determination they may eventually become good ones. *To Make Sauces.* All sauces must be made with good butter, preferably not salted. Whenever possible, they should be made immediately before serving. Only sauces made with water can be allowed to remain boiling on a slow fire. A good sauce should be thick. Do not forget that it becomes thinner when adding the yolk of an egg or cream. When adding the yolk of an egg to a sauce already made, put the egg in a sauceboat and add the boiling sauce gently, stirring well. Serve at once.

## White Sauces

The general principles of sauce making can best be given in the recipe for the commonest of all sauces, White Sauce. The French version calls for 1 tablespoon butter in a saucepan. When it begins to melt, add 2 tablespoons flour, $\frac{1}{2}$ teaspoon salt, and $\frac{1}{4}$ teaspoon pepper. Heat gently, stirring with a wooden spoon. When the butter and flour are well mixed, but before they are brown, add about 1 cup hot water slowly, continuing to stir, until the required consistency is obtained. If the sauce is lumpy, it is because the water has been added too quickly. For this there is a simple remedy: boil it again, stirring vigorously, until the excess of water has evaporated and a smooth paste obtained. Recommence adding hot water slowly to thin. If egg is to be added, pour the sauce on to the yolk of an egg as explained above. This makes about 1 cup sauce.

## MILK SAUCE SAUCE AU LAIT

Proceed as for White Sauce, but add hot milk instead of water. Omit the egg or use, as preferred.

## CAPER SAUCE SAUCE AUX CÂPRES

Prepare White Sauce. Add about 1 tablespoon capers and the yolk of an egg before serving.

## CHEESE SAUCE SAUCE AU FROMAGE

To Milk Sauce add 2 tablespoons grated Gruyère or other cheese.

## CREAM SAUCE SAUCE À LA CRÈME

Make Milk Sauce, and when ready add 1 or 2 tablespoons heavy cream. Do not boil.

## CURRY SAUCE SAUCE AU CURRY

Make Milk Sauce and add 1 teaspoon curry powder. Mix smoothly and boil 5 minutes. Add 1 tablespoon heavy cream and $\frac{1}{2}$ teaspoon salt. Heat again, but do not boil.

## GREEN SAUCE SAUCE VERTE AUX FINES HERBES

*Cream Sauce*                                          ½ *cup chopped fresh herbs*
1 *tbs. mixed dried herbs or*

Use a mixture of parsley, chervil, tarragon, according to the flavour desired, chop very finely. This makes about 1½ cups sauce when the fresh herbs are used.

## JELLIED SAUCE SAUCE CHAUD-FROID

1 *cup warmed meat jelly or gelatine*      ¼ *cup cold water*
   *made with*                           ¼ *cup boiling water or bouillon*
1 *tbs. plain unflavoured gelatine*        *Cream Sauce*

If meat jelly is not available, soak the gelatine in the cold water until softened, then stir the boiling water in until dissolved. Add to the hot sauce. Mix well. The sauce thickens as it cools.

## MUSHROOM SAUCE SAUCE AUX CHAMPIGNONS

Prepare Cream Sauce. Add ¼ cup chopped cooked mushrooms.

## ONION SAUCE SAUCE AUX OIGNONS

¼ *cup chopped onions*                     ¼ *tsp. salt*
*water to cover*                           ⅛ *tsp. pepper*
1 *tbs. butter*                            *Cream Sauce*

Cook the onions, uncovered, in enough water to cover. When the water has boiled away, stir in the butter, salt, and pepper. Mix and add the Cream Sauce.

## SHRIMP SAUCE SAUCE ROSE AUX QUEUES DE CREVETTES

¼ *cup chopped cooked, cleaned*           1 *cup Cream Sauce*
   *shrimps*                 *red food colouring*

Add the shrimps to the sauce and serve. Or add 1 or 2 drops red food colouring, then add the shrimps.

## THERMIDOR SAUCE SAUCE THERMIDOR

1 tbs. butter
1 tbs. chopped shallots
1 cup dry white wine
1 cup hot Milk Sauce

½ cup heavy cream
½ tsp. salt
¼ tsp. pepper

Melt the butter; stir the shallots into it. Add the wine; reduce to half the volume. Stir into the Milk Sauce. Stir the cream in; add seasoning if needed.

## TRUFFLE SAUCE SAUCE AUX TRUFFES

1 tbs. chopped truffles or canned
   truffles
1 cup hot Cream Sauce

salt
pepper

Add the truffles to Cream Sauce. Season as needed. Heat and stir 2 minutes and serve at once.

# Other Sauces

## BÉARNAISE SAUCE BÉARNAISE

¾ cup vinegar
¼ tsp. salt
⅛ tsp. pepper

2 shallots, chopped
Hollandaise Sauce

Heat the vinegar, salt, pepper, and shallots together in a glass, or enamel saucepan until reduced to about 1 tablespoonful. Add the vinegar mixture drop by drop to Hollandaise Sauce and serve.

## CHANTILLY SAUCE SAUCE CHANTILLY

1 cup mayonnaise
Mix and serve.

½ cup whipped cream

## GARLIC SAUCE AILLOLI

5 cloves garlic
½ tsp. salt
¼ tsp. pepper

1 egg yolk
1 cup oil
¼ lemon, juice only

Chop garlic fine with the salt and pepper. Beat the egg yolk in a bowl. Add the garlic, then beat and add oil drop by drop, stirring or beating always in the same direction. Add lemon juice. Mix and serve.

## HERB SAUCE SAUCE VERTE

½ cup chopped mixed fresh herbs
1 slice French bread soaked in
   bouillon or meat extract
1 yolk hard-boiled egg
2 yolks raw eggs

½ tsp. salt
¼ tsp. pepper
½ tsp. dry mustard
½ cup oil
½ tsp. vinegar

Wash the parsley and chop fine. Squeeze the liquid from the bread; mash bread with the cooked egg yolk. Add to the herbs with the raw yolks and beat until smooth. Season; then add oil and vinegar alternately, beating until mixture has the consistency of mayonnaise.

## HOLLANDAISE SAUCE SAUCE HOLLANDAISE

½ cup butter
2 egg yolks, slightly beaten

1 tbs. lemon juice
⅛ tsp. cayenne

Divide the butter in 2 portions. Put one in the upper part of a double boiler with the yolks and lemon juice. Set pan over hot but not boiling water, and stir constantly until the butter is melted. Add the remaining butter and stir until the sauce thickens. Remove from the heat. Season with cayenne. Serve at once.

NOTE: If the water is too hot or by mistake begins to boil, the sauce may curdle. If it does, add heavy cream (about 1 tablespoon) drop by drop.

## MADEIRA SAUCE SAUCE MADÈRE

| | |
|---|---|
| 1 tbs. butter | ½ cup Madeira wine |
| 2 tbs. flour | pepper |
| ½ cup hot water | 12 olives, seeds removed |

Melt the butter in a saucepan. Stir the flour smoothly in; add the water, stirring slowly, and the wine and pepper. Stir and cook until thickened. Add the olives; cook 5 minutes and serve.

## MARINADE SAUCE SAUCE MARINADE

See Game and Poultry chapter.

## MAYONNAISE SAUCE MAYONNAISE

| | |
|---|---|
| 1 egg yolk | ¼ tsp. salt |
| ½ cup olive oil | ⅛ tsp. pepper |
| 1 or 2 tsp. vinegar | |

Stir the yolk, always in the same direction, adding a drop or two of oil at a time. Stir until 'as thick as butter'. Add a few drops of vinegar, stirring smoothly; and continue until all is used. Stir in the salt and pepper. Makes 1 cup of mayonnaise or more.

Vinegar can, if preferred, be replaced by mustard; the sauce is improved by adding a teaspoon of dried herbs, or 1 or 2 tablespoons of mixed fresh herbs dried with a cloth and finely chopped.

Principles to be remembered in making mayonnaise:

1. The oil, egg, and vinegar must be the same temperature, but whether warm or cold matters little. To ensure this equal temperature, place the ingredients near each other an hour before starting to make the sauce.

2. Eggs must be fresh, but not too new-laid; the yolk of a new-laid egg does not coagulate easily.

3. For preference use an earthenware bowl and see that both it

and the spoon used for stirring are clean and of the same temperature as the ingredients.

4. The oil used must be of good quality, preferably olive oil.

## MOUSSELINE SAUCE SAUCE MOUSSELINE

*Hollandaise Sauce*                    ½ *cup whipped cream*

Combine ingredients and serve at once.

## NORMANDY SAUCE SAUCE NORMANDE

½ *cup butter*                         ¼ *tsp. salt*
½ *cup heavy cream*                    ⅛ *tsp. pepper*
2 *egg yolks*

Melt the butter in a saucepan. Add the cream; mix. Beat the yolks lightly in the upper part of a double boiler; stir the butter mixture in slowly, adding salt and pepper. Set the pan over hot but not boiling water. Heat and stir until thickened. Do not boil. Serve at once.

## PIQUANT SAUCE SAUCE PIQUANTE

1 *tbs. butter*                        ⅛ *tsp. pepper*
2 *tbs. flour*                         3 *tbs. vinegar*
1 *cup hot water*                      3 *shallots, chopped*
¼ *tsp. salt*

Brown the butter; stir the flour smoothly in and cook until browned. Stir the water in slowly; add seasonings and boil, stirring until slightly thickened.

In another enamel, glass, or pan heat the vinegar and shallots, cooking until the liquid is reduced to 1 tablespoonful. Add this slowly to the first sauce; stir, heat, and serve.

# Sauces : Other

## TARTARE SAUCE SAUCE TARTARE

2 *hard-boiled eggs*  
1 *cup olive oil*  
1 *or* 2 *tbs. vinegar*

½ *tsp. salt*  
¼ *tsp. pepper*  
1 *tsp. prepared mustard*

Mash the yolks fine. Chop the whites as fine as possible. To the yolks and whites add oil drop by drop, stirring smoothly until almost all the oil is added. Then vinegar and oil, stirring smoothly. Add the seasonings; blend and serve.

## TOMATO SAUCE SAUCE TOMATE

3 *or* 4 *tomatoes*  
½ *tsp. salt*  
¼ *tsp. pepper*  
*garlic*

1 *cup water*  
1 *tbs. butter*  
1 *tbs. flour*

Slice the tomatoes into an enamel saucepan. Season; add a small sliver of garlic and the water. Cover and cook slowly until the tomatoes are softened, 25 or 30 minutes. Press through a sieve. Heat the butter, blend the flour smoothly with it, and stir the tomatoes in. Stir and cook until thickened.

NOTE: Add more water for large tomatoes. There should be about 2 cups of tomato purée after straining.

# PÂTÉS

Although nearly everyone is familiar with pâté de foie gras, the simpler bourgeois pâtés made by French housewives may come as a surprise. They are easily prepared, economical, and a welcome addition to the reserve shelf in the pantry or refrigerator.

## BRAWN PÂTÉ DE TÊTE

| | |
|---|---|
| ½ *pig's head* | *sprig thyme* |
| 2 *carrots* | *bay leaf* |
| 2 *turnips* | *parsley* |
| 2 *leeks* | *salt and pepper* |
| 1 *onion* | 2 *shallots, chopped* |
| 2 *cloves* | 1 *tbs. chopped parsley* |
| 1 *clove garlic* | ¼ *cup cognac* |

Have the butcher clean and cut the pig's head. Rinse it; drain. Place in a 2-quart saucepan. Wash, scrape or peel, and slice the carrots, turnips, leeks, and onion. Add to the saucepan; add the cloves, garlic, herbs, salt, and freshly ground pepper. Cover with water. Cook slowly 2 to 3 hours, or until the meat is so tender it falls from the bones. Skim the boiling liquid from time to time during the cooking period.

When the meat is done, remove it; discard the bone but save the soup. Chop the meat. Mix with the shallots and about 1 tablespoon chopped parsley. Roll into the shape of a ball. Tie tightly in a clean cloth. Place in a bowl, cover with a weighted lid, and let stand in the refrigerator 12 hours. Turn out on a chilled serving dish. Cook the soup in the saucepan until reduced to about 1½ cups. Add the cognac. Pour this over the meat. Chill again. Serve sliced. Serves 6.

# Pâtés

## DUCK PÂTÉ PÂTÉ DE CANARD

| | |
|---|---|
| 1 *young roasting duck* | 3 *tbs. bouillon* |
| 1 *slice fat pork* | 3 *tbs. tomato juice* |
| 1 *tbs. butter* | |

STUFFING

| | |
|---|---|
| 1 *carrot* | ½ *cup heavy cream* |
| 1 *onion* | *duck's liver, minced* |
| 2 *leeks* | ¼ *cup pâté de foie gras (small* |
| 1 *quart water* | *tin)* |
| ½ *lb. calf's liver, sliced* | 1 *or 2 truffles, chopped (small* |
| 5 *slices bacon* | *tin)* |
| 1 *slice bread* | 1 *tsp. salt* |
| 2 *egg yolks* | ½ *tsp. pepper* |

Clean the duck. Make an incision the length of the backbone, laying back the flesh on each side, and remove the backbone and ribs. Fill the inside of the duck with the stuffing. Press the bird back to its original shape. Wrap the piece of uncooked pork around it and tie to hold in place. Brown the duck in the butter in a fireproof dish. Add the bouillon and tomato juice. Cover and cook in a moderate oven (350° F.) or on top of the range 1½ hours, or 20 minutes per pound. Remove from the heat. Let cool and then place in the refrigerator overnight.

The stuffing is prepared as follows:

Slice vegetables into a 2-quart saucepan. Add the water and boil 45 minutes. Add the calf's liver and bacon and boil 5 minutes. Remove the meat and mince it with the bread (soaked in a little of the liquid from the saucepan). Beat until smooth; add the egg yolks, cream, duck's liver, pâté de foie gras, and truffles. Season; mix and let stand about 1 hour in a cool place before using in the bird.

The stuffed duck slices smoothly and serves 8 or more.

## GOOSE PÂTÉ CONFIT D'OIE

| | |
|---|---|
| 1 *fat goose* | *coarse salt* |

Cut the cleaned and drawn goose at the joints. Remove the best pieces of meat; use the rest for stew. Cover the selected meat with coarse salt and let stand in the refrigerator 24 hours. Remove the salt carefully and dry the meat with a clean cloth.

Melt the goose fat; filter it by passing it through a piece of clean muslin. Heat it to boiling; add the goose flesh and cook. Simmer 3 to 4 hours. To know when the meat is cooked, insert a pointed knife; if no blood adheres, it is ready.

Place the meat in a bowl; pour the fat in which it cooked over it. If not enough to cover, add a little melted lard. Cover the dish tightly; seal with pastry made of flour and water or an adhesive cloth strip. Keep in the refrigerator. Serves 10 to 20.


## HARE PÂTÉ PÂTÉ DE LIÈVRE

| | |
|---|---|
| *hindquarters of a hare* | *pepper* |
| 1 *lb. sausage meat* | *crackling* |
| 3 *oz. lean veal* | 3 *oz. fat pork* |
| 3 *oz. shin of veal* | 1 *sprig thyme* |
| *liver and heart of the hare* | 1 *bay leaf* |
| *hare's blood* | $\frac{1}{2}$ *calf's shinbone* |
| *salt* | $\frac{1}{4}$ *lb. pork dripping* |

Skin and clean a hare, keeping as much of the blood as possible. Cut the hare in two parts at the middle of the back, over the kidneys. The hind quarters only should be used for the pâté, the remainder being used for jugged hare.

Remove all the bones very carefully from the hind-quarters and mince the meat with 1 lb. of sausage meat, 3 oz. lean veal, 3 oz. shin of veal, the liver and heart of the hare, the blood which has been saved, salt, and pepper.

Cover the bottom of an earthenware dish with a piece of crackling; fill the dish with the minced meat, placing strips of fat pork here and there. On top place a thin slice of uncooked pork fat, a sprig of thyme, and a bay leaf. Sprinkle with $\frac{1}{2}$ cup of meat jelly made by boiling together for 2 hours in a little water the bones of the hare, some crackling, and $\frac{1}{2}$ calf's shinbone. Put the cover on the dish and place in a moderate oven (350° F.) 45 minutes. The pâté is properly cooked when it no longer adheres to the sides of the dish.

When the pâté is cold, pour over it ¼ lb. hot pork dripping. If the pâté is to be kept for several months, increase the quantity of dripping so as to seal it completely. When cold, replace the lid on the dish and seal with a pastry made of flour and water.

## LARK PÂTÉ PÂTÉ D'ALOUETTES

| | |
|---|---|
| 20 *larks* | *short pastry* |
| ¼ *lb. calf's liver* | *sausage meat as required* |
| ¼ *lb. belly of pork* | 1 *bay leaf* |
| *salt, pepper* | 1 *slice pork fat if necessary* |

Pluck, singe, and clean some 20 larks. Remove the heads and fill the bodies with a mixture made of ¼ lb. calf's liver, ¼ lb. belly of pork, both minced, and salt and pepper.

Place the larks in a fireproof dish or pie dish lined with short pastry. Fill the empty spaces with sausage meat mixed with any of the stuffing left over. Add salt, pepper, and a bay leaf. If a fireproof dish is used, cover with a thin slice of uncooked pork fat before putting the lid on. If, however, a pie dish is used, cover with pastry. Bake in slow oven (300° F.) about 1 hour.

## LIVER PÂTÉ PÂTÉ DE FOIE DE PORC

| | |
|---|---|
| 2 *slices fat pork* | 1½ *tsp. salt* |
| 1 *lb. pork liver, minced fine* | ½ *tsp. pepper.* |
| 1 *lb. minced fat pork* | *bay leaf* |
| 1 *egg* | ¼ *cup cognac* |

Place 1 slice of the fat pork in a deep pâté dish. Fill the dish with the minced liver, fat pork and 1 beaten egg. Season. Cover with the second slice of fat pork. Add the bay leaf and pour the brandy over. Cover and bake in a moderate oven (350° F.) 45 minutes or longer, depending on the size of the dish. Let cool. Serve sliced. Serves 10 or more.

NOTE: The pâté mould cover should have holes in it to let the steam escape.

# Pâtés

## PEASANT PÂTÉ PÂTÉ PAYSANNE OU DE CAMPAGNE

1 *lb. rump of beef, minced*
1 *lb. sausage meat*
½ *cup white wine*
1 *egg, beaten*
1½ *tsp. salt*

½ *tsp. pepper*
1 *slice fat pork*
1 *onion, sliced*
*bay leaf*
*thyme*

Mix the beef and sausage well together. Stir the wine, egg, salt and pepper into the meat. Mix smoothly. Place the slice of fat pork in the bottom of the pâté mould or deep earthenware dish. Add the onion and herbs, then the meat mixture. Cover and seal with adhesive tape, or with flour-and-water pastry, leaving only the airhole in the lid free. Set in a shallow pan half filled with water. Bake in a moderate oven (350° F.) 1½ hours. Do not remove the lid until the pâté has cooled. Serves 10 or more.

## RABBIT PÂTÉ PÂTÉ DE LAPIN

1 *cleaned and drawn rabbit, cut in*
   *pieces at the joints*
*rabbit liver*
1½ *lb. sausage meat*
1½ *tsp. salt*
½ *tsp. pepper*
*cracklings or 4 to 6 slices fat*
   *pork or bacon*

*sprig thyme*
*bay leaf*
1 *cup meat jelly (boiled-down*
   *bouillon allowed to chill and*
   *thicken)*
4 *tbs. melted lard*

Remove any splinters of bone. Mince the liver with the sausage; add the seasonings. Cover the bottom of an earthenware dish with cracklings or 2 slices bacon; add a layer of rabbit, then a layer of sausage. Repeat, placing the remaining strips of bacon or pork in these layers. Lay 1 strip on top. Add the thyme and bay leaf. Pour the jellied meat broth over. Cover and seal as for other pâtés. Set in a shallow pan half filled with water. Bake in a moderate oven (350° F.) 1 hour. When cooked, pour the melted lard or pork drippings over the pâté. Let cool. Serves 10 to 20.

## RILLETTE PÂTÉ RILLETTES

| | |
|---|---|
| 1 *lb. beef, goose, or rabbit* | 1 *tsp. thyme* |
| 1 *lb. fat pork* | 1 *tbs. minced parsley* |
| 1½ *tsp. salt* | *bay leaf* |
| ½ *tsp. pepper* | ½ *cup or more melted lard* |

Cut the meat in small pieces and do likewise with the same quantity of fat pork. To the meat add salt, pepper, thyme, parsley and bay leaf. Cover with water. Simmer for 5 to 6 hours until the meat is reduced to a pulp and the water is nearly evaporated. Turn it out on a large plate. Remove the bones and mash meat well. Shape in a loaf or place in an earthenware mould. If the pâté is to be kept for any length of time, cover with melted lard. Chill. Serves 20 or more.

## VEAL AND HAM PÂTÉ PÂTÉ DE VEAU ET JAMBON

| | |
|---|---|
| *rich pastry for deep pie dish* | ½ *lb. cooked ham, cubed* |
| ½ *lb. sausage meat* | *bay leaf* |
| *salt and pepper* | 1 *egg yolk* |
| ½ *lb. veal, cubed* | |

Line a deep earthenware or glass pie dish or loaf tin with rich pastry. Crimp an edge around the dish. Spread a layer of sausage meat in the bottom; season. Add alternate layers of veal, ham, and sausage. Season each layer. Put the bay leaf on top. Cover the dish with pastry. Cut a small hole in the centre to allow steam to escape. Crimp a decorative edge around the dish. Brush the pastry with the beaten yolk. Bake in a slow oven (300° F.) about 1 hour. The pastry should be golden. Serves 8.

## WILD DUCK PÂTÉ PÂTÉ DE GRIVES

Use the same recipe as for Lark Pâté.

## WOODCOCK PÂTÉ PÂTÉ DE BÉCASSE

Proceed as for Lark Pâté, but reduce by ½ the amount of belly of pork used for the stuffing.

# VEGETABLES

The French use practically every vegetable known to English cooks, but it is the humble varieties that play an all-important role in French cookery. It is the poor but honest onion—the shallot in particular—leeks, carrots, beans, and cabbage that make their appearance again and again on the French table. How could a ragoût be made without them? And the custom of serving certain vegetables as a separate course is one with many advantages.

## JERUSALEM ARTICHOKES TOPINAMBOURS

*2 or 3 lbs. Jerusalem artichokes*  　*Cream Sauce or*
*boiling salted water*  　*Mayonnaise*

Select firm unwrinkled tubers. About 3 pounds serves 6 people. Wash the vegetables, scrub with a brush, and pare. Cover with boiling salted water (1 teaspoon salt to 1 quart water). Boil 20 to 35 minutes. Drain and serve covered with cream sauce. Or chill and serve with mayonnaise. Serves 4 to 6.

## ASPARAGUS SERVED COLD ASPERGES FROIDES

Cook the asparagus as described below. Let cool, then chill. Serve with mayonnaise seasoned with a little mustard. Or mix whipped cream and mayonnaise and pour over the cold asparagus.

## ASPARAGUS ASPERGES

*16 to 20 stalks green asparagus*  　*Hollandaise Sauce or*
*boiling salted water*  　*Mousseline Sauce or*
　*White Sauce*

# Vegetables

Wash the asparagus; snap off each stalk as far up as it will break easily. Remove scales. Tie in bunch and stand in a saucepan or asparagus cooker. Add boiling salted water (1 teaspoon salt to 1 quart water) or steam over boiling water; 15 to 20 minutes for boiling, 25 to 30 minutes for steaming. Drain. Serve hot or cold with Hollandaise or Mousseline Sauce; hot with White Sauce. Or make the special sauce below. Serves 4 or 5.

SPECIAL SAUCE

| | |
|---|---|
| 2 or 3 hard-boiled eggs | ½ tsp. salt |
| melted butter | ¼ tsp. pepper |

Remove the yolks from the eggs while still warm. Mash and beat melted butter into them until the mixture has the consistency of mayonnaise. Season and serve. Allow 1 or 2 tablespoons of sauce per serving.

## ASPARAGUS TIPS I POINTES D'ASPERGES

The tips are cooked and served like the longer stalks. Mix into scrambled eggs or use in an omelet.

## ASPARAGUS TIPS II

| | |
|---|---|
| 16 to 20 green tips | 2 cups hot water |
| boiling water | 1 tbs. cornstarch |
| 1 tbs. butter | 1 egg yolk |

Wash the asparagus; drain. Cover with boiling water and boil 5 minutes. Drain and place in a saucepan with the butter and hot water. Cover and boil gently for about 30 minutes. Remove the asparagus. Sprinkle the cornflour into the water in which the asparagus boiled; stir smoothly until thickened. Remove from the heat; pour slowly over the egg yolk, beating slowly until mixed. Pour over the asparagus and serve. Serves 4 or 5.

## BROAD BEANS FÈVES

3 *lb.* (2½ *qts.*) *young broad beans*  ½ *tsp. pepper*
*boiling salted water*  1 *tbs. sugar*
1 *tbs. butter*  1 *cup water*
2 *tbs. flour*  2 *egg yolks*
1 *tsp. salt*

Cover the beans with the boiling salted water (1 teaspoonful salt to 1 quart of water) and cook covered until they are tender, about 30 to 45 minutes. If the beans are large, their skins must be removed after boiling and discarded. Drain off water.

Heat the butter, stir in the flour smoothly, add the seasonings, and mix. Add the water gradually. Bring to boil; stir until thickened. Remove from heat and stir in the yolks. Pour over the beans and serve. Serves 4 or more.

NOTE: About 5 quarts of beans in the pod make 1 quart shelled beans, to serve 6 to 8.

If the pods are not tender, green, and juicy, shell the beans and cook them as described. If the pods are very young and tender, leave them on, cook, and serve.

## FRENCH BEANS HARICOTS VERTS

These are the kidney beans whose pods are picked just after the bean begins to form. The whole pod is cooked and eaten. Yellow and green varieties may or may not have strings. Remove tips and strings if any.

1½ *lb. beans*  1 *tbs. butter*
*boiling salted water*  1 *tbs. chopped fresh herbs*
½ *cup heavy cream*

Cover prepared beans with boiling salted water (1 teaspoon salt to 1 quart water). Boil about 45 minutes, or until tender. Drain. Stir the cream and butter into the beans; sprinkle with herbs and serve. Serves 6.

# BUTTER BEANS WITH TOMATOES HARICOTS BLANCS À LA PURÉE DE TOMATES

| | |
|---|---|
| 2 *cups dried beans* | 2 *tbs. tomato paste* |
| 2 *qts. cold water* | 2 *tsp. salt* |
| 1 *tbs. butter* | ½ *tsp. pepper* |
| 1 *tbs. heavy cream* | |

Cover the beans with cold water and let soak overnight. Drain. Cover with the 2 quarts of water and boil until tender. Cook slowly, about 1½ to 2 hours. Drain; mix with the butter, cream, tomato paste, and seasonings. Reheat and serve. Serves 6.

# CABBAGE WITH CHEESE CHOU AU FROMAGE

| | |
|---|---|
| 1 *head cabbage* | ¼ *cup grated cheese* |
| *boiling water* | ¼ *cup butter, melted* |
| 1 *cup White Sauce* | ¼ *cup bread crumbs* |

Boil cabbage as described in the following recipe. Drain; cut in quarters or chop. Mix the White Sauce and cheese. Pour over the cabbage and mix well. Pour into a buttered baking dish. Sprinkle the top with crumbs and the remaining butter. Brown in a moderate over (350° F.) 20 minutes. Serves 4 to 6.

# CABBAGE À LA BOURGEOISE CHOU À LA BOURGEOISE

| | |
|---|---|
| 1 *head cabbage* | *sprig thyme* |
| *boiling water* | *bay leaf* |
| 2 *cups bouillon* | ½ *lb. bacon cut in chunks* |
| 1 *carrot* | 1 *sausage* |
| 1 *onion* | |

Cabbage can be a delicious vegetable if it is properly cooked. It is, however, somewhat indigestible. To make it more digestible, after having washed it, immerse in boiling water for 10 minutes. Drain and then continue with the recipe. The smell of cabbage when boiling is reduced by placing a crust of bread on the top of the vegetable and covering the pan with a lid.

Place the drained, parboiled vegetable in a saucepan with the bouillon, vegetables, herbs, and meat. Cover and simmer 1½ hours. Add a little more bouillon during the cooking if needed. Serve hot. Serves 4 or more.

## FLANDERS RED CABBAGE CHOU ROUGE À LA FLAMANDE

| | |
|---|---|
| 1 *red cabbage* | ½ *tsp. pepper* |
| *cold salted water* | 2 *cloves* |
| 5 *apples, peeled and sliced* | 1 *tbs. flour* |
| 2 *tbs. butter* | 1 *tbs. red currant jelly* |
| 1 *tsp. salt* | |

Cover prepared cabbage with cold salted water (1 teaspoon salt to 1 quart water). Add the apples, 1 tablespoon of the butter, seasonings, and cloves. Cover and cook slowly for 2 hours.

Melt the other tablespoon of butter in a saucepan. Stir the flour in; mix. Add 1 cup of liquid from the cabbage saucepan. Stir and boil until thickened like gravy. Add the jelly. Drain the cabbage and serve with the sauce. Serves 4 to 6.

## PICKLED RED CABBAGE CHOU ROUGE MARINÉ

| | |
|---|---|
| 2 *or* 3 *heads red cabbage* | 8 *or* 10 *small onions* |
| *salt* | 2 *or* 3 *sweet red peppers* |
| *cloves* | *vinegar* |

Cut prepared cabbage in chunks, or chop fine with a cabbage slicer. Place in a stone jar which has a cover. Cover with salt. Stir and turn the cabbage every hour or so. At the end of 24 hours drain off the water. Arrange in layers with cloves, onions, and very small red peppers or strips of sweet red pepper. Pour vinegar over to cover. Lay a clean cloth over the jar and place its lid on. Let stand in a cool place for one month. Serves 12 to 20.

## CARROTS WITH BUTTER CAROTTES NOUVELLES

| | |
|---|---|
| 8 *to* 12 *small carrots* | 1 *tsp. salt* |
| 2 *tbs. butter* | 1 *tbs. minced herbs* |
| ¼ *cup hot water* | |

Heat the butter, add the prepared carrots. Cover and cook slowly about 10 minutes, shaking the pan frequently. Add the water and continue to cook 20 minutes. Season and serve. Serves 6.

## CARROTS VICHY CAROTTES À LA VICHY

| | |
|---|---|
| 8 *small carrots* | 1 *tsp. salt* |
| 1 *tbs. butter* | ½ *tsp. pepper* |
| 1 *tbs. flour* | 1 *cup water* |

Slice the carrots thinly. Heat the butter in a saucepan. Add the carrots; toss and mix. Sprinkle with the flour; mix well and cook 5 minutes. Season. Add the water. Cover and cook gently 30 to 45 minutes, or until the carrots are tender. Serves 4.

## CAULIFLOWER WITH CHEESE CHOUFLEUR AU GRATIN

| | |
|---|---|
| 1 *medium-sized cauliflower* | ¼ *cup grated cheese* |
| 1 *tsp. salt* | ¼ *cup bread crumbs* |
| 1 *cup White Sauce* | |

Cover cauliflower with cold water; add salt. Boil until tender, about 30 minutes. Drain; break or cut into small sections. Mix the White Sauce with 2 tablespoons of the cheese. Place the cauliflower in a buttered baking dish. Pour the cheese sauce over it. Sprinkle with the rest of the cheese and the crumbs. Brown in a moderate oven (375° F.) until bubbly and golden, about 15 minutes. Serves 6.

# CAULIFLOWER WITH TOMATO SAUCE PAIN DE CHOUFLEUR

1 *head cauliflower*
*boiling salted water*
2 *eggs, beaten*
½ *tsp. salt*

¼ *tsp. pepper*
1 *cup White Sauce*
*Tomato Sauce*

Cook cauliflower in boiling salted water (1 teaspoon salt to 1 quart water) until tender, about 30 minutes. Drain. Cut apart and press through a colander or sieve.

Mix the eggs and seasoning into the slightly cooled White Sauce. Combine with the cauliflower. Pour into a buttered mould. Cover and cook over boiling water or in a moderate oven (350° F.) 45 minutes. Serve hot with hot Tomato Sauce. Serves 6.


# BRAISED CELERY CÉLERI BRAISÉ

6 *good stalks celery*
1 *tbs. butter*
1 *cup water*

1 *tsp. salt*
½ *tsp. pepper*

Wash the celery; cut off leafy tops. Cut into 2-inch lengths or smaller. Heat the butter in a saucepan; stir the celery into it and cook about 10 minutes. Add the water and seasoning. Cover the pan and cook slowly 35 minutes, or until the celery is tender. Serves 4 to 6.


# CHESTNUT PURÉE PURÉE DE MARRONS

2 *lb. chestnuts*
*olive oil*
*boiling water*

*salt and pepper*
*hot milk or cream*
*butter*

The easiest way to shell chestnuts is as follows: with a sharp paring knife make a slit in each shell. Put the chestnuts in a pan, adding ½ teaspoon of oil for each cup of nuts. Shake the pan over the heat 5 minutes, then set it in a hot oven 5 minutes. Take from the oven.

Remove the shells with the aid of a sharp knife, and the skin will come off with the shell.

Cover with boiling salted water (1½ teaspoons of salt to 1 quart water) and boil gently 20 minutes, or until tender. Put chestnuts through a ricer or mash them. To every cup of mashed chestnuts mix in ¼ teaspoon salt, a little pepper, 2 tablespoons hot milk or cream, and 1 tablespoon butter. Mix and beat smoothly. Serve at once. Serves 6.

## FRIED EGGPLANT AUBERGINES FRITES

| | |
|---|---|
| 2 *medium-sized eggplants* | ½ *tsp. pepper* |
| 1 *cup milk* | *oil for frying* |
| ½ *cup flour* | 1 *lemon, quartered* |
| 1 *tsp salt* | 2 *tomatoes, sliced* |

Slice eggplants lengthwise but do not peel. Dip the slices in milk and seasoned flour. Sauté in hot olive oil until the slices are golden and tender. Serve garnished with lemon and tomato slices. Serves 6 to 8.

## EGGPLANT WITH TOMATOES AUBERGINES À LA TOMATE

Prepare eggplant as in the preceding recipe. Serve with Tomato Sauce.

## BRAISED ENDIVE ENDIVES BRAISÉES

| | |
|---|---|
| 4 *heads Belgian endive* | ½ *tsp. pepper* |
| 1 *tbs. butter* | 1 *tsp. sugar* |
| 1 *tsp. salt* | *hot water* |

Cut each endive in half lengthwise. Heat the butter in a frying pan. Lay the endive halves in the hot butter. Season; add the sugar and cover the pan. Cook slowly, adding a little hot water if necessary, until the endive is tender, about 30 minutes. Serves 4 to 8.

## LENTIL STEW LENTILLES

| | |
|---|---|
| 1 *lb.*(2 *cups*) *lentils* | ¼ *lb. bacon, cut in chunks* |
| 1 *qt. bouillon* | 12 *small onions* |
| 1 *tbs. butter* | 1 *tsp. salt* |
| ½ *calf's foot* | ½ *tsp. pepper* |

Cover lentils with water. Boil 30 minutes. Drain. Rinse in cold water; drain. Add the bouillon.

Heat the butter; brown the calf's foot in it with the bacon, peeled onions, and seasonings. Cook 10 minutes. Add to the lentils and continue to cook gently 1½ to 2 hours. Serves 6.

## MUSHROOMS IN SAUCE CHAMPIGNONS À LA SAUCE

| | |
|---|---|
| 1 *lb. fresh mushrooms* | 1 *tbs. butter* |
| *cold water* | 1½ *cups Cream Sauce* |

Trim off earth end of stalk. Break stems from caps and wash in water. Put caps and stems in cold water with the butter and boil 5 minutes. Drain. Mix with hot sauce and serve. Serves 6.

## MUSHROOMS WITH CHEESE CHAMPIGNONS AU FRO-MAGE

| | |
|---|---|
| 1 *lb. fresh mushrooms* | 2 *shallots, minced* |
| *boiling water* | 1 *hard-boiled egg, minced* |
| 4 *tbs. butter* | ¼ *cup grated cheese* |
| 1 *slice bread* | ¼ *cup bread crumbs* |
| 2 *tbs. minced parsley* | 1 *tsp. salt* |
| 1 *small section garlic, minced* | ½ *tsp pepper* |

Wash and boil the mushrooms as described in the preceding recipe Drain them and place in a casserole rubbed with butter.

Mix the crumbled bread, parsley, garlic, shallots, and egg together. Spread this over the mushrooms. Top with cheese, crumbs, seasoning, and dabs of butter. Bake in a moderate oven (350° F.) 30 minutes. Serves 6.

# Vegetables

## SMALL ONIONS WITH RAISINS LES PETITS OIGNONS

2 lb. small onions
4 oz. seedless sultanas (dry)
4 oz. sugar
1 cup water

¼ cup vinegar
6 tbs. tomato purée
3 tbs. oil
½ tsp. salt
⅛ tsp. cayenne

Leave onions whole. Place in a 2-quart enamel saucepan; add the sultanas sugar, water, vinegar, and all other ingredients. Mix. Cover and cook slowly about 45 minutes, longer if necessary. Serves 5 to 6.

## BRAISED ONIONS PURÉE D'OIGNONS

2 lb. onions (8 medium)
2 tbs. butter
1 tsp. salt

½ tsp. pepper
boiling water

Slice or chop the onions fine. Heat the butter in a saucepan; brown the onions in it, stirring well. Add the seasonings. Cover the pan and cook slowly about 30 minutes. Add a little boiling water if necessary. Serves 5 to 6.

## FRIED PARSNIPS PANAIS

12 small parsnips
vinegar
cold water

salt
batter for frying
fat for deep frying

Scrape the parsnips; wash; drain. Cover with cold water to which about 1 tablespoon of vinegar has been added. Drain. Place in a saucepan; cover with cold salted water (1 teaspoon salt to 1 quart water). Cover and cook until the parsnips are tender, 30 to 50 minutes. Drain. Cut in strips or quarters. Dip in batter and fry in deep hot fat. Or dip in flour and sauté in a little oil or butter until browned. Serves 6.

# Vegetables

*Fritter Batter.* To make a simple fritter batter use:

| | |
|---|---|
| 1 *cup flour* | 2 *tbs. olive oil* |
| ¼ *tsp. salt* | 1 *egg white, beaten* |
| ⅔ *cup water or beer* | |

Mix and sift the dry ingredients. Add beer or water; beat until smooth (about 3 minutes). Add the oil. Fold in the stiffly beaten white. Use as directed.

## GREEN PEAS PETITS POIS

| | |
|---|---|
| 2 *qts. (lb) peas in the shell* | ½ *tsp. pepper* |
| 2 *tbs. butter* | 1 *onion, sliced* |
| 1 *head lettuce* | 1 *tbs. sugar* |
| 1 *tsp. salt* | |

Select young, green, juicy peas. Shell them and place in a 2½-quart saucepan with the butter. Wash the lettuce and cut in quarters. Add to the pan. Season and add the onion and sugar. Cover and cook over low heat 30 minutes. Very small new potatoes may be added and cooked at the same time. Serves 6.

## PURÉE OF DRIED PEAS PURÉE DE POIS CASSÉS

| | |
|---|---|
| ½ *lb. (1 cup) dried peas* | ½ *tsp. pepper* |
| 2 *cups cold water* | 1 *tbs. butter* |
| 1 *onion, sliced* | 2 *slices fried bread* |
| 1 *tsp. salt* | |

Cover peas with water and let soak overnight. To cook them, drain, cover with cold water, and add the onion and seasonings. Cover and cook slowly until the peas are soft and the water boiled down, about 1½ hours or longer. Put through a sieve. Mix with the butter. Serve garnished with strips of fried bread. Serves 4.

## FRIED POTATOES POMMES DE TERRE FRITES

2 *lb. potatoes*                              salt
1 *qt. olive oil or other fat*

Slice peeled potatoes thinly or cut in matchsticks. Heat the oil;
before it begins to smoke, fry a small quantity of the potatoes.
Use a frying basket lowered into the hot oil. Remove the basket
just as the potatoes begin to turn golden. Drain them on thick paper.
Repeat the process until all have had their first frying. Then replace
the half-fried potatoes in the hot oil and cook until browned and
crisp. Drain on thick paper . Serve sprinkled with salt. Serves 6.

## POTATOES CHAMONIX POMMES DE TERRE CHAMONIX

2 *lb. potatoes, steamed*                    ¼ *tsp. grated nutmeg*
1 *cup milk*                                  5 *oz. flour*
2 *tbs. butter*                               4 *eggs*
1 *tsp. salt*                                 3 *oz. grated cheese*
½ *tsp. pepper*                              *oil or fat for deep frying*

Mash and keep warm the potatoes. Put one cup of milk, the butter,
salt, pepper and nutmeg in a saucepan and boil. Remove from fire,
and mix gradually with 5 oz. of flour. Replace on fire and stir
until the mixture is dry. Remove from fire and mix with 4 eggs,
one at a time. Mix with the potatoes, add 3 oz. of grated cheese,
roll into balls the size of a large walnut and fry a few at a time in
a moderately hot oil bath, increasing the heat.

## MASHED POTATOES POMMES DE TERRE EN PURÉE

2 *lb. (8) potatoes*                          ½ *tsp. pepper*
1 *tbs. butter*                               1 *cup rich milk*
1 *tsp. salt*

Cover peeled potatoes with cold water and boil 30 minutes, or
until the potatoes are tender. Drain; press through a ricer. Beat
into the potatoes the butter and seasonings. Stir vigorously; add
the milk and mix well. Serve at once. Serves 4.

# *Vegetables*

## POTATO PANCAKES CRÊPES PARMENTIER

2 *cups mashed potatoes*  
½ *cup flour*  
2 *tbs. oil*  

1 *cup water*  
*rich milk*  
2 *tbs. butter*

Beat the potatoes and flour together; gradually add the oil, then the water. Add enough milk to make the consistency of thick cream. Heat the butter in a pancake pan. Pour the batter in as for any other pancake. Brown on both sides. Serves 6.

## NEW POTATOES WITH BUTTER POMMES DE TERRE
### NOUVELLES AU BEURRE

2 *lb. very small new potatoes*  
2 *tbs. butter*  

1 *tsp. salt*  
1 *tbs. minced green herbs*

Scrape potatoes a little but do not peel them. Heat the butter in a heavy pan; add the potatoes and cook slowly 30 minutes. Sprinkle with salt and herbs and serve. Serves 6.

## POTATOES WITH BACON POMMES DE TERRE AU LARD

1 *tbs. butter*  
½ *lb. bacon, cubed*  
2 *onions, sliced*  
1 *tsp. salt*  

½ *tsp. pepper*  
2 *lbs. potatoes, sliced*  
*water*

Heat the butter in a heavy deep frying-pan. Add the bacon and cook 5 minutes. Add the onions and seasonings. Stir, then add the potatoes. Season lightly. Pour in water barely to cover. Cover the pan and cook slowly 30 minutes, or until the potatoes are tender and the liquid absorbed. Serves 6.

## POTATOES WITH CHEESE POMMES DE TERRE AU FROMAGE

3 *large boiled potatoes*  
1 *cup grated cheese*  
¼ *cup cream*  

1 *tsp. salt*  
½ *tsp. pepper*  
2 *tbs. butter, melted*

Cut the potatoes in halves, lengthwise. Scoop out some of the centre of each half. Mash this scooped-out portion with the cheese, cream,

145

and seasonings. Pile back into the halves and place in a buttered baking dish. Pour the melted butter over them and brown in a moderate oven (350° F.) 20 minutes, or until golden. Serves 6.

## SLICED POTATOES IN TOMATO SAUCE POMMES DE TERRE EN RONDELLES

| | |
|---|---|
| 2 *lb. potatoes* | 2 *tbs. tomato paste* |
| 1 *onion, sliced* | 1 *cup milk* |
| 1 *tbs. butter* | 1 *tsp. salt* |
| 2 *tbs. flour* | ½ *tsp. pepper* |

Peel the potatoes and slice thinly. Cook the onion in the butter; add the potatoes. Sprinkle with flour. Add the tomato paste and pour the milk over. Season. Cover and cook gently 25 minutes. Serve hot. Serves 4 or 6.

## POTATOES WITH TOMATOES AND ONIONS POMMES DE TERRE AUX TOMATES

| | |
|---|---|
| 2 *lb. potatoes* | 1 *tbs. butter* |
| 2 *lb. (5 to 7 medium) tomatoes* | 1 *tsp. salt* |
| 8 *small onions* | ½ *tsp. pepper* |
| | ½ *cup heavy cream* |

Slice the potatoes and tomatoes. Arrange in layers in a baking dish. Skin the onions and brown them in the butter. Scatter them over the dish; add the seasonings. Pour the cream over. Cook covered in a moderate oven (350° F.) about 45 minutes, or until the potatoes are tender. Uncover the dish for the last 10 minutes of cooking. Serves 8.

## POTATOES WITH CHEESE SAUCE POMMES DE TERRE À LA CRÈME

| | |
|---|---|
| 2 *lb. potatoes, boiled* | ¼ *cup grated cheese* |
| 1½ *cups Cheese Sauce* | ¼ *cup bread crumbs* |

146

Slice the potatoes into a buttered baking dish. Pour the Cheese Sauce over them. Sprinkle thickly with cheese and crumbs. Brown in a moderate oven (350° F.) about 20 minutes, or until bubbly and browned. Serves 6.


## FRIED SALSIFY SALSIFIS FRITS

| | |
|---|---|
| 6 *salsify roots* | *salt* |
| *vinegar* | *Fritter Batter* |
| *cold water* | *oil or fat for deep frying* |

Select small, firm roots. Cut off tops; wash well. Drain. Cover with cold water to which 1 tablespoon of vinegar has been added. Drain, scrape, and slice in strips. Put into cold water. Boil 45 to 60 minutes. Drain, dip in batter, then fry in deep hot oil or fat. Drain on thick paper towelling. Serve hot, salted or plain. Serves 6.


## SPINACH EPINARDS

| | |
|---|---|
| 2½ *to* 3 *lb.* (1 *peck*) *spinach* | 1 *tsp. salt* |
| 1 *cup boiling water* | ½ *tsp. pepper* |
| ¼ *tsp. salt* | ½ *tsp. sugar* |
| 2 *tbs. butter* | ¼ *tsp. grated nutmeg* |
| ½ *cup hot White Sauce* | 3 *small bananas* |
| 2 *egg yolks* | |

Wash the spinach under running cold water several times. Place in a saucepan; add boiling water and salt. Cover and boil 5 minutes. Drain; chop fine. Heat in a saucepan with 1 tablespoon butter. Stir and cook 5 minutes. Add the beaten yolks and seasonings to the White Sauce. Turn this over the spinach; mix and serve. Garnish the dish with halves of small bananas sautéed in 1 tablespoon of butter. Serves 6.

## BAKED SPINACH EPINARDS AU GRATIN

2½ to 3 *lb. spinach*              ¼ *cup bread crumbs*
*boiling water*                    2 *tbs. olive oil*

Wash and boil the spinach as described in the preceding recipe. Drain, mince, and place in a buttered baking dish. Sprinkle with crumbs and oil. Bake in a moderate oven (350° F.) 15 minutes, or until browned on top. Serves 6.

## CREAMED SPINACH EPINARDS À LA CRÈME

1 *qt. boiled spinach*             1 *tsp. salt*
   (*see preceding recipe*)        ½ *tsp. pepper*
1 *cup heavy cream*                1 *tbs. butter*

Drain the boiled spinach; pass it through a sieve. Mix with the cream, seasonings, and butter. Reheat a few minutes and serve. Serves 6.

## SPINACH WITH EGGS PAIN D'EPINARDS

1 *qt. boiled spinach*             1 *tsp. salt*
*thick Cream Sauce*                ½ *tsp. pepper*
2 *eggs, beaten*                   ½ *cup heavy cream*

Drain the hot boiled spinach. Mince it; mix with enough Cream Sauce (about 1 cup) to make a smooth, thick mixture. Add the eggs and seasoning. Pour into a buttered mould. Cook above boiling water 20 minutes, or until hot and thick. Pour into a warmed serving dish. Dash the top with a little heavy cream and serve. Serves 6.

## TURNIP PURÉE NAVETS EN PURÉE

2 *lb.* (4 *to* 6 *medium*) *turnips*    1 *cup hot water*
1 *tbs. butter.*                         *cream*
1 *tsp. salt*                            *grated nutmeg* (*optional*)
½ *tsp. pepper*

Peel the turnips and cut in quarters or slice them. Brown in heated butter. Season, then add the water. Cook covered until the turnips are soft, 45 minutes. Reheat and serve. Add a sprinkling of nutmeg or leave plain. Serves 6.

## VEGETABLE STEW RAGOÛT DE LÉGUMES

| | |
|---|---|
| 2 *slices bacon* | 2 *tomatoes, sliced* |
| 1 *onion, sliced* | 8 *small young potatoes* |
| 1 *tbs. butter* | 8 *small young carrots* |
| 1 *cup green peas* | 1 *cup young broad beans* |
| 1 *cup sliced marrow* | 1 *cup water* |

Brown the bacon in a heavy saucepan. Add the onion and brown it. Add the butter, then the vegetables. Add water to half cover. Cover the pan and cook slowly 2 hours or longer. More water may be needed, but the mixture should be a thick stew. Serves 6 or more.

# SALADS

No French meal would be considered complete without a salad. Usually it consists of various greens in combination with a simple oil dressing. And no French salad would be complete without its *chapon*, a piece of bread rubbed with garlic, added to the bowl. You can, of course, rub the sides of the bowl with a cut clove of garlic, but many believe the *chapon* to be the best bit of the entire salad. The various mixtures and concoctions served under the name of French Dressing are not always a French salad dressing. To be really French the dressing must be simple; the simpler the better. The rule is one part of vinegar to two parts of oil, plus varied seasonings.

## CHICORY SALAD SALADE DE CHICORÉE

| | |
|---|---|
| 1 *or* 2 *bunches chicory* | ½ *tsp. salt* |
| *crust of French or Italian bread* | ¼ *tsp. black pepper* |
| 1 *garlic bud, cut in half* | 1 *tbs. vinegar* |
| 4 *warm boiled potatoes, sliced* | 2 *tbs. olive oil* |

Rub the crust of bread with the garlic and toss with the cleaned chicory. Or rub the garlic on the bowl. Add the potatoes. Put the salt and pepper in a tablespoon; fill the spoon with vinegar and sprinkle this on the salad. Then sprinkle the oil over the salad. Mix and serve at once. Serves 4 to 6.

# CUCUMBER SALAD WITH CREAM SALADE DE CON-
## COMBRES À LA CRÈME

| | |
|---|---|
| 2 *or* 4 *cucumbers* | *lemon juice* |
| *salt* | 1 *tbs. chopped tarragon or* |
| *heavy sweet or sour cream* | *parsley* |

Peel the cucumbers and slice thin. Sprinkle with salt. Cover and place in the refrigerator overnight. To serve, drain the cucumbers and mix with enough cream to coat. Add a few drops of lemon juice. Season with chopped herbs and serve. Serves 2 to 4.

## ENDIVE SALAD SALADE D'ENDIVES

| | |
|---|---|
| 4 *bunches Belgian endive* | 1 *tsp. salt* |
| 1 *cooked or pickled beet, sliced* | $\frac{1}{2}$ *tsp. pepper* |
| 1 *or* 2 *onions, sliced* | 1 *tbs. vinegar* |
| 1 *hard-boiled egg, sliced* | 2 *tbs. olive oil* |

Cut the bunches of endive and add slices of cooked beet, onion, and egg. To prepare the dressing put the salt and pepper in a tablespoon, fill with vinegar, and sprinkle over the salad. Then sprinkle the oil over all. Serve at once. Serves 4 to 8.

## GREEN SALAD WITH OLIVES SALADE AUX OLIVES

| | |
|---|---|
| 1 *head lettuce* | $\frac{1}{2}$ *tsp. pepper* |
| 1 *bunch chicory* | $1\frac{1}{2}$ *tbs. vinegar* |
| 2 *tomatoes, sliced* | 3 *tbs. olive oil* |
| 2 *hard-boiled eggs, sliced* | 2 *tbs. chopped chives and* |
| 30 *olives, seeds removed* | *parsley* |
| 1 *tsp. salt* | |

Slice or quarter the tomatoes. Combine lettuce, chicory, tomato, eggs, and olives. To make the dressing, put the salt and pepper in a tablespoon, add the vinegar, and sprinkle almost all of it over the salad; then add about $\frac{1}{2}$ tablespoon additional of vinegar and sprinkle over the salad. Then sprinkle with the oil. Mix, add the herbs, and serve. Serves 6.

# Salads

## LETTUCE AND FRUIT SALAD SALADE AUX POMMES

1 *head cabbage lettuce*
2 *apples*

1 *cup walnut kernels*
*mayonnaise*

Wash and peel the apples. Slice or chop them; mix with the nuts and enough mayonnaise to coat. Pile on the washed and drained lettuce to serve. Serves 4.

## LETTUCE SALAD SALADE DE LAITUE

1 *head cabbage lettuce*
1 *tsp. each minced parsley, chives,*
  *tarragon*
1 *small onion, sliced or chopped*
1 *hard-boiled egg, sliced*

1 *tsp. salt*
½ *tsp. pepper*
1½ *tbs. vinegar*
3 *tbs. olive oil*

Place the cleaned lettuce leaves in a bowl; sprinkle with the herbs, onion, and sliced egg. Prepare the dressing by placing the salt and pepper in a tablespoon; fill with vinegar and sprinkle over the salad. Then sprinkle the oil over the salad. Mix. Serve at once. Serves 4 or more.

## RUSSIAN SALAD SALADE RUSSE

4 *cooked carrots*
2 *cooked turnips*
1 *cup cooked French beans*
1 *cup cooked peas*
2 *or 3 boiled potatoes*
1 *cup boiled cauliflower*

*mayonnaise*
*crisp lettuce leaves*
2 *tomatoes, sliced*
1 *tbs. chopped chives*
1 *tbs. chopped parsley*

Have all ingredients chilled. Slice the carrots and turnips; mix with the beans and peas; cut the potatoes in small cubes; break cauliflower in small pieces. Mix with mayonnaise to coat. Pile on crisp lettuce leaves. Garnish with tomatoes and the herbs. Serves 6 to 8.

# DESSERTS

Here is the basic recipe referred to in following recipes as Vanilla Cream.

## Creams

### VANILLA CREAM CRÈME À LA VANILLE

3 egg, yolks
3 tbs. sugar

1 pt. scalding milk
1 tsp. vanilla essence

Use a 1-quart double boiler. Mix the yolk of eggs, sugar. Pour over this slowly the scalding milk, stirring until the sugar is fully dissolved. Heat over boiling water until the custard coats a metal spoon, 6 to 8 minutes, but it should not boil. Stir constantly, slowly, and smoothly. Remove from the heat; add the flavouring. Use as directed in these recipes. Makes 4 servings.

### ALMOND CREAM GÂTEAU AUX AMANDES

4 oz. ground almonds
4 oz. butter, softened
4 oz. sugar

Vanilla Cream
12 to 18 sponge fingers or sliced sponge cake

Mix the almonds and butter; beat the sugar smoothly in. Add 4 tablespoons of cold Vanilla Cream and mix well. Line a deep buttered baking dish or mould with ladyfingers or sliced sponge cake. Pour the mixture into it. Cover with fingers or thin slices of cake. Cover and place in the refrigerator for 2 hours or longer.

To serve, turn out on a serving dish and cover with the rest of the cold Vanilla Cream. Or put servings in individual dishes, and top with Vanilla Cream. This may be made a day before using. Serves 6.

## BISCUIT CAKE WITH CHOCOLATE CREAM CRÈME AU BEURRE AU CHOCOLAT

| | |
|---|---|
| 3 oz.(squares) chocolate | ¼ lb. butter, softened |
| 1 tbs. sugar | 12 vanilla wafers |
| 2 egg yolks | extra chocolate and butter |

Soften the chocolate over hot water; mix with it the sugar, beaten yolks, and butter. Stir 15 minutes and then place covered in the refrigerator.

Place a layer of biscuits in the bottom of a serving dish; cover with the chocolate mixture; repeat layers of wafers and chocolate mixture, finishing with biscuits. Melt 1 or 2 squares of chocolate and mix with the same amount of melted butter. Pour over the dish and chill 12 hours or overnight. Serves 6.

## BISCUIT CAKE WITH COFFEE CREAM CRÈME AU BEURRE AU CAFÉ

| | |
|---|---|
| 4 oz. sugar | 2 egg yolks |
| 2 tbs. water | 12 or more thin biscuits or |
| ¼ lb. butter | sponge fingers |
| 3 tbs. coffee essence | |

Mix the sugar and water in a saucepan; cook, stirring with a wooden spoon until the sugar melts. Let cook until thickened and syrupy. Cool. Mix the butter, coffee essence, and egg yolks, beating well. Add the syrup slowly and stir 15 minutes. Chill covered in the refrigerator for 2 hours. Make a layer of biscuits in a serving dish. Cover with a layer of the coffee sauce; repeat layers of biscuits and sauce, finishing with biscuits. Spread remaining coffee sauce over the top and down the sides. Serves 6.

## CARAMEL CREAM CRÈME AU CARAMEL

| | |
|---|---|
| *Vanilla Cream* | *2 tbs. water* |
| *4 tbs. sugar* | |

When the Vanilla Cream is removed from the heat, pour it into a serving dish or 4 to 6 individual dishes. Heat the sugar and water together until it browns. When boiling, remove; pour a little over each serving or over the large custard. Let cool. The custard should be served very cold. Serves 4 to 6.

## BAKED CHESTNUT PURÉE PURÉE DE MARRONS

| | |
|---|---|
| *1 lb chestnuts* | *2 oz. sugar* |
| *boiling water* | *2 oz. butter* |
| *1 cup hot milk or cream* | *2 eggs* |

Slit the shells of the chestnuts. Cover them with boiling water and cook slowly 30 minutes. Drain and shell them. Pour boiling water on the nuts. Let stand 30 minutes. Drain. Rub off the brown skins. Mash the nuts or put through a mincer. To every cup add 2 tablespoons hot milk or cream, sugar, and 1 tablespoon butter. Beat 3 minutes. Beat the eggs in. Pour into buttered individual baking dishes. Bake in a moderate oven (350° F.) 10 to 15 minutes. Serves 6 or more.

## CHESTNUT CHARLOTTE CHARLOTTE AUX MARRONS

| | |
|---|---|
| *Chestnut Purée* | *½ pt. cream, whipped* |
| *½ lb. butter* | *sponge fingers or sponge cake* |
| *3 oz. sugar* | *4 tbs. grated chocolate* |
| *3 tbs. rum or* | *4 tbs. butter* |
| *1 tsp. vanilla* | |

While the Chestnut Purée is still warm beat in the butter, sugar, and flavouring. When smooth, stir in the whipped cream. Line a baking dish or mould with fingers or sliced sponge cake. Fill with the mixture. Cover the top with fingers or sliced cake. Cover.

Chill overnight in the refrigerator. To serve, turn out on a chilled plate. Melt the chocolate and butter together, allow to cool and pour over servings. Serves 6 or 8.

## CHESTNUT CREAM MONT BLANC MARRONS MONT BLANC

| | |
|---|---|
| *Chestnut Purée* | 1 *cup hot milk* |
| 3 *oz. sugar* | *vanilla essence* |
| 2 *oz. butter* | 2 *egg yolks, beaten* |
| *Cream Chantilly* | |

Beat the purée with the milk, sugar, and vanilla essence; add butter, the egg yolks and stir all to the consistency of thick cream. Pour into a serving dish. Cool. Pour Cream Chantilly over it and serve. Serves 4 to 6.

## CHESTNUT CREAM MOUSSE AUX MARRONS

| | |
|---|---|
| *Chestnut Purée* | 1 *tsp. vanilla* |
| ½ *cup hot milk* | 3 *eggs, separated* |
| 3 *tbs. sugar* | 1 *pt. cream, whipped* |

To the warm Chestnut Purée add the milk in which the sugar has been dissolved. Stir; add the vanilla. Mix smoothly. Beat the yolks slightly and mix into the purée. Whip the egg whites until stiff and mix in. Stir the whipped cream smoothly in and mix well. Pour into a lightly buttered mould. Cover and place in the refrigerator overnight. To serve, turn it out on a chilled serving dish. Top with cream or leave plain. Serves 6 or more.

## CHESTNUT CREAM AUVERGNAT GÂTEAU AUVERGNAT

In the preceding recipe omit the whipped cream. Pour 3 or 4 tablespoons Caramel Syrup into an ungreased mould; tilt it to coat the sides of the mould. Pour the Chestnut Purée mixture into it. Set in a shallow pan half filled with water. Bake in a slow oven (275° F.) 30 minutes. Serve with Vanilla Cream. Serves 6.

## CHESTNUT CREAM CHANTILLY GÂTEAUX AUX MARRONS CHANTILLY

| | |
|---|---|
| *Chestnut Purée* | *4 egg yolks* |
| *3 tbs. sugar* | *4 stiffly whipped egg whites* |
| *½ tsp. vanilla* | *Caramel Syrup* |
| *1 cup milk* | |

Into the freshly made Chestnut Purée beat the sugar and vanilla dissolved in the milk; mix smoothly. Beat in the yolks and finally the stiffly whipped whites. Pour the caramel (3 or 4 tablespoons) into a cake tin (small Turk's-head pan, preferably). Pour the chestnut mixture into it and bake in a slow oven (275° F.) 1 hour. Serve covered with Cream Chantilly. Serves 6.

NOTE: Make this dessert the day before it is to be served.

## CHESTNUT CREAM MAGDA GÂTEAU MAGDA

| | |
|---|---|
| *Chestnut Purée* | *½ lb. butter, softened* |
| *½ cup milk* | *½ lb. sugar* |
| *½ tsp. vanilla* | |

Mix into the freshly made purée the milk in which the vanilla has been stirred. Gradually beat into the purée the butter and sugar. The stirring must continue 'until it becomes white'. Butter a fancy mould. Pour the mixture into it. Chill 12 hours or overnight. Turn out on a chilled serving dish. Serves 6.

## CHESTNUT AND CHOCOLATE CREAM GÂTEAU AUX MARRONS AU CHOCOLAT

| | |
|---|---|
| *2 lb. chestnuts* | *3 eggs* |
| *3 oz. (squares) chocolate, melted* | *2 tbs cognac* |
| *3 tbs. water* | *Caramel Syrup* |
| *4 oz. butter, melted* | *Cream Chantilly* |
| *4 tbs sugar* | |

To shell, blanch, and mash the nuts, follow directions for Baked Chestnut Purée. Melt the chocolate with the water. Mix the butter and sugar and add to the chocolate; beat in the yolks and brandy. Stir well for 10 minutes. Whip the egg whites until stiff and fold in.

Pour Caramel Syrup into a mould or cake tin. Tilt it to coat the sides and bottom. Pour the mixture in. Cover with waxed paper and a plate with a weight on it. Chill overnight. Turn out on a chilled serving dish. Garnish with Cream Chantilly. Serves 6.

## CHOCOLATE CHARLOTTE charlotte au chocolat

| | |
|---|---|
| 3 oz. (squares) chocolate | 3 tbs. sugar |
| 2 tbs. hot water | liqueurglassful of rum |
| 4 oz. butter | ¼ lb. sponge fingers |
| 3 eggs | |

Melt the chocolate in two tablespoonfuls of water. Add the butter piece by piece, followed by the yolks of eggs one by one, the sugar and rum. Stir with a wooden spoon for ten minutes and then add the whipped whites of eggs.

Butter a cake tin, cover the bottom and sides with sponge fingers, pour in the mixture and cover with a layer of biscuits. Place a plate with a weight on top and keep in a cold place for the night. Turn out on to a serving dish. A vanilla cream may be poured over it.

## CHOCOLATE CREAM crème au chocolat

| | |
|---|---|
| *Vanilla Cream* | 4 oz. (squares) chocolate, melted |

Flavour the Vanilla Cream with the melted chocolate. Mix as directed.

## CHOCOLATE CREAM DESSERT crème au chocolat

| | |
|---|---|
| 4 oz. (squares) chocolate | 4 eggs, separated |
| 2 tbs. hot water | 1 tbs. sugar |

Stir the chocolate and hot water together with a wooden spoon until creamy. Add the egg yolks one at a time, stirring steadily. Add the sugar. Whip the egg whites until stiff; add a tablespoon at a time, beating well. As soon as cold, serve piled in dessert glasses, with or without cream. Serves 6.

## CHOCOLATE MOUSSE MOUSSE AU CHOCOLAT

This variation of Chocolate Cream Dessert is called Mousse au Chocolat. Omit the eggs from Chocolate Cream Dessert. When the chocolate, hot water, and sugar have been stirred to the consistency of heavy cream, pour slowly into 2 cups of heavy cream, beating vigorously to a froth with a fork. Serve cold in a glass bowl. Serves 6 to 8.

## CHOCOLATE CORNETS CORNETS AU CHOCOLAT

| | |
|---|---|
| *2 egg whites* | *2 tbs. butter, melted* |
| *2 oz. sugar* | *1 oz. ground almonds* |
| *1 oz. flour* | |

Mix the egg whites and sugar; combine with the flour and butter, beating smoothly together. Add the almonds. Spread in a thin layer on lightly floured waxed paper. Cut into 2-inch squares. Carefully lift them to a buttered baking pan. Bake in a moderate oven (350° F.) 10 minutes. Remove from the pan. Roll each into a little cone or cornucopia. Wrap with waxed paper and tie to hold the shape. When cooled, remove the string and paper and fill the cones with Chocolate Cream. Makes 2 to 3 dozen cornets.

## CHOCOLATE SURPRISE CRÈME GLACÉE

| | |
|---|---|
| *4 oz. (squares) chocolate* | *2 tbs. castor sugar* |
| *2 tbs. water* | *2 eggs* |
| *4 oz. butter* | *extra sugar* |

Melt the chocolate in a saucepan with two tablespoonfuls of water and stir until the consistency of cream is obtained. Place the butter, sugar and yolks of eggs in a basin, add the chocolate slowly and stir for threequarters of an hour. Add the whipped whites of eggs and stir for a further quarter of an hour.

Sprinkle a white cloth with sugar and water, pour the mixture into the centre, shape like a ball, tie the cloth and place in a pudding basin. Leave in a cold place for twelve hours. Two hours before requiring place on ice. Serve on a dish suitably garnished with wafer biscuits, crystallized cherries or almonds, according to taste.

## CHOCOLATE CREAM CHANTILLY CRÈME CHANTILLY
### AU CHOCOLAT

1 *pt. heavy cream*                           2 *tbs. hot water*
4 *oz. (squares) chocolate*

Whip the cream. Melt the chocolate by stirring with the hot water
10 minutes. When cool, mix slowly with the cream. Use as cake
icing, filling, and in other desserts as directed. Serves 6 to 8 as a
dessert.

## CHOCOLATE PUDDING WITH CREAM SAUCE
### BISCOTTES AU CHOCOLAT

3 *oz. (squares) chocolate*                *milk*
2 *tbs. water*                             2 *eggs, separated*
4 *rusks*                                  *Chocolate Cream*

Melt the chocolate in the water, stirring until smooth. Add the rusks
soaked in milk; mix. Add the yolks. Stir well. Whip the egg whites
until stiff; stir into the chocolate mixture. Pour into a buttered mould.
Set in a shallow pan half full of water and bake in a moderate oven
(350° F.) 30 minutes. Or set the mould in a steamer; add a little
water to the bottom of the steamer. Cover and cook 30 minutes.
Turn out on a hot serving dish. Serve with warm Chocolate Cream.
Serves 6.

## CHOCOLATE SPONGE FINGERS BISCUITS AU CHOCOLAT

*sponge fingers*                          *heavy cream*
*Chocolate Cream*                         *sugar*

Cover the bottom of a serving dish with fingers. Pour in a layer of
cold Chocolate Cream. Repeat layers. Finish with a layer of the
fingers. Chill. Serve with sweetened cream poured over it.

## CHOCOLATE MARQUISE MARQUISE AU CHOCOLAT

4 *oz. (squares) chocolate, grated*      *Vanilla Cream*
¼ *cup butter, melted*

Mix the chocolate and butter smoothly together until creamy. Stir into the slightly cooled Vanilla Cream. Mix smoothly. Pour into a serving dish. Cover with waxed paper. Chill and serve. Serves 4 to 6.

## COCONUT CREAM CRÈME À LA NOIX DE COCO

6 *oz. grated coconut*          *port wine*
3 *egg yolks*              *cream*
*vanilla wafers*            *grated coconut*

Mix the coconut and yolks together, stirring to a smooth, creamy mixture. Moisten the wafers lightly with the wine. Line a buttered mould with the wafers. Spread a layer of the coconut in the mould; cover with wafers. Repeat until all is used. Cover the top with the remaining wafers. Lay waxed paper over it; place a plate and weight on top. Chill overnight. To serve, turn out on a chilled serving plate. Cover with cream and grated coconut. Serves 6.

## COFFEE CREAM CHANTILLY CRÈME CHANTILLY AU CAFÉ

1 *pt. heavy cream*          3 *tbs. coffee essence*
3 *tbs. sugar*

Whip the cream; add the sugar and coffee essence. When smoothly mixed, use as directed in other recipes, or serve heaped in dessert glasses as a dessert. Serves 6 to 8.

*Variation.* Coffee and Chocolate Mousse (*Mousse de Café au Chocolat*). Add 2 tablespoons melted chocolate to Coffee Cream Chantilly.

## COFFEE MOUSSE WITH BISCUITS GÂTEAU AU CAFÉ

32 *sponge finger biscuits*
5 *oz. butter*
5 *oz. sugar*

2 *yolks of egg*
2 *tbs. coffee essence*
I *cup cold strong coffee*

Put the butter and sugar in a bowl and stir well. Incorporate the yolk of egg and coffee essence.

Dip the biscuits quickly, one by one, in the strong coffee. The biscuits must not be left to soak or they will lose their shape. Arrange a layer of eight biscuits side by side on a flat dish, then a layer of cream, so continuing until all the biscuits have been used. Add a final layer of cream and sprinkle with sugar.


## COFFEE CREAM CRÈME AU CAFÉ
*Vanilla Cream*                     2 *tsp. coffee essence*

Flavour Vanilla Cream with coffee essence. Serve very cold.


## CREAM CAKES CHOUX À LA CRÈME

2 *oz. butter*
½ *tsp. sugar*
*a pinch of salt*

½ *tsp. water*
2 *oz. flour*
2 *eggs*

Boil the butter, sugar and salt in the water. When boiling add the whole of the flour at once and the same time stirring well. When the paste is so thick that it can be removed whole, remove from fire and add the eggs one by one, stirring vigorously as each is added.

Place heaped tespoonfuls of the mixture at intervals of about three inches on a buttered tray and allow to stand for a quarter of an hour. Bake in a moderate oven for thirty to forty minutes, taking care not to open the oven door for the first quarter of an hour.

When cool remove the tops of the cakes and fill the centres with Cream Chantilly.

## CREAM CHANTILLY CRÈME CHANTILLY

1 *pt. heavy cream*               2 *tbs. sugar*
2 *tbs. milk*

Place the cream in a bowl and add the milk slowly, stirring well. Add the sugar, whipping to obtain a frothy mixture. Drain through a muslin cloth. Use as directed in various recipes.

## CREAM MERINGUE ILE FLOTTANTE

3 *egg whites*               *Caramel Syrup*
3 *tbs. sugar*               *Vanilla Cream*

Whip the egg whites until stiff, adding the sugar gradually. Line a metal mould with the Caramel Syrup. Tilt the mould to coat the sides. Pile the egg whites in. Place the mould in a saucepan of boiling water for 30 minutes. Turn it out at once on to a serving dish. Surround with chilled Vanilla Cream and serve. Serves 4 to 6.

## CREAMED PRALINES CRÈME PRALINÉE

Add ¼ lb. chopped browned almonds to the whipped egg whites and sugar in the preceding recipe. Pour the mixture into the caramel-lined mould and cook 45 minutes over boiling water. Turn out while still hot on to a serving dish. Garnish with cold Vanilla Cream and serve. Serves 4 to 6.

## CUSTARD CRÈME RENVERSÉE

Boil one pint of milk with three tablespoonfuls of sugar and a few drops of vanilla essence. Pour slowly on to two beaten eggs, mixing well.

Brown three tablespoonfuls of sugar with a little water in a metal mould, line the sides with the caramel and pour in the milk and eggs. Bake in a hot oven for twenty minutes and turn out while still hot. Serve hot or cold.

## CREAMED BISCUITS BISCUITS À LA CRÈME

| | |
|---|---|
| *sponge fingers* | *raspberry or other jam* |
| *water* | *Vanilla Cream* |
| *kirsch* | *candied cherries* |

Dip the fingers in an equal mixture of water and kirsch. Make a layer in a buttered mould. Spread the layer thickly with jam. Repeat for 4 to 6 layers. Make the top layer biscuits. Chill. Pour the Vanilla Cream over and around it. Garnish with candied cherries. Serves 6.

## FRANGIPANE Filling for cakes

Mix 3 oz. flour with cold milk to form a paste, then add 3 yolks of eggs, 1 whole egg, 2 oz. sugar, and a pinch of salt. Stir with a wooden spoon for 5 minutes, afterwards slowly adding 1 pint of hot milk and 1 oz. butter in small pieces. Mix for 5 minutes. Place in a saucepan on the fire, stir all the time but do not allow to boil. When the consistency of cream is obtained, add 3 oz. of ground almonds.

## MOCHA CREAM CRÈME MOKA

| | |
|---|---|
| $\frac{1}{2}$ *lb. butter* | $1\frac{1}{2}$ *tbs. coffee essence* |
| $\frac{1}{2}$ *lb. sugar* | *4 egg yolks* |

Place the butter in a warmed bowl. Beat with the sugar until creamy. Add the coffee essence. Beat 5 minutes. Beat in 1 egg at a time. Use as filling for cakes, toppings, puddings, etc. Makes $2\frac{1}{2}$ cups.

## RICE CARAMEL WITH VANILLA CREAM GÂTEAU DE RIZ

| | |
|---|---|
| *6 tbs. rice* | *1 egg, separated* |
| *2 cups of water* | *3 tbs. sugar* |
| *1 pint milk* | *2 tbs. water* |
| *4 tps. sugar* | *Vanilla Cream* |

Put 6 tablespoonfuls of rice in cold water and boil. Drain off the water. Heat one pint of milk with the sugar, add the rice and boil for 20 minutes or $\frac{1}{2}$ hour. Cool and add one yolk of egg and one whipped white of egg.

Brown 3 tablespoonfuls of sugar with two of water in a metal mould. Line the sides of the mould with the caramel and fill the centre with the rice. Place the mould in a pan of boiling water, or in the oven, for half an hour. Turn into a dish and surround with Vanilla Cream.


## PASTRY CREAM CRÈME PÂTISSIÈRE

For use as a filling with cakes or pastry.

Mix well together 2 whole eggs, 5 yolks of eggs, 2 oz. flour, and 8 oz. sugar.

Heat $1\frac{1}{2}$ pints of milk in a saucepan with a few drops of vanilla essence and pour slowly on the first mixture. Put in a saucepan on the fire, stir well and remove the moment it comes to the boil.


## SEMOLINA MOULD WITH VANILLA CREAM GÂTEAU DE SEMOULE

| | |
|---|---|
| 1 *pt. milk* | 1 *egg* |
| 3 *tbs. sugar* | 3 *tbs. sugar* |
| 6 *tbs. semolina (Cream of Wheat* | 2 *tbs. water* |
| *or farina)* | *Vanilla Cream* |

Heat the milk with the sugar to boiling. Stir the semolina in and boil 6 to 8 minutes, stirring all the time. Cool. Add the egg. Proceed as in the recipe for Rice Caramel. Serves 6.


## SNOW EGGS OEUFS À LA NEIGE

| | |
|---|---|
| 3 *cups milk* | 4 *egg whites* |
| 4 *tbs. sugar* | *Vanilla Cream* |
| 1 *tsp. vanilla* | |

Heat the milk in a double boiler with the sugar and vanilla. Beat the egg whites until stiff. When the milk is boiling, immerse 1 rounded tablespoon of egg white at a time in the milk; turn the 'egg' after half a minute. Let it cook another half minute. Place on a serving dish and cover with Vanilla Cream. Serves 6.

## SYLVABELLA SYLVABELLA

| | |
|---|---|
| 6 *oz. butter* | 4 *lumps (or 1 tbs.) sugar* |
| 5 *oz. sugar* | ¼ *cup rum* |
| 4 *eggs, separated* | ½ *cup water* |
| 4 *oz. (squares) chocolate* | 12 *or more ladyfingers* |
| 2 *tbs. water* | |

Stir butter with the sugar and beaten yolks for 10 minutes. Mix the chocolate with the 2 tablespoons of water and slowly heat, stirring to the consistency of cream. Add this slowly to the first mixture, then fold the stiffly beaten egg whites.

Stir the 4 lumps of sugar into the rum and water mixed together. Dip the ladyfingers in this liquid and line a fancy mould with them. Pour the chocolate mixture into the middle of the mould and cover with a layer of the soaked ladyfingers. Place a plate on top with a weight on it; chill in the refrigerator at least 6 hours. Turn it out on a chilled plate. Serves 8.

## YULE LOG WITH COFFEE CREAM BÛCHE DE NOËL

| | |
|---|---|
| ½ *lb. sponge fingers* | ½ *cup butter* |
| 3 *tbs. rum* | *Mocha Cream* |

Crumble the fingers; sprinkle with rum and mix with softened butter; work until smooth. Spread in a thick layer on a piece of buttered waxed paper. Roll lightly with rolling pin or pat, then roll like a jelly roll. Wrap in the waxed paper, closing the ends. Chill overnight. Unwrap and serve covered with Mocha Cream. Serves 6.

# Cakes

Here are some suggestions for baking those cakes which are so delicious when we select them from the French pastry tray; and which are so different and surprising to handle when we try them in an English kitchen.

1. Stir the paste until bubbles appear. The more the paste is stirred, the better the cake will be.

2. Use a clean tin.

3. Warm the cake tin before use and butter it well.

4. Stand the cake tin in the oven on a hot brick or tile. This ensures that the bottom of the cake will be well baked. (Not needed in modern ovens.)

5. Open the door as rarely as possible.

6. The cake is sufficiently baked when a knitting needle or knife comes out dry.

## FRENCH CAKE ICING

Melt 1 cup icing sugar in a saucepan with about 1½ tablespoons boiling water, adding desired flavouring such as lemon, orange, kirsch, etc. Stir smoothly and steadily until the right consistency to spread. To spread the icing on the cake, use a knife first dipped in boiling water. The icing should be spread on the cake while the cake and the icing are warm. The icing will harden on standing and should be used on cakes which are to be eaten the same day they are made.

## AFTERNOON CAKE GÂTEAU POUR LE THÉ

| | |
|---|---|
| 8 *oz. flour* | 5 *oz. sugar* |
| 1 *tsp. baking powder* | 5 *oz. butter* |
| 2 *eggs* | |

Mix the flour and baking powder in a bowl and make a hole in the centre to receive the eggs, sugar, and melted butter. Stir for 10 minutes. Put the mixture in a buttered tin and bake in a moderate oven for half an hour.

## AFTERNOON CAKE GÂTEAU AU BEURRE

| | |
|---|---|
| 8 oz. flour | 1 oz. yeast |
| 3 eggs | pinch of salt |
| 5 oz. butter | |

Put the flour in a bowl, make a hole in the centre and in it place the eggs, butter, crumbled yeast and salt. Work well with the fingers into the form of a ball and allow to stand for one hour. Put in a buttered tin and bake in a moderate oven three quarters of an hour.

## ARDENNES CAKE GÂTEAU DES ARDENNES

| | |
|---|---|
| 1 oz. yeast | 8 oz. flour |
| 3 tbs. milk | 1 oz. sugar |
| 3 eggs | 4 oz. butter |

Dissolve the yeast in the milk and allow to stand for ten minutes. Mix the remaining ingredients in the order given, finally adding the yeast and milk. Stand the mixture in a warm place for one hour, put in a buttered tin and bake in a moderate oven for 30 to 40 minutes.

## BÉARN CAKE GÂTEAU BÉARNAIS

| | |
|---|---|
| 6 eggs | 2 oz. sifted flour |
| $\frac{1}{8}$ tsp. salt | 2 tbs. chopped blanched almonds |
| $\frac{1}{2}$ lemon, grated peel only | 8 or 10 whole almonds |
| $\frac{1}{2}$ tsp. vanilla | 2 or 3 tbs. milk |
| 2 oz. sugar | 2 tbs. sugar |

Beat the eggs in a bowl as for an omelette. Add the salt, lemon peel, and vanilla and stir well. Add the sugar; stir well. Gradually mix in the flour. Add the almonds. Pour into a buttered round cake tin (small). Decorate the top with the whole almonds. Brush with the milk mixed with the sugar. Bake in a moderate oven (325° F.) 20 to 30 minutes. Serves 6.

## HASTY CAKE TÔT FAIT

*2 oz. sifted flour*
*2 oz. potato flour*
*7 oz. sugar*

*3 oz. butter*
*6 egg whites*

Sift the flour, potato flour, sugar, and butter, mixing well. Beat 10 minutes. Whip the egg whites until stiff; fold into the flour mixture. Pour at once into a buttered round cake tin. Bake in a moderate oven (325° F.) 25 minutes. Serves 6.

## CHOCOLATE CAKE GÂTEAU AU CHOCOLAT

*3 oz. chocolate*
*3 eggs*

*equivalent weight of 2 eggs of*
*flour, butter and sugar*

Heat the chocolate to soften it, place in a bowl, add first the eggs and then the butter, flour, and sugar, stirring all the time. Beat the mixture for ten minutes. Place in a buttered cake tin and bake in the oven for a quarter of an hour.

## CHOCOLATE CAKE II. GÂTEAU AU CHOCOLAT

*6 oz. chocolate*
*3 tbs. milk*
*few drops of vanilla essence*
*3½ oz. butter*
*4 eggs*

*5 oz. sugar*
*1½ oz. ordinary flour*
*1½ oz. potato flour*
*2 oz. melted chocolate*
*1 tsp. butter*

Divide the sugar, flour, and potato flour into four equal parts. Dissolve the chocolate in three tablespoonfuls of milk and the vanilla, add the butter and pour into a bowl. Add one yolk of egg and one part each of sugar, flour, and potato flour. Stir until well mixed and repeat the operation, using one yolk of egg and part of the other ingredients at one time, until the four yolks of eggs are used. Stir for 5 minutes, and then add the 4 whipped whites of eggs. Mix well. Pour into a buttered cake tin and bake in a moderate oven for three-quarters of an hour. When cold, cover the cake with a cream made by mixing 2 oz. melted chocolate with a teaspoonful of butter.

## CHOCOLATE CAKE III BISCUIT AU CHOCOLAT

3 eggs, separated
6 oz. sugar
3½ oz. potato flour

2 tbs. butter
2 oz. (squares) chocolate

Beat the yolks with the sugar 20 minutes. Add the potato flour and 1 tablespoon butter and continue beating for 10 more minutes. Whip the egg whites until stiff and fold in; mix and pour into a buttered oblong tin. Bake in a slow oven (300° F.) 50 minutes. Cool. Cover with the chocolate melted with the other tablespoon of butter. Serves 6 to 10.

## CHOCOLATE CAKE IV GÂTEAU DIABOLO

3 oz. (squares) chocolate
½ cup water
4 oz. sifted flour

4 oz. butter
6 oz. sugar
5 eggs, separated

Melt the chocolate with the water in a saucepan. Remove from heat and stir in the flour, softened butter, sugar, and the egg yolks. Stir 10 minutes. Whip the egg whites until stiff. Fold in and mix. Pour into a buttered cake tin and bake in a slow oven (275° F.) 1 hour. Serves 6 to 10.

## COFFEE CREAM CAKE GÂTEAU MOKA

5 eggs, separated
7 oz. sugar

2 tsp. grated lemon peel
4 oz. potato flour

Beat the yolks. Sift in the sugar slowly, beating steadily. Add the peel, the flour, then fold in the stiffly beaten whites. Turn into a greased pan and bake in a moderate oven (325° F.) 1 hour. When done, invert the pan on a cake rack (support the pan on 4 teacups) and let the cake come down of its own weight. Let it stand several hours. Cut horizontally. Fill with Coffee Cream. Serves 8 or more.

COFFEE CREAM FILLING

4 oz. butter

4 oz. sugar

2 tsp. coffee essence

2 egg yolks

1 or 2 tbs. sugar

Stir the butter in a warmed bowl until it is like thick cream. Gradually add the sugar, then the coffee essence. Add the yolks one at a time. Mix and use as directed in the cake. Pour any remainder over the cake. Sprinkle with sugar.

WALNUT CREAM FILLING GÂTEAU AUX NOIX

Mix one cup grated walnuts with ¼ cup sugar and 1 cup cream, whipped. Use as filling for Coffee Cream Cake.

## KOUGLOFF KOUGLOFF

1½ lb. sifted flour

8 oz. butter

1 egg, beaten

1 cup sugar

1 pint hot milk

1 cup boiling water or milk

1 cake compressed yeast

8 oz. seedless raisins

Mix the flour and butter in a mixing bowl; add the egg. Stir. Then the sugar and milk. Add the crumbled yeast softened in the hot water or milk; mix well. Work with the hands until smooth and well mixed. Shape into a round ball in the mixing bowl; cover lightly with a folded towel. Let rise in a warm, not hot place until doubled. Knead or mix with a wooden spoon, working the raisins in. Shape into a loaf in a greased cake or loaf pan. Cover lightly with the cloth; let rise again, about 1 hour. Poke down in the pan, then bake in a moderate oven (350° F.) 45 minutes. Makes 1 large loaf, 12 or more servings.

## FOUR QUARTERS QUATRE-QUARTS

2 eggs and their weight each in

butter

sugar

flour

1 tsp. baking powder

⅓ cup dried currants, soaked in

⅓ cup rum

Soften the butter; put in a mixing bowl and combine with the sugar. Add 1 egg; beat well. Add the second egg and beat. Sift the flour and baking powder together and add slowly to the mixture. Add the drained soaked currants gradually. Beat well. Pour into a greased loaf tin. Bake in a moderate oven (350° F.) ·30 minutes. Serves 8 to 10.


## GENOA CAKE PAIN DE GÈNES

5 oz. shelled almonds
boiling water
5 oz. sugar
3 eggs

1 tsp. rum or kirsch
3 oz. flour, sifted
3 oz. butter, melted

Pour boiling water over the almonds. Let them stand 5 minutes. Drain. Rub the brown skins off. Mince and mix with the sugar. Beat 2 eggs and the yolk of the third egg together and mix with the almonds and sugar, 10 minutes. Add the rum or kirsch, then beat in the flour and butter. Add the remaining egg white beaten stiffly. Stir well together 10 minutes. Line the cake pan with waxed paper rubbed with a little butter or margarine. Fill three-fourths full. Bake in a moderate oven (325° F.) about 50 minutes. Serves 6 or more.


## POLISH CAKE GÂTEAU POLONAIS

8 oz. butter
8 oz. sugar
8 egg yolks

8 oz. sifted flour
4 oz. (squares) chocolate, grated

Soften the butter and stir with a wooden spoon until it is like cream. Add the sugar. Beat the egg yolks until they are white; add to the butter and sugar. Stir well and add the flour and grated chocolate gradually, beating well after each addition. Stir 10 minutes more. Pour into a buttered cake tin. Bake in a moderate oven (350° F.) 30 to 40 minutes. Serves 6 to 8.

## RUM BABA SAVARIN SAVARIN

| | |
|---|---|
| 1½ oz. butter | 2 eggs, separated |
| 2 tbs. milk | 4 oz. pastry flour, sifted |
| 2 tbs. sugar | 2 tsp. baking powder |

Heat the butter in a saucepan with the milk. Remove from the heat; add the sugar, beaten yolks, and then, very slowly, the flour and the baking powder. Stir slowly and smoothly for 10 minutes. Add the stiffly beaten whites. Pour the mixture in a buttered ring mould and bake in a moderate oven (350° F.) 30 minutes. Cool. Turn out on a serving plate. Serves 6.

SYRUP

| | |
|---|---|
| 1 cup sugar | rum |
| 1 cup water | sweetened whipped cream |

Boil the sugar and water together 5 minutes. Just before serving pour over the cake while the syrup is still hot. Sprinkle with rum. Fill the centre with sweetened whipped cream.

## RUM BABA SAVOY BABA SAVOIE AU RHUM

Add the grated peel of 1 lemon to the Rum Baba Savarin recipe; increase the eggs to 3 or 4. Sprinkle a buttered round mould with sugar; pour in the batter. Bake in a moderately slow oven (300° F.) about ½ hour. Cool. Cut in thick slices. Spread apricot jam or candied pineapple between the slices. Pour the syrup and rum over them. Fill the centre with fresh or preserved fruit and sprinkle all with granulated sugar.

## RUM FRUIT CAKE GÂTEAU AUX FRUITS

| | |
|---|---|
| 7 oz. sugar | 4 oz. currants |
| 3 eggs | 4 oz. seedless raisins |
| 10 oz. sifted flour | ¼ cup chopped lemon and orange |
| 1 pinch salt | peel |
| 7 oz. butter or margarine | 3 tbs. rum |
| | 1 tsp. baking powder |

173

Mix the sugar and eggs, add the flour gradually, then the butter melted, but not hot, the fruit previously soaked in warm water or rum and the chopped peel. Stir well and, when bubbles appear on the surface, add the rum and baking powder. Stir well again. Pour into a buttered cake tin lined with greased paper, cover the tin and bake in a moderate oven for one hour.

## GINGERBREAD. SPICE CAKE PAIN D'ÉPICE

10 oz. honey
1 pinch aniseed
1 lb. flour

1 tsp. bicarbonate soda
some milk

Mix the honey and aniseed together.

Mix the bicarbonate of soda and flour, place in a bowl and make a hole in the centre of the mixture. Pour in enough milk to make a paste, afterwards adding the honey and aniseed. Stir for ten minutes.

Half fill one or more buttered cake tins with the mixture. Cover and allow to stand for a quarter of an hour before baking. The tin should remain covered during the first threequarters of an hour of the full baking period of one to one and a half hours. As soon as baked, turn out on to a dish, but do not eat for forty-eight hours.

## SPICE CAKE WITH MARMALADE PAIN D'ÉPICE FOURRÉ

Make like Spice Cake; when baked and cool, cut horizontally in slices and fill with marmalade.

## SPONGE CAKE GÂTEAU MOUSSE

4 oz. butter
4 oz. sugar
4 oz. rice flour

2 tbs. chopped candied orange
  peel
2 eggs, separated
icing

Soften the butter and beat until creamy. Slowly add the sugar and flour; mix well. Add the peel; mix. Add the beaten yolks. Whip the whites until stiff and beat in. Pour into a greased cake tin. Bake in a moderately hot oven (375° F.) 20 minutes. When cool, cover with the plain icing described on page 167, or with any favourite icing. Serves 6 to 8.

## SPONGECAKE MADELEINE GÂTEAU MADELEINE

2 oz. butter
4 oz. sifted flour
5 oz. sugar

½ lemon peel, grated
3 eggs, separated

Soften or melt the butter. Add the ingredients in the order given. Add the peel, then the beaten yolks. Stir 10 minutes. Whip the whites and add. Mix and pour into a buttered tin. Bake in a slow oven (300° F.) 20 minutes. Serves 8.

## SPONGECAKE MOUSSELINE GÂTEAU MOUSSELINE

2 oz. rice flour
4 oz. sugar

2 eggs, separated

Sift the flour and sugar together. Beat the yolks and combine with the dry mixture. Whip the whites until stiff and combine with the yolk mixture. Pour into a greased cake tin, filling it only half full. Bake in a slow oven (300° F.) 20 minutes. Serves 4 to 6.

## SPONGECAKE SAVOY GÂTEAU DE SAVOIE

1½ oz. potato flour
2 eggs, separated

5 oz. sugar
extra sugar

Stir together 5 minutes the flour, egg yolks, and one-third of the sugar. Whip the egg whites until stiff and mix with the rest of the sugar. Combine with the first mixture. Sprinkle the greased cake tin with sugar and add cake mixture. Mixture should half fill the tin. Bake in a slow oven (300° F.) 45 minutes. Let cool in the tin. Serves 4 to 6.

### SWISS ROLL GÂTEAU DE SAVOIE ROULÉ

| | |
|---|---|
| 2 *eggs, separated* | ½ *cup potato flour* |
| ½ *cup sugar* | 1 *lemon peel, grated* |
| ⅛ *tsp. salt* | *sugar* |
| ½ *cup sifted flour* | *jam or marmalade* |

Beat the yolks, sugar, and salt together. Stir in the flour and potato flour, mixing smoothly. Whip the egg whites until stiff and fold in with the lemon peel. Pour into an oblong tin, 4 by 8 inches, which has been lined with waxed paper. Bake in a moderate oven (350° F.) about 20 minutes, or until done. Remove the tin at once. Carefully lift the cake by the paper. Spread thickly with jam or marmalade. Pull the paper off at one end and roll the cake, pulling off the paper at the same time. Sprinkle with sugar. Let cool. Slice and serve. Serves 8 to 12.

To remove paper wet with a damp cloth.

### WALNUT CAKE GÂTEAU AUX NOIX

| | |
|---|---|
| 7 *oz. grated walnuts* | 4 *eggs, separated* |
| 7 *oz. sugar* | 3½ *oz. sifted flour* |
| ½ *cup heavy cream* | |

Mix two-thirds of the grated walnuts with one-third of the sugar and all of the cream. Mix the rest of the walnuts and sugar with the egg yolks. Beat and add the flour slowly, stirring well. Whip the egg whites until stiff and fold into this batter. Pour into a buttered cake tin. Bake in moderate oven (350° F.) 45 minutes. When cool, slice the cake in two horizontally. Fill with the walnut and cream mixture. Serves 6 to 8.

# Small Cakes

### ALMOND CAKES PAINS D'AMANDES

2 oz. butter
8 oz. pastry flour, sifted
½ tsp. powdered cinnamon
6 oz. brown sugar

⅛ tsp. baking soda
1 egg, separated
6 oz. blanched and ground or
    chopped almonds

Melt the butter; sift the flour, cinnamon, sugar, and soda together. Add gradually to the butter. Beat the yolk into the mixture. Add the nuts. Whip the egg white until stiff and add. Drop by spoonfuls about 2 inches apart on to a buttered baking sheet. Bake in a moderate oven (350° F.) 8 to 12 minutes. Makes about 3 dozen cakes.

### ALMOND TURNOVERS TUILES AUX AMANDES

3 oz. sugar
2 egg whites, stiffly beaten

2 oz. pastry flour, sifted
few chopped blanched almonds

Combine the sugar, egg whites, and flour, mixing smoothly. Drop by spoonfuls about 3 inches apart on a greased baking sheet. Place a few chopped almonds on each. Bake in a moderate oven (350° F.) 6 minutes, then lift each cake with a spatula and turn half of it over, making a turnover or 'pocket-book'. Continue the baking 4 to 6 minutes. Makes 2½ dozen turnovers.

### BRIOCHE

1 oz. yeast
some warm water
8 oz. flour
6 oz. butter

pinch of salt
1 tsp. sugar
3 eggs

Place the yeast in a bowl, add a little warm water slowly, and then enough flour to make a thin paste. Cover with a cloth and leave in a warm room for two hours. Add the rest of the flour, the butter, salt, sugar, and finally, the eggs one by one, stirring for a quarter of an hour, when bubbles will appear on the surface. Leave the paste in a bowl, put in a warm place and leave until the next morning.

Well butter a deep cake tin, or small tins, half fill and bake in a moderate oven for about ¾ of an hour.

## BRIOCHE SULTANA BRIOCHE AUX RAISINS

Add one-third cup washed and drained seedless raisins to the brioche when adding the flour.

## CATS' TONGUES I LANGUES DE CHATS

Make a rich butter-cake batter such as Genoa Cake. Omit the rum. Bake in the special baking pans designed for Cats' Tongues. Or spread in a buttered baking pan and cut in long narrow strips. Bake in a moderate oven (350° F.) until browned, about 15 minutes. The recipe makes 5 or 6 dozen tongues.

## CATS' TONGUES II LANGUES DE CHATS

*2 oz. butter*　　　　　　　*2 oz. sugar*
*1 oz. sifted flour*　　　　　*1 egg white*
*1 oz. rice flour*

Soften the butter; stir the flour and rice flour in smoothly. Add the sugar. Stir 5 minutes. Add the stiffly whipped egg white. Pour into greased baking tray or spread in a baking pan and cut in long narrow strips (4 in. by 1 in.). Bake in a moderate oven (350° F.) until browned, about 15 minutes. Makes 5 to 6 dozen tongues.

# Desserts : Small Cakes

## MERINGUES I MERINGUES

3 *whites of egg*                     8 *oz. sugar*

Using an egg whisk, beat the egg whites until stiff. Whisk in the sugar, stirring for 10 minutes.

Put tablespoonfuls of the mixture on a buttered or oiled tray at intervals of about 3 inches and bake in a very slow oven about 1 hour.

## CHOCOLATE MERINGUES MERINGUES AU CHOCOLAT

3 *whites of egg*                     ½ *coffee spoonful vinegar, prefer-*
8 *oz. sugar*                              *ably white*
2 *tbs. cocoa or grated chocolate*

Beat the egg whites and sugar until very stiff. Add the cocoa and vinegar and stir well again. Put tablespoonfuls of the mixture on a buttered tray at intervals of about 3 inches and bake in a very slow oven, about 1 hour.

## CREAM BISCUITS I PETITES SÉCHES

6 *tbs. cream*                        *sifted flour*
1 *tbs. sugar*                         *butter*
2 *oz. butter*                         ¼ *cup powdered sugar*
⅛ *tsp. salt*

Mix the cream, sugar, butter, and salt, beating well together. Sift in gradually enough flour to make a dough. Roll as thin as possible. Place the sheet of dough on a buttered baking sheet. Cut squares without separating them. On each put a dab of butter and a little powdered sugar. Bake in a hot oven (450° F.) about 10 minutes. Makes 24 or more biscuits.

## CREAM BISCUITS II BISCUITS À LA CRÈME

8 *oz. sifted flour*                   ½ *cup cream*
2 *oz. butter, melted*              ⅛ *tsp. salt*

Mix the ingredients smoothly together. Let stand 2 hours in the refrigerator. Roll as thin as possible on a lightly floured board. Cut with a pastry cutter. Bake on a lightly greased baking sheet in a hot oven (400° F.) until golden, about 15 minutes. Makes 20 to 30 biscuits.

## CREAM BUNS PETITS GÂTEAUX À LA CRÈME DE LAIT

| | |
|---|---|
| 4 *heaped tbs. cream from milk that has been boiled and cooled* | 4 *oz. sugar* |
| | 1 *tbs. butter* |
| 4 *oz. flour* | *few drops of vanilla essence* |

Mix the ingredients in the order given, stirring for 5 minutes. Butter a baking tray and arrange heaped teaspoonfuls of the mixture at intervals of about 3 inches. Bake in a hot oven until golden brown. Store the cakes in a tin container until required.

## DOLLAR BISCUITS DOLLARS

| | |
|---|---|
| 4 *oz. flour, sifted* | 4 *oz. butter* |
| 4 *oz. cornflour* | 2 *tbs. water* |
| 4 *oz. sugar* | |

Sift the dry ingredients together; work the butter and water in. Mix well. Roll out to $\frac{1}{4}$-inch thickness on a floured board. Cut in rounds about $1\frac{1}{4}$ inches in diameter. Bake on a lightly buttered pan in a hot oven (400° F.) 15 minutes. Makes about 50 biscuits.

## HAZELNUT BISCUITS CROQUETS AUX NOISETTES

| | |
|---|---|
| 8 *oz. ground hazelnuts or almonds* | 4 *oz. sugar* |
| 4 *oz. butter* | *flour, sifted* |

Mix the nuts with the butter and sugar; add sufficient flour to form a dough stiff enough to roll. Roll on a lightly floured board to

¼-inch thickness. Cut with a biscuit cutter. Place on a greased baking sheet or pan. Bake in a moderate oven (350° F.) 15 minutes. Makes 3 dozen biscuits.

## HONEY CAKES NONNETTES

These should be baked in small pans. Use well-greased cupcake or muffin pans.

| | |
|---|---|
| 1 *lb. liquid honey* | ½ *oz. powdered cinnamon* |
| 7 *oz. rye flour* | ½ *oz. ground cloves* |
| ½ *cake compressed yeast* | ¼ *cup rum* |
| ½ *cup milk* | 1 *egg white* |
| ½ *oz. ground aniseed* | 4 *tbs. icing sugar* |

Heat the honey to boiling in the upper part of a double boiler over boiling water; remove any scum. Pour into the mixing bowl. Stir the flour into it to form a thick paste. There should be enough flour to make a dough stiff enough to roll. Roll out in a thick layer on a lightly floured board. Let stand 30 minutes.

Dissolve the yeast in the milk; add the aniseed, cinnamon, and cloves all pounded together and mixed with the rum. Work into the dough and knead well 15 minutes. Pull off pieces and place in the baking pans, shaping them into rounds. Bake in a slow oven (275° F.) about 10 minutes, or until risen, delicately browned, and light. Set the pan on the drop door of the oven if you have one, or somewhere close at hand. Brush the tops of the cakes with beaten egg white mixed with sugar, and put back in the oven for 1 or 2 minutes. Makes 12 to 18 Nonnettes.

## JAM BISCUITS LAMPIONS

| | |
|---|---|
| 8 *oz. flour* | *salt* |
| 4 *oz. butter* | *some jam* |
| *water* | *caster sugar for dusting* |

Mix the flour and butter with enough slightly salted water to form a thick paste. Roll out to the thickness of about a quarter of an inch. Cut half into rounds with a plain biscuit cutter. Cut the other half with a round doughnut cutter and remove the centres. Bake in a moderate oven for 10 minutes. When the biscuits are nearly cool spread the plain rounds with raspberry jam or red currant jelly. Place the ring biscuits on top. Dust lightly with sugar.

## JAM SABLES SABLÉS À LA CONFITURE

4 oz. sugar
4 oz. softened butter
8 oz. flour

4 tbs. white wine
some currant jelly

Mix the ingredients in the order given, stirring until they are thoroughly mixed. Roll out the paste with a rolling pin and cut into biscuit shapes with a pastry cutter or glass. Bake in a slow oven. When cool place a layer of red currant jelly between two biscuits.

## LEMON TURNOVERS TUILES AU CITRON

2 egg whites
2 tbs. flour

2 tbs. sugar
1 tbs. lemon juice

Whip the whites until stiff; mix with the flour, sugar, and lemon juice. Drop by spoonfuls on a baking sheet about 3 inches apart. Bake in a moderate oven (350° F.) about 8 to 10 minutes. When done and still warm, partially fold over like pocket-book rolls. Makes 8 to 10 turnovers.

## MACAROONS MASSEPAINS

2 oz. ground almonds
2 oz. caster sugar

1 egg white, stiffly beaten
granulated sugar

Beat the almonds and sugar together smoothly. Gradually fold in the stiffly beaten egg white. Knead until smooth. Arrange spoonfuls on a greased baking sheet covered with waxed paper. Place ½ to 1 inch apart. Bake in a slow oven (275° F.) about 20 minutes. Remove the pan from the oven; invert the paper and wet it with a damp cloth. The macaroons will slip off. Makes 2 dozen.

## COCONUT MACAROONS MACARONS À LA NOIX DE COCO

Use freshly grated (or canned grated) coconut in place of the ground almonds. Mix and bake as described.

## HONEY MACAROONS MACARONS AU MIEL

Use liquid honey in place of sugar to mix with the almonds in the plain Macaroons recipe.

## MACAROONS. MALINES MACARONS DE MALINES

*4 oz. grated almonds*              *4 oz. sugar*
*1½ oz. rice flour*              *2 whipped whites of eggs*

Mix together the almonds, rice flour and sugar. Then add the whites of egg. Butter a baking tray and arrange dessertspoonfuls of the mixture at intervals. Bake in a very slow oven. When baked sprinkle with caster sugar and place in a very hot oven for a few moments until the sugar is brown.

## MADELEINE CAKES MADELEINES

Madeleines are small shell-shaped cakes. Bake any rich cake mixture in buttered shell-shaped pans in a moderately slow oven (300° F.) about 15 minutes, gradually increasing the temperature to 350° F.

A pleasant variation is the addition of grated lemon peel.

The cake should be evenly baked, rich, and delicious. Here is a cake mixture for Madeleines or other small cakes:

| | |
|---|---|
| 2 oz. butter | 3 yolks of eggs |
| 4 oz. flour | 3 whipped whites of eggs |
| 5 oz. sugar | grated rind of ½ lemon |

Melt the butter, add the flour, sugar, yolk of egg and lemon rind. Stir for 5 minutes and add the whipped whites of egg. Bake in the shell-shaped pans in a slow oven, increasing the temperature.

## SHORTBREAD BISCUITS GALETTES FONDANTES

| | |
|---|---|
| 4 oz. flour | 2 tbs. cream taken from boiled |
| 3 oz. butter | milk |
| heaped tbs. sugar | few drops vanilla essence |

Mix the ingredients into a paste, roll and cut biscuit shape with a pastry cutter or tumbler. Prick with a fork and bake on a buttered tray for 20 minutes.

## SULTANA CAKES PALAIS DE DAMES

| | |
|---|---|
| 4 oz. butter | 1 tbs. sultanas |
| 4 oz. sugar | 4 oz. flour |
| 2 eggs | |

Stir the butter and sugar together for 10 minutes. Beat the eggs lightly and mix with the first mixture. Add the sultanas. Mix well and add the flour to form a paste.

Butter a tray and arrange at intervals small quantities of the mixture about the size of a walnut. Bake in a slow oven until a golden colour. Allow to cool and then brush with a mixture made with two ounces of sugar and a white of egg.

## SULTANA BUNS BISCUITS AUX RAISINS

| | |
|---|---|
| 1 *lb. flour, sifted* | 2 *tbs. sugar* |
| ⅛ *tsp. salt* | 1 *egg* |
| 1 *tsp. baking powder* | ½ *cup milk* |
| 2 *tbs. butter* | *extra milk and flour* |
| 4 *oz. seedless raisins or currants* | |

Sift the flour with the salt and baking powder. Make a hole in the middle and add the softened butter, raisins, and sugar. Mix and work together. Beat the egg in the milk and add to the first mixture. Work to a good dough consistency. Roll out on a lightly floured pastry board to ¼-inch thickness. Cut with a large biscuit or cake cutter. Brush with milk. Bake on a floured baking sheet in a hot oven (450° F.) 15 to 20 minutes, or until risen and delicately browned. May be eaten warm. Makes 12 to 18 buns.

## SWISS CAKES PETITS GÂTEAUX SUISSES

| | |
|---|---|
| 4 *eggs* | ¼ *cup rum* |
| ½ *lb. (1 cup) sugar* | 1 *lb. sifted flour* |
| 4 *oz. butter, melted* | *oil or fat for deep frying* |

Beat the eggs with the sugar, melted butter, and rum. Slowly add the flour, mixing and stirring. Work the dough with the hands; shape in walnut-size pieces. Fry a few at a time in deep hot oil or fat. Makes 40 to 50 small cakes.

# Fritters and Doughnuts

## APPLE FRITTERS I BEIGNETS DE POMMES
FILLING

| | |
|---|---|
| 3 *or* 4 *apples, peeled and sliced* | *kirsch or other liqueur* |

BATTER

| | |
|---|---|
| ¾ *lb. sifted flour* | 2 *tbs. olive oil* |
| ¼ *tsp. salt* | 2 *eggs* |
| *milk* | |

Cover peeled and sliced apples with a mixture of equal parts of water and kirsch or other liqueur and let stand while the batter is prepared.

Sift the flour and salt together; add milk gradually and beat smoothly (about 3 minutes). Stir the oil in; mix well. Add the eggs.

Dip the apples in the batter. Fry a few at a time in the deep hot oil or fat. Fry 5 to 7 minutes. Drain on thick paper towelling only until the batch is ready to serve. Sprinkle with sugar and serve at once. Makes 18 or more fritters.


## APPLE FRITTERS II BEIGNETS DE POMMES

2 eggs

⅛ tsp. salt

¼ cup cognac

¼ cup olive oil

1 cup ale or beer

10 oz. sifted flour

3 or 4 apples, peeled and sliced

oil or fat for frying

sugar

Beat the eggs with the salt, cognac, oil, and ale or beer. Slowly stir in the flour; stir slowly for 5 minutes. Let stand in a warm, not hot, place about 6 hours.

When ready to fry the fritters, dip apple slices in the mixture and fry a few at a time in the hot, smoking oil or fat. Drain on thick paper towelling; serve sprinkled with sugar. Makes 18 or more fritters.


## BREAD FRITTERS PAIN PERDU

2 eggs

2 tbs. sugar

1 cup milk

8 slices bread

2 tbs. butter

sugar

Beat the eggs, sugar, and milk together. Dip the bread slices in, then fry in the hot butter. Turn each slice to brown other side. Serve hot sprinkled with sugar. Serves 4.

## MAIZE FRITTERS BEIGNETS DE MAÏS

1 qt. water
⅛ tsp. salt
2 tbs. sugar
1 lemon peel, sliced thin
2 oz. butter

10 oz. cornflour
1 tbs. rum
flour
oil or fat for deep frying
sugar

Heat the water, salt, sugar, lemon, and butter together in a saucepan. When boiling, remove from the heat. Pour slowly into the cornflour, stirring well until smooth. Return the mixture to the saucepan; heat again for 2 minutes, stirring continually. Remove from the heat and stir the rum in. Let the pan stand in a warm place until the batter is very thick.

Place spoonfuls of the mixture side by side on a thick cloth, sprinkle with flour, then drop a few at a time into the smoking hot oil or fat. Fry until golden. Drain on thick paper towelling. Sprinkle with sugar and serve. Makes 24 or more fritters.


## VIENNESE FRITTERS BEIGNETS VIENNOIS OU KRAPFEN

2 eggs
1 cup sugar
1 cup milk
2 oz. butter
½ lb. sifted flour

1 tsp. baking powder
½ to 1 tsp. salt
apricot jam
oil or fat for deep frying
caster sugar

Beat the yolks with the sugar; gradually add the milk, the melted butter and the flour which has been sifted with the baking powder and salt. Mix well after each addition. Shape the dough in a ball in the mixing bowl. Cover and chill 1 or 2 hours.

Roll the dough out on a lightly floured board to ¼-inch thickness. Cut with a biscuit cutter in 2-inch or a little larger sizes. Put 2 together with apricot jam between. Press the edges of the upper and lower dough together. Fry a few at a time in deep hot oil or fat for 2 minutes, or until the dough is cooked and browned. Drain on thick paper towelling. Sprinkle with powdered sugar. Makes 18 or more Krapfen.

## FRENCH DOUGHNUTS BEIGNETS À LA LEVURE

1 oz. yeast
1 cup of milk
2 eggs

¾ lb. flour
oil for frying

Mix the yeast with a little warm milk, and put in a basin with 2 eggs and all the flour at once. Stir well with a wooden spoon until the mixture does not adhere to it. The basin should not be more than half full. Cover with a cloth and put aside in a warm place for two hours, when it will have risen to fill the basin.

Drop a few teaspoonfuls of the mixture at a time into moderately hot oil and leave until a golden brown colour. Remove, drain, place in a dish lined with absorbent paper and sprinkle with castor sugar.

## SOUFFLÉ FRITTERS BEIGNETS SOUFFLÉS

1 cup of water
3 oz. butter
pinch of salt

4 oz. flour
3 eggs

Put one cup of water, the butter, and a pinch of salt in a saucepan and boil until the butter is melted. Remove from fire and add 4 oz. of flour all at once, stirring the mixture until it holds together in a ball. Place on the fire for 3 minutes, stirring well. Remove and add 3 eggs one after the other. Allow to cool. Drop portions of the paste, about the size of a walnut, in moderately hot oil and fry until a golden brown colour. Drain and serve sprinkled with castor sugar.

## *Fruit*

## APPLES ALSACIENNE POMMES À L'ALSACIENNE

6 medium-sized apples
4 egg yolks
1 tsp. flour
1 cup heavy cream

½ cup milk
4 oz. sugar
¼ cup kirsch

Peel, slice, and remove cores. Place in a buttered baking dish. Mix the eggs and flour smoothly; stir in the cream, milk, sugar, and kirsch. Pour over the apples. Bake in a moderate oven (350° F.) 40 minutes. Serve hot or cold. Serves 6.


## BAKED APPLES POMMES CUITES AU FOUR

| | |
|---|---|
| *6 apples* | *6 slices bread fried in butter* |
| *3 tbs. sugar* | *2 or 3 tbs. butter* |
| *6 tbs. butter or currant jelly* | *1 or 2 tbs. water* |

Peel; remove the cores. Stuff the core cavity with butter and sugar or currant jelly. In a baking pan place the 6 slices of bread. Place an apple on each. Add dabs of butter to the apples and bread and spoon the water into the pan. Bake in a moderate oven (375° F.) about 40 minutes. Serves 6.


## APPLE CRUMBLE POMMES À LA CASSONADE

| | |
|---|---|
| *1 cup brown sugar* | *4 apples, peeled and sliced* |
| *1 cup sifted flour* | *½ cup water* |
| *1 oz. butter* | *1 tbs. sugar* |

Mix the sugar and flour and combine with dabs of butter. Cook the apples in the water with the sugar until the water is absorbed. Pour the apples in a buttered baking dish. Cover with the sugar mixture. Bake in a moderate oven (350° F.) until browned, about 30 minutes. Serves 4 or 5.


## APPLE DUMPLINGS POMMES EN PÂTE

| | |
|---|---|
| *6 apples* | *4 tbs. sugar* |
| *6 tbs. butter* | *rich pie pastry* |

Peel, and core the apples. Stuff the core cavity with mixed butter and sugar. Roll out pastry to ¼-inch thickness. Cut in 5- or 6-inch circles. Place an apple in each circle and wrap the pastry around it;

pinch the edges together at the top. Bake in a moderate oven (325° F.) 50 minutes. Serves 6.

NOTE: If the apples are hard, parboil them 5 minutes before wrapping with the pastry.

## APPLES BORDALONE POMMES À LA BOURDALOUE

*Apple crumble*                    *Vanilla Cream*
*kirsch*

Add a few drops of kirsch to the Apple Crumble when putting it in the oven. Serve it warm with very cold Vanilla Cream on it. Serves 4 or 5.

## APPLE CHARLOTTE CHARLOTTE AU PAIN

*12 slices bread*                  *grated nutmeg*
*butter*                           *sugar*
*4 to 6 apples*                    *Vanilla Cream*

Butter enough slices of bread to line a greased baking dish along the sides and bottom. Peel, core, and slice the apples. Dip them in nutmeg and sugar and fill the dish. Add dabs of butter. Cover the top with slices of buttered bread. Bake in a moderate oven (350° F.) 45 minutes. If the top slices brown too quickly, cover them with greased paper for the last few minutes of baking. Serve plain, with or without Vanilla Cream. Serves 6.

## APPLE JELLY POMMES AU SUCRE

*1 tbs. grated lemon peel*          *1 tbs. plain unflavoured gelatine*
*Apple Compote as below*           *2 tbs. warm water*

Add the lemon peel to the Apple Compote a few minutes before removing from the heat. Stir the gelatine into the warm water to soften. When the compote has cooled almost to lukewarm, stir the gelatine in. Beat gently with a fork 15 minutes. Pour into an oiled mould. Let stand in the refrigerator 3 hours or longer. Turn out just before serving. Serves 6 to 8.

## APPLE COMPOTE COMPOTE DE POMMES

*4 or 5 apples*                    *3 tbs. brown sugar*
*½ cup water*

Peel, core, and slice the apples. Cook in an enamel saucepan with the water and sugar until the apples are soft and the liquid absorbed. Use low heat, about 15 to 25 minutes. Remove from the heat and mash with a fork. Serve warm or cold. Serves 6 to 8.

## APPLE CUSTARD FLAN AUX POMMES

*4 apples*                    *Vanilla Cream*

Wash, peel, and core the apples. Slice them into buttered baking dish. Cover with cold Vanilla Cream. Bake in a moderate oven (350° F.) 20 minutes. Serves 6.

## APPLE CREAM POMMES CHEZ-SOI

*Vanilla Cream*                 1 *cup cake crumbs or macaroons*
*Apple Compote*                    *crumbled*
1 *tsp. kirsch*                 1 *tbs. butter, melted*

Let the Vanilla Cream cool. Stir the kirsch into the cream just as it is removed from the heat. Pour the compote into a buttered baking dish. Pour the Vanilla Cream over the apples. Sprinkle with crumbs and pour the melted butter over all. Bake in a moderate oven (350° F.) about 20 minutes. Serves 6.

## APPLE MERINGUES POMMES MERINGUÉES

*Apple Compote*                 3 *oz. butter*
3 *tbs. rice*                    4 *eggs, separated*
2 *cups milk*                    1 *tbs. sugar*
6 *oz. sugar*

While the Apple Compote is cooking, cook the rice in the milk with the sugar and butter. When the rice is soft, about 20 minutes, remove from the heat; let cool a few minutes. Beat the yolks and add. Pour into the buttered baking dish. Put the Apple Compote on top of the rice. Whip the whites until stiff; add the tablespoon of sugar. Pile the meringue on top. Bake in a slow oven (250° F.) until the meringue is golden, about 15 minutes. Serves 6.


## APPLE RICE POMMES AU RIZ

| | |
|---|---|
| *6 apples* | *1½ cups cooked rice* |
| *1 cup water* | *3 eggs* |
| *3 tbs. sugar* | *cream* |
| *Apple Compote* | |

Wash, peel, and core the apples. Boil in the water with the sugar until tender, 15 to 25 minutes. Place in a buttered baking dish. Fill the centres with Apple Compote and use the rest of the compote over the top of the apples. Beat the eggs and a spoonful of cream into the cooked rice. Pile it around the apples. Brown in a hot oven (425° F.) 10 to 20 minutes. Serve hot or cold. Serves 6.


## APPLE TURNOVERS CHAUSSONS DE POMMES

| | |
|---|---|
| *flaky pastry* | *Apple Compote* |
| *sliced raw apples or* | *sugar* |

Roll out pastry to ¼-inch thickness. Cut in 4- or 5-inch squares. On one corner place several slices of sugared apple or a generous spoonful of Apple Compote. Fold the opposite corner over. Press the edges together. Place on a buttered baking sheet and bake in a hot oven (450° F.) 10 to 15 minutes, or until the pastry is golden.

# Desserts : Fruit

## ORANGE JELLY GELÉE D'ORANGE DANS LES PEAUX

2 tbs. plain gelatine
½ cup warm water
3 tbs. sugar
4 oranges, juice only

1 lemon, juice only
orange shells
extra orange juice
curaçao

Stir the gelatine into the warm water and let it dissolve. Set the dissolved gelatine over boiling water and stir the sugar into it; remove from the heat. Add the strained fruit juice and pour into the orange shells, which have been kept as nearly whole as possible. Chill until the gelatine is firm. To serve, sprinkle with a few drops of fresh orange juice and curaçao. Serves 4.

## ORANGE MOUSSE MOUSSE À L'ORANGE

Vanilla Cream
orange essence

grated peel 2 oranges
4 egg whites

Flavour the Vanilla Cream with orange essence instead of vanilla. Add the grated orange peel. Let cool. Whip the egg whites until stiff. Fold into the orange custard. Chill in a covered bowl or pack in ice for 4 to 6 hours. Serves 6.

## PEACHES CONDÉ PÊCHES À LA CONDÉ MERINGUÉES

1½ cups hot cooked, creamed
    rice
3 eggs, separated

6 or 8 tender ripe peach halves,
    fresh or canned
5 tbs. sugar

To cook creamed rice follow direction under Strawberry Rice. When the rice has cooled a little, beat the yolks into it and spread in buttered pie dish. Place the peach halves on the rice. If fresh peaches are used, peel. Whip the egg whites until stiff; beat the sugar in. Pile on the peaches. Bake in a moderate oven (300° F.) 10 minutes, or until the meringue is golden. Serves 6.

# Desserts : Fruit

## PEACHES PARISIENNE PÊCHES À LA PARISIENNE

6 *tender ripe peaches (fresh or* 1 *qt. ripe strawberries, washea*
 *canned)*      *and hulled*
*boiling Sugar Syrup*

Peel the peaches. Dip each in boiling Sugar Syrup. Place on a serving dish. Dip the berries in the same syrup and arrange around the
peaches. Serve warm. Serves 6.

## PEARS IN WINE POIRES AU VIN

6 *small ripe pears*    $\frac{1}{2}$ *cup water*
$\frac{1}{2}$ *cup red wine*     3 *tbs. sugar*

Wash the pears. Leave whole with the stem on, but peel them. Mix
the wine, water, and sugar in an enamel saucepan. Place the pears
in the pan; boil gently until cooked, about 10 minutes. Let cool
in the liquid. Serves 6.

## PEARS, SNAPDRAGON POIRES FLAMBÉES

*Stewed pear halves*    $\frac{1}{4}$ *cup cognac, rum, or kirsch*
Place the freshly stewed pears in a flameproof serving dish. Cook
the juice down until thickened. Pour it over the pears. Dash with
the cognac or rum; ignite and serve.

## RHUBARB CREAM CRÈME DE RHUBARBE

2 *lb. rhubarb*     2 *eggs*
1$\frac{1}{2}$ *lb. sugar*     1 *tbs. rice flour*
$\frac{1}{2}$ *cup water*     1 *lemon, juice only*

Wash the rhubarb and skin it; cut in small pieces. Place in an
enamel or glass saucepan with the sugar and a little water—usually
only enough to cover the bottom of the pan. Cook slowly until
tender and smooth, like a purée. Cool. Beat the eggs with the rice
flour and lemon juice. Stir into the cooled purée. Return to the
heat and cook until thickened, but do not boil. Let cool and serve.
Serves 6 to 8.

## STRAWBERRY RICE FRAISES AU RIZ

1½ cups hot cooked, creamed rice
1 egg, separated
Caramel Syrup

1 qt. hulled strawberries
rum or kirsch
½ cup chopped almonds

To make the creamed rice for this recipe, use 4 tablespoonsful of rice; cover with 4 cups milk. Cook 20 minutes, or until the rice is tender and the liquid absorbed.

Beat the yolk into the rice. Whip the egg white until stiff; fold in. Line a mould with the Caramel Syrup. Tilt the mould to coat the sides and bottom. Pour the rice in. Set mould in a shallow pan half filled with water. Bake in a moderate oven (350° F.) 30 minutes. Turn out on to a dessert dish. Surround with strawberries sprinkled with rum or kirsch. Top with almonds and serve. Serves 6.

# Ice Creams

## CHOCOLATE ICE CREAM GLACE AU CHOCOLAT

7 oz. (squares) chocolate
hot water
2 qts. scalding milk

1 tsp. vanilla
7 egg yolks, beaten
6 oz. sugar

Soften the chocolate in a bowl over boiling water. Stir into the scalding milk in the upper part of a double boiler. Add the vanilla. Remove from the heat. Beat the eggs and sugar together, then add the milk slowly. Reheat over very low heat; do not boil. When thick, remove from the heat. Let cool slowly. Freeze well. Makes about 2 quarts.

## COFFEE ICE CREAM GLACE AU CAFÉ

Make as for Chocolate Ice Cream. In place of chocolate, stir 1½ cups strong cold coffee into the milk.

## Desserts : Ice Creams

### COFFEE ICE CREAM LIÉGEOIS CAFÉ LIÉGEOIS

1 *cup strong cold coffee*
1 *cup sugar*

1 *cup heavy cream*
*whipped cream*

Mix coffee, sugar, and cream together; freeze in paper cups in the coldest part of the refrigerator. Or place the cups in a mould, close it securely, and pack it in ice for 4 or 5 hours. When ready to serve, top each cup with a whirl of whipped cream. Serves 6.


### COUPE JACQUES

*Vanilla Ice Cream*
*fresh peaches, halved*

*sweetened whipped cream*

Half fill champagne glasses with Vanilla Ice Cream. Place a fine peach half (peeled, stone removed) in the centre of each. Top with sweetened whipped cream.


### FRUIT ICE CREAM GLACE PLOMBIÈRES

*Vanilla Ice Cream*
*chopped candied pineapple*

*candied orange slices, apricots,*
 *dates*

When ready to freeze Vanilla Ice Cream, add 1 or 2 cups chopped cooked or candied fruit; or berries or cherries.


### ICE CREAM WITH HOT CHOCOLATE SAUCE GLACE
### CHAUD-FROID

Serve Vanilla Ice Cream with hot chocolate sauce.


### PEACH MELBA PÊCHE MELBA

*Vanilla Ice Cream*
*fresh peaches*

*clear raspberry syrup or other*
 *sweet syrup*
 *sweet whipped cream*

Add syrup before topping with cream. See Coupe Jacques.

## PISTACHIO ICE CREAM GLACE À LA PISTACHE

*Vanilla Ice Cream*
*¼ cup chopped pistachio nuts*

1 or 2 drops light green food
   colouring

Mix the nuts and delicate colouring into the Vanilla Ice Cream
mixture just before freezing.

## PEAR MELBA POIRE MELBA

See Coupe Jacques. Use halves of ripe pears, peeled and sweetened.

## PRALINE ICE CREAM GLACE AU PRALINÉ

**4 tbs. sugar**
**1 tbs. water**

½ cup chopped toasted almonds
*Vanilla Ice Cream*

Melt the sugar in a heavy pan; stir the water in and let boil until
slightly caramelized. Add the nuts. Stir 1 minute. Add to Vanilla
Ice Cream mixture just before freezing. Stir and freeze.

## VANILLA ICE CREAM GLACE À LA VANILLE

1 qt. milk
1 cup sugar
6 egg yolks, slightly beaten

1 tsp. vanilla
1 pt. cream

Scald the milk in the upper part of a double boiler. Add the sugar
to the egg yolks; pour the hot milk on to the eggs gradually, stirring
constantly. Return to the double boiler and cook over hot water
until mixture coats a metal spoon (about 8 minutes). Let cool gradually. Add the flavouring and cream and freeze. Makes about 2 quarts.

# *Omelettes and Pancakes*

## JAM OMELETTE OMELETTE À LA CONFITURE

Make an omelette. Put any favourite jam on it; roll, sprinkle with
powdered sugar, and serve on a hot dish.

## Desserts : Omelettes and Pancakes

### RUM OMELETTE OMELETTE AU RHUM

Proceed as in the previous recipe. When the omelette is cooked and rolled on a hot dish, sprinkle with caster sugar, pour rum or cognac on, and ignite.

### PANCAKES

| | |
|---|---|
| 4 oz. sifted flour | 1 egg |
| ½ tbs. sugar | 2 egg yolks |
| ⅛ tsp. salt | 1 oz. butter |
| 1 oz. butter, melted | sugar |
| 1 cup milk | lemon juice |

When making Pancakes, the batter must have the consistency of thick cream.

Sift the flour, sugar, and salt together. Mix with the melted butter. Add the milk slowly, then the 1 egg, beaten slightly, and the 2 yolks. Beat with a wooden spoon until bubbles appear on top.

Brown 1 teaspoon butter or margarine in a frying pan. Tilt the pan so the fat covers the whole pan. Pour in 2 tablespoons of the mixture. Brown each side in turn. Serve hot sprinkled with sugar and lemon juice. Makes 12 pancakes.

### PANCAKES BOULONNAIS CRÊPES BOULONNAISES

Use cream in place of milk; whip the white of the egg until stiff and beat into the batter. Make the pancakes twice as thick as usual.

### SUZETTE PANCAKES CRÊPES SUZETTE

Make Pancake batter. Fry as described. Roll each and place side by side in a flameproof serving dish. Pour over them ¼ cup cognac and a little kirsch and anisette. Sprinkle with caster sugar and ignite. Serves 12.

## JAM PANCAKES crêpes à la confiture

Make Pancakes as usual. When baked, cover each with a spoonful of jam. Roll, sprinkle with caster sugar, and serve hot.

## ORANGE PANCAKES crêpes à l'orange

Make Pancakes as usual. When baked, cover each with 1 teaspoon heavy cream and 1 tablespoon orange marmalade. Roll, put on a hot dish, sprinkle with Grand Marnier, and ignite.

# Soufflés

In the chapter on entrées is good advice on the making of soufflés. This instruction applies to sweet soufflés also.

## APPLE SOUFFLÉ soufflé aux pommes

| | |
|---|---|
| *Apple Compote* | *1 tbs. butter* |
| *½ lemon, juice or grated Peel* | *½ tbs. potato flour* |
| *pinch of cinnamon* | *3 eggs, separated* |
| *3 tbs. caster sugar* | *breadcrumbs* |

Let the Apple Compote cool a little, then add the lemon juice or peel, cinnamon, sugar, butter, and flour. Beat with a wooden spoon. Beat the egg yolks and mix. Then add the 3 whipped whites of egg. Butter a soufflé mould, sprinkle with bread crumbs, pour in the mixture and bake in a slow oven for threequarters of an hour.

## CHOCOLATE SOUFFLÉ soufflé au chocolat

| | |
|---|---|
| *3 oz. chocolate* | *2 tbs. flour* |
| *1 cup milk* | *knob of butter* |
| *2 tbs. sugar* | *2 egg yolks* |
| *few drops vanilla essence* | *2 egg whites* |

Grate the chocolate and put in a saucepan on the fire with 3 table-spoonsful of milk. When well mixed add the remainder of the milk, the sugar, and the vanilla essence. Bring to the boil and allow to cool. Pour slowly on to the flour. Replace mixture in a saucepan and stir until thick. Remove from fire, add the butter and pour slowly on the egg yolks, stirring for a few minutes. Add the whipped egg whites and pour into a buttered earthenware dish. Bake in a medium oven for 20 minutes.

## COFFEE SOUFFLÉ SOUFFLÉ AU CAFÉ

Add 2 tablespoons coffee essence to the milk in place of the chocolate in the above recipe.

## LIQUEUR SOUFFLÉ SOUFFLÉ À LA LIQUEUR

Follow directions for Vanilla Soufflé, using cognac or kirsch as flavouring. Beat 1 tablespoon of liqueur into the egg yolks.

## RHUBARB SOUFFLÉ SOUFFLÉ À LA RHUBARBE

| | |
|---|---|
| 1 *lb. rhubarb* | 2 *eggs, separated* |
| ¾ *lb. sugar* | 1 *tbs. rice flour* |
| ½ *cup water* | ½ *lemon, juice only* |

Prepare rhubarb and cut in small pieces. Place with the sugar in a glass or enamel saucepan. Add the water, just enough to cover the bottom of the pan. Cook slowly until very soft. Mash with a wooden spoon. Cool. Beat the egg yolks with the rice flour and lemon juice and stir into the rhubarb. Heat, but do not boil. Stir smoothly until thickened. Cool again. Whip the egg whites until stiff and fold into the rhubarb. Pour into a buttered soufflé dish set in a shallow pan of water. Bake in a moderate oven (325° F.) 30 minutes. Carry at once to the table and serve. Serves 6.

## VANILLA SOUFFLÉ SOUFFLÉ À LA VANILLE

| | |
|---|---|
| 1 *cup milk* | 2 *tbs. flour* |
| *few drops vanilla essence* | *knob of butter* |
| 2 *tbs. sugar* | 2 *eggs* |

Put the milk, sugar, and essence of vanilla in a saucepan, bring to the boil and allow to cool. Pour slowly on to the flour. Replace the mixture in a saucepan on the fire and stir until thick. Remove from fire, add the butter and pour slowly on the egg yolks, stirring for a few minutes. One teaspoonful of baking powder will help the soufflé to rise. Add the whipped egg whites and pour into a buttered earthenware dish. Bake in a medium oven for 20 minutes.

# PASTRY, PIES AND TARTS

Here are six pointers on how a French housewife goes about her pastry making:

1. Mix the paste well, first stirring with a wooden spoon and then working with the hands for 10 minutes altogether.

2. Roll several times on a pastry board sprinkled with flour.

3. When baking, place the tin or pie dish on a hot brick in the oven. (Not needed in regulated, thermal-controlled modern ovens.)

4. The paste will become a nice golden colour if brushed with egg, beer, or butter before baking.

5. It is best to use a special tart tin with a removable centre.

6. If the tart is to be filled after baking, while the pastry is in the oven the centre should be weighted with small stones or dried haricot beans to prevent its puffing. Other cooks use a layer of rice for the same purpose; or prick the unbaked pastry with a sharp fork.

## Pastry

### PLAIN PASTRY PÂTE POUSSÉE

| | |
|---|---|
| 1 *lb. flour* | 3 *oz. sugar* |
| 1½ *cupfuls milk* | 3 *oz. melted butter* |
| 1 *oz. yeast* | *grated peel of ½ lemon* |
| *pinch of salt* | 1 *egg* |

Put 12 oz. flour in a basin and make a hole in the centre.

Pour a cupful of milk slowly over the yeast, stirring well. Add

# *Pastry*

a pinch of salt and pour into the centre of the flour. Mix well and stand in a hot place until the paste rises.

Mix the sugar with half a cupful of milk. Add the melted butter, the grated lemon peel, the remainder of the flour and the first mixture. Add the egg and work the paste for ¼ hour. Allow to stand. Line a buttered tart tin and again allow to stand for 20 minutes before baking. Prick with a fork before placing in oven.


## PUFF OR FLAKY PASTRY PÂTE FEUILLETÉE

½ *lb. butter*                    ¾ *cup ice water*
½ *lb. pastry flour*

Mash the butter with a wooden spoon; shape half the flour into a flat cake about ½-inch thick. Stir 1 tablespoon of butter into the flour; moisten gradually with just enough water to make a stiff dough. Knead on a lightly floured board until smooth and elastic. Cover and let stand a few minutes.

Roll out ¼-inch thick and rectangular in shape. Place 1 tbs. of butter in the centre of the lower half of the paste. Sprinkle lightly with flour. Fold the upper half of the paste down over the butter; press the edges firmly together. Fold the right side of the paste under the butter and fold the left side over the butter. Press the edges together; cover and let stand 5 minutes. Turn halfway around and roll as before. Repeat 3 times. Use as little flour as possible on the board and rolling pin. If possible, between rollings chill the dough in a pan set on ice, then roll as described for any recipe and chill.

It should be ice cold when placed in the oven. Bake on a tin sheet covered with a double thickness of paper towelling or brown paper in a hot oven (475° to 500° F.). The time of baking is given in each recipe. For a baked shell allow 15 to 20 minutes; the pastry should be a pale gold colour when done. This makes pastry for 10 4-inch tarts or 2 double-crust pies or large shells.

# Pastry

### SHORT PASTRY I PÂTE SABLÉE

½ *lb. flour*  
4 *oz. sugar*  
2 *yolks of egg*

*water*  
6 *oz. butter*

Mix the flour and sugar in a bowl. Make a hole in the centre and in it place the yolks of egg and enough water to form a paste. When well mixed add the butter cut in small pieces. Work well with the fingers. Allow the paste to stand for half an hour before using.

### SHORT PASTRY II PÂTE BRISÉE

½ *lb. sifted flour*  
4 *oz. butter*  
⅛ *tsp. salt*

*water*  
*flour*

Sift the flour into a mixing bowl. Make a hole in the centre and add the butter, salt, and a very little water. Gradually mix, adding enough water to form a stiff paste. (Use only 3 or 4 tablespoons of water in all.) Mix well, first with a spoon, then with the fingers. Let the paste stand for 1 hour in a cool place, then roll lightly on a floured pastry board; fold and roll again several times.

Line a buttered tart tin with the pastry; trim the edge and crimp it high, using thumb and forefinger. Prick with a fork or fill with dried beans, rice, or small pebbles. Bake in a hot oven (475° F.) 20 minutes, or until the pastry is golden. (Shake out the beans, rice, or pebbles.) Makes 2 pastry shells or 1 2-crust tart or pie.

### SHORT PASTRY III PÂTE BRISÉE

½ *lb. sifted flour*  
2 *oz. butter*  
3 *ozs. sugar*

1 *egg yolk*  
2 *tbs. cream*  
¼ *cup cognac, rum, or kirsch*

Sift the flour into the mixing bowl. Add the butter, sugar, and egg yolk and mix well together. Add the cream and liqueur, mixing smoothly. Let stand 1 hour in the refrigerator. Roll and line a buttered tart tin. Prick well with a sharp fork. Bake in a hot oven (475° F.) 15 to 20 minutes. Makes 2 tart shells or a 2-crusted pie.

## TART PASTRY I PÂTE À TARTE

| | |
|---|---|
| 4 oz. flour | pinch of salt |
| 3 oz. butter | some milk |

Put the flour in a bowl, make a hole in the centre and in it place the butter, salt, and enough milk to form a paste. Mix well with a wooden spoon, then work with the fingers, roll, form a ball, sprinkle with flour and allow to stand for 2 hours before using.

## TART PASTRY II PÂTE À TARTE

| | |
|---|---|
| 7 oz. sifted flour | 1 egg |
| 3 oz. butter | ½ lemon, grated peel only |
| 1 cup ground almonds | ¼ tsp. powdered cinnamon |
| 6 tbs. sugar | ⅛ tsp. salt |

Sift the flour into a mixing bowl; soften or melt the butter and put into the centre of the bowl. Add the almonds, sugar, beaten egg, and lemon peel; mix. Add cinnamon and salt. Beat and mix until smooth. Let stand in the refrigerator 1 hour. Roll lightly. Line a buttered tart tin. Prick with a sharp fork. Bake in a hot oven (475° F.) 15 to 20 minutes. Makes 2 tart shells or a 2-crust pie.

# Pies and Tarts

## ALSATIAN TART TARTE ALSACIENNE

| | |
|---|---|
| 1½ cups cooked dried or canned apricots or other fruit | ¼ cup heavy cream |
| baked tart shell | 1 tbs. sugar |
| 2 egg yolks, beaten | ⅛ tsp. powdered cinnamon |
| | grated peel of 1 lemon |

Place the fruit, drained of excess juice, in the shell. Mix the yolks, cream, sugar, cinnamon, and peel. Pour over the fruit. Bake in a moderate oven (325° F.) about 15 minutes, or until the custard on the fruit is cooked. Serves 4 to 6.

## APPLE PIE PLÂTRÉE DE POMMES

| | |
|---|---|
| 4 *or* 5 *apples* | *cognac* |
| *sugar* | *flaky Pastry* |
| *butter* | *heavy cream* |

Peel, core, and slice the apples. Place a layer of apples in a buttered pie dish; sprinkle with sugar and dabs of butter. Repeat until the dish is full. Sprinkle a little brandy on top. Cover with a flaky pastry crust. Prick in several places with a sharp fork. Brush with the cream. Bake in a moderate oven (350° F.) 50 minutes to 1 hour. Serve warm. Serves 6.

## APPLE TART TARTE AUX POMMES

See Apple Pie.

## APRICOT TART TARTE AUX ABRICOTS

See Alsatian Tart.

## BANANA TART TARTE AUX BANANES

| | |
|---|---|
| 1 *cup apricot jam* | ¼ *cup cognac, curaçao, or rum* |
| *baked pastry shell* | *toasted almonds* |
| 2 *or* 3 *ripe bananas, sliced* | |

Spread a layer of jam in the baked pastry shell. Fill threequarters full with sliced bananas. Pour the liqueur over the fruit. Spread another layer of jam. Bake in a moderate oven (325° F.) 10 minutes, or until the jam is melted. Garnish with almonds. Serves 6.

# Pies and Tarts

## BILBERRY TART TARTE AUX MYRTILLES

pastry
2 to 3 cups whortleberries or
   blueberries

$\frac{1}{2}$ to $\frac{3}{4}$ cup sugar
2 to 3 tbs. flour
sugar

Here are two methods for making this delicious tart. Either plain or puff pastry may be used. With the simple pastry, the pan should be lined, the edge crimped handsomely, the berries placed in it and sprinkled with sugar and a little flour. Cover with pastry; prick the top. Bake in a hot oven (about 450° F.) 20 minutes; reduce to moderate (350° F.) and bake 25 minutes more. Serve sprinkled with sugar.

When Puff Pastry or a rich pastry is used, bake the shell first, as described in the pastry recipes. When it has cooled, fill with berries which have been stewed a little with the sugar. Let cool and serve. A tart, or pie, serves 6.


## TARTLETS

Small or individual tarts are made like the larger ones, with unbaked or baked shells. The baked shells may be filled with cooked fruits and a spoonful of Vanilla Cream and require no further baking.

A delicious tartlet may be made with thick Vanilla Cream, grated walnuts, and seedless raisins, with a little rum added. Fill the baked shells of Plain or Tart Pastry just before serving.


## CHERRY TART TARTE AUX CERISES

Tart Pastry
cherries, stones removed

caster sugar

Mix the pastry and line the tin. Almost fill the shell with layers of juicy ripe cherries and powdered sugar. Bake in a hot oven (425° F.) 30 minutes, or until the cherries are cooked down and the shell golden. Serve cold.

Strawberry Tart and other berry tarts are made the same way.

## Pies and Tarts

### GRAPE TART TARTE AUX RAISINS

1 *lb. seedless grapes*
¼ *cup sugar*
*Vanilla Cream*

1 *cup grated or chopped walnuts*
1 *tsp. rum*
*baked tart shell*

Wash the grapes; remove stems. Place in an enamel or glass sauce-pan with 1 cup water and the sugar. Boil 5 minutes. Drain and mix with the Vanilla Cream, to which the walnuts and rum have been added. The Vanilla Cream should be thick and cold. Mix and fill the tart just before serving. Serves 6.

### LEMON TART TARTE AU CITRON

*Vanilla Cream*
*lemon peel and essence*

*pastry for tart shell*

Flavour the Vanilla Cream with grated lemon peel and lemon essence instead of vanilla. Let the custard cool a little. Pour into the pastry-lined pan. Bake in a moderate oven (350° F.) 25 to 30 minutes. Serves 6.

### CORNFLOUR CUSTARD TART TARTE AU MAÏS

*Short Pastry for* 1-*crust pie*
2 *cups milk*
3 *tbs. sugar*
½ *tsp. vanilla*
3 *tbs. cornflour*

1 *tbs. cream*
2 *tbs. butter*
1 *egg, separated*
*sugar*

Line a tart tin with the pastry. Heat the milk in the upper part of a double boiler over boiling water. Add the sugar and vanilla. Stir, and when the milk is boiling, slowly add the cornflour mixed to a smooth paste with a little cold milk. Continue to stir until thickened. Remove from the hot water and let the custard cool to lukewarm. Add the cream, butter, and egg yolk, beating in smoothly. Whip the egg white until stiff and fold in. Pour at once into the pastry-lined tart tin; sprinkle the top with sugar. Bake in a moderate oven (350° F.) about 30 minutes, until the custard is set and the top delicately browned. Let cool before serving. Serves 6.

## Pies and Tarts

### PEACH TART TARTE AUX PÊCHES

*Vanilla Cream*
*baked pastry tart shell*

*sliced ripe or canned peaches*
*juice or Sugar Syrup*

Pour cooled Vanilla Cream into the baked shell. Arrange peaches closely all over it. Cook the liquid from the canned peaches until thickened and pour a few tablespoons over the peaches; or use a little thick Sugar Syrup. Serves 6.

### PEAR FLAN FLAN AUX POIRES

*Tart Pastry*
*red currant jelly or jam*
*3 or 4 ripe pears*

*1 cup water*
*2 tbs. sugar*
*2 tbs. red currant jelly*

Line a pie dish with the pastry. Spread a thick layer of jam in the bottom. Wash, peel, and core the pears. Cook them in the water with the sugar about 10 minutes, or until tender. Drain. Arrange in the pie dish, cut side up. Bake in a moderate oven (375°F.) 35 to 45 minutes. Boil the pear juice down; add 2 tablespoons red currant jelly. When thick, pour over the baked tart. Serve cold. Serves 6.

### PEAR TART TARTE AUX POIRES

*baked pastry shell*
*1 cup red currant jelly*
*Vanilla Cream*

*2 or 3 cooked pears*
*1 cup cream, whipped*
*8 or 10 walnuts*

Into the cooled pastry shell spread the currant jelly. Pour over this the thick Vanilla Cream (about 1 cup, unless the tart tin is very deep; then use 1½ cups). Arrange quartered pears in the Vanilla Cream. Add the whipped cream, spreading it smoothly to fill the shell. Decorate the top with walnut halves. Serves 6.

# Pies and Tarts

## PLUM TART I TARTE AUX PRUNES

1 *lb. ripe plums*
1½ *cups sugar*

*Short Pastry for 2-crust pie or tart*

Prepare the plums the day before. Wash them, cut in halves, and remove stones. Place in a bowl and cover with the sugar. Let stand covered in the refrigerator overnight, turning them several times.

To bake, line a tart or pie pan with the pastry; trim the edge. Fill with the drained plum halves. Pour a little of the juice over them and sprinkle with a little sugar. Cut the remaining pastry in strips about ¾-inch wide and cover the tart with crisscrossed strips. Bake in a hot oven (450° F.) 20 minutes; reduce the heat to moderate (350° F.) and bake 25 minutes longer. Just before serving, pour a little of the remaining sweet juice into the pie. Serves 6.

## PLUM TART II TARTE AUX QUETSCHES

*baked pastry shell*
*sweetened plums*

2 *egg whites*
1 *tbs. sugar*

Fill the baked tart shell with the drained plums prepared as in the preceding recipe. Whip the egg whites until stiff, whisking the sugar into them. Pile the meringue on top of the plums. Set the tart in a moderate oven (300° F.) until the meringue is set and the tips golden. Serves 6.

## RICE TARTLETS TARTELETTES AU RIZ

*baked tartlet shells*
*boiled, creamed rice*

*peach or apricot halves boiled in Sugar Syrup*

Fill baked tartlet shells with creamed rice. Place a peach or apricot half, cut side up, on each. Pour a little syrup over.

## RASPBERRY TART TARTE AUX FRAMBOISES

*Puff Pastry*
*raspberry jam*

1 *egg, beaten*

# Pies and Tarts

Line a tart tin with Puff Paste. Chill. Fill with jam. Crisscross strips of pastry over the tart. Brush these with egg. Bake at once in a hot oven (500° F.) 20 minutes. Serves 6.

*Variations.* Use red currant jam and other jams in the same way.

# SAVOURIES AND SAVOURY BISCUITS

The delicious result of combining very rich pastry with good cheese, baked to crisp tenderness, is detailed in these savouries. They could be served with salads; the biscuits, enlarged a little, with Cheese Sauce as luncheon entrées.

## HOT CHEESE SANDWICH GALETTES AU CHESTER

5 tbs. flour
2 tbs. grated cheese
yolk of an egg

heaped tbs. butter
pinch each of salt, pepper and
   cayenne pepper
egg for browning

FOR THE FILLING:
3 tbs. grated cheese
½ cupful thick milk sauce

yolk of an egg

Knead the first ingredients together, make the paste into a ball and leave to stand for half an hour. Roll out to biscuit thickness and cut to biscuit shape with a pastry cutter. Brush with a beaten egg, place on a buttered tray and bake for ten minutes.

Make half a cupful of thick milk sauce and add the three table-spoonsful grated cheese and the yolk of egg. Use as a filling between two cakes. Serve very hot.

## CHEESE BEIGNETS BEIGNETS SOUFFLÉS

1 cup water
3 oz. butter
4 oz. sifted flour
1 tsp. salt

3 eggs
5 oz. grated cheese
oil or fat for deep frying

Heat the water to boiling. Stir the butter in, remove from the heat, then stir in the flour sifted with the salt. Mix to a smooth paste. Replace on the heat; stir. Remove; add 1 egg at a time, stirring well. Add the cheese. Drop the dough by the teaspoonful into hot oil or fat. Fry until puffed and golden, 8 to 10 minutes. Drain on thick paper towelling. Serve hot. Serves 10 or more.

## CHEESE BISCUITS CAKES AU CHESTER

5 oz. butter
4 oz. sifted flour
⅛ tsp. cayenne

4 oz. grated Gruyère or Parmesan
   cheese

FILLING

3 oz. butter
4 oz. grated cheese

⅛ tsp. cayenne

Mix the butter and flour smoothly together, gradually adding the cheese. Add the cayenne. Beat 10 minutes. Roll out to about ¼-inch thickness on a lightly floured board. Cut in biscuit shapes. Place on a buttered pan. Chill. Mix a filling of the other ingredients. Bake the biscuits in a very hot oven (475° F.) 10 minutes. Put together with cheese filling and serve. Serves 16 or more.

## CHEESE STRAWS I PETITS BÂTONS AU FROMAGE

3 oz. sifted flour
3 oz. grated Gruyère or Parmesan
   cheese

¼ tsp. salt
3 oz. butter
2 tbs. milk

Mix the flour, cheese, and salt smoothly together to form a paste. Add the butter and knead 10 minutes. Roll out about ½-inch thick on a pastry board. Chill. When ready to bake, cut the dough in small sticks, place on a greased pan, and brush with milk. Bake in a hot oven (450° F.) 12 minutes. Serve hot or cold. Serves 10 or more.

## CHEESE STRAWS II BÂTONS AU FROMAGE

Mix the recipe above as directed; add the well-beaten yolks of 2 eggs and increase the salt to ½ teaspoon. Roll the pastry and let it chill at least 1 hour. Brush with beaten egg yolk in place of milk. Bake as directed.

## CHEESE STRAWS III ALLUMETTES AU FROMAGE

Mix the recipe above; sift 1 teaspoon baking powder with the flour. Omit eggs altogether. Bake as directed.

## CHEESE STRAWS IV BÂTONNETS À LA MOUTARDE

Add 1 teaspoon dry mustard to the Cheese Straws recipe. Sift it with the flour. Mix and bake as directed. Brush the straws with milk before baking in a moderate oven (350° F.) 15 minutes.

## CHEESE EGGS BOULES SOUFFLÉES

2 egg whites                    oil or fat for deep frying
1 cup grated cheese

Whip the egg whites until stiff. Mix the cheese in. Form small balls and drop them in the hot oil or fat. Fry until browned. Drain on thick paper towelling. Serves 12 or more.

## CHEESE PASTIES RAMEQUINS

recipe for Cheese Beignets            Cheddar cheese cut very thin

Drop the Beignet paste by teaspoonfuls on a buttered baking pan. Chill. When ready to bake, lay a piece of cheese on each. Bake in a slow oven 10 minutes. Serve hot. Serves 10 or more.

## Savouries and Savoury Biscuits

### CHEESE SQUARES PÂTE FEUILLETÉE AU FROMAGE

*Flaky Pastry*
*1 cup thick cold White Sauce*

*1 cup grated cheese*
*cayenne*

Cut Flaky Pastry in squares or oblongs and place on a buttered baking sheet. Chill. When ready to bake, put a spoonful of thick White Sauce on each and a generous sprinkling of cheese. Add a dash of cayenne. Bake in a hot oven (450° F.) 10 to 12 minutes. Serve hot. Serves 12 to 16.

### CHEESE TOASTIES TOAST AU FROMAGE

*loaf of bread*
*butter*

*grated cheese*
*grated nutmeg*

Cut very thin slices of bread; spread with softened butter. Spread generously with cheese. Sprinkle with nutmeg. Brown in a slow oven (300° F.) until the cheese is browned.

### SALTED BISCUITS BISCUITS SALÉS

*4 oz. sifted flour*
*2½ oz. butter*
*3 or 4 tbs. cold milk*

*½ tsp. salt*
*1 egg yolk, beaten*

Combine the flour, butter, milk, and salt. Knead together 10 minutes. Roll paste very thin. Cut with a biscuit cutter. Prick with a sharp fork. Chill. When ready to bake, brush the biscuits with the beaten egg yolk. Bake in a hot oven (475° F.) 8 to 10 minutes. Serves 30 or more.

### SALTED ALMONDS AMANDES SALÉES

*almonds*
*boiling water*
*butter*

*plain gelatine*
*salt*

Plunge shelled almonds into boiling water. Let stand 5 minutes. Drain. Rub the brown skins off. Scatter the almonds in a big shallow pan and place in a hot oven (475° F.) 3 minutes. Melt a little butter in a saucepan; stir the almonds in it over heat. Dip them in a plain gelatine solution (follow directions on gelatine package; use while the gelatine is warm). Roll in fine salt.

# SANDWICHES

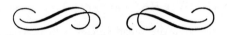

The variety of sandwiches may be increased almost indefinitely. A perusal of the hors-d'oeuvre section will suggest many additional ideas. The sandwiches do not normally have bread on top, as in English sandwiches, if served at table.

## CHEESE SANDWICHES SANDWICHES AU CHESTER

Place thin slices of Cheddar cheese on thin slices of buttered bread; garnish with sliced almonds, walnuts, or hazelnuts.

## CREAM CHEESE SANDWICHES SANDWICHES AU PAIN COMPLET

On thin slices of buttered brown bread spread cream cheese or cottage cheese mixed with chopped chives. Garnish with chopped walnuts.

## EGG SANDWICHES SANDWICHES AUX OEUFS

Butter thin slices of toast. Sprinkle with chopped chives or estragon, and on each place one or more slices of hard-boiled egg. Garnish with capers.

## LETTUCE SANDWICHES SANDWICHES À LA SALADE

Cover thin slices of buttered white bread with lettuce spread with mayonnaise.

# Sandwiches

## MUSTARD SANDWICHES sandwiches à la moutarde

Cover thin slices of buttered white bread with mayonnaise mixed with mustard. Garnish with thin slices of gherkins.


## SHRIMP SANDWICHES crevette à la mayonnaise

On thin squares of white bread spread with mayonnaise arrange cleaned shrimps and capers.


## TOMATO SANDWICHES sandwiches aux tomates

On thin squares of buttered white bread arrange lettuce and slices of tomato; sprinkle with pepper and salt.


## TUNA FISH SANDWICHES sandwiches au thon

Butter thin squares of white bread and cover with lettuce and minced tuna fish. Sprinkle with cayenne or paprika.


## WALNUT SANDWICHES sandwiches aux noix

Grate 4 tablespoons of shelled walnuts and mix with 4 tablespoons of butter and 2 tablespoons of powdered sugar. Spread on thin squares of buttered white bread.

# CONSERVES, JAMS AND
## ~ JELLIES ~

### TOMATOES, BOTTLED CONSERVES DE TOMATES

Cut some large tomatoes in four and place in a pan filled with cold water. Heat gently. Before the water boils, the tomatoes, if good, will rise to the surface, those that do not should be rejected. Remove from pan, drain, and plunge immediately in cold water to cool. Drain. Place in quart preserving jars with two cloves, a sprig of thyme, half a bay leaf and a small peeled onion. Fill up the bottles with salt water, dissolving 2 oz. salt in each quart of water. Close hermetically and place in a water bath, allowing half an hour from the time the water comes to the boil.

### TOMATO PURÉE, BOTTLED CONSERVES DE TO-
#### MATES EN PURÉE

Peel the tomatoes and remove any parts that are hard or unripe. Crush to a pulp. Add 1 gram. of salicylic acid for each 2 lb. of tomatoes. Place in preserving bottles. Cover with ½-inch of olive oil and seal hermetically.

### PEAS, GREEN, BOTTLED CONSERVE DE POIS

Shell a small amount of peas at a time. Peas in quantity ferment. Place the peas in salted boiling water and boil for five minutes. Remove, drain, and leave for 2 or 3 days. Repeat the operation and boil for 20 minutes. Put in preserving bottles and boil in a water bath, allowing 1½ hours for bottles containing 1 quart and 1 hour for ½ pint.

## BEANS, FRENCH, BOTTLED HARICOTS VERTS EN CONSERVE

Choose French beans that have been picked the previous day. Top and tail them, wash and boil for 6 to 8 minutes. Cool in cold water and closely pack in preserving bottles. Cover with cold water containing a teaspoonful of salt and a pinch of bicarbonate of soda to each quart. Seal the bottles hermetically and boil in a water bath for 2 hours from the time the water first comes to the boil. Before using the French beans soak for 3 hours in frequent changes of cold water.

# *Jams and Jellies*

## SOME HINTS ON JAM MAKING

1. A copper pan should be used: the pan should be scrupulously clean.
2. The fruit should be picked in dry weather.
3. The jam pots should be washed in clean hot water.
4. It is better to make jam when nothing else is cooking. Any smell, even of tobacco, may spoil it.
5. Jam pots should be filled as soon as the jam is ready.
6. Jam pots should be hermetically sealed.

## APPLE JAM CONFITURE DE POMMES

Take some apples and threequarters of their weight of sugar. Peel and slice the fruit. Place the fruit, sugar, 1 cup of water and the juice of a lemon in a preserving pan. Boil slowly at first, increasing the heat. Remove the scum and boil until the apples become transparent. Put in pots and seal immediately.

# Jams and Jellies

## APRICOT JAM CONFITURE D'ABRICOTS

Take clean, dry fruit, removing the stones and stalks. Remove the kernels from the stones. Weigh the fruit and put threequarters of its weight of sugar in a preserving pan with a tumblerful of water for every 4 lb. sugar. Boil for 20 minutes, add the fruit, boil for a further 20 minutes, then add the kernels. Scum should be removed as it forms.

## BRAMBLE JELLY CONFITURE DE MÛRES

Place the fruit in a pan with a tumblerful of water and boil quickly for a few minutes. Remove from fire and extract the juice of the fruit by squeezing through a damp cloth. Weigh the juice and boil for 15 minutes in a preserving pan with threequarters of its weight of sugar, stirring well.

## CHESTNUT JAM CONFITURE DE MARRONS

Take boiled chestnuts from which the inner skin has been removed and mash. Weigh. Put threequarters of their weight of sugar in a preserving pan with a cupful of water for every 4 lb. of sugar, adding a few drops of vanilla essence. Boil for 20 minutes, remove the scum, add the chestnuts and boil for a further 20 minutes.

## PEAR JAM CONFITURE DE POIRES ENTIÈRES

Peel some small ripe pears and as they are peeled place in water to which some lemon juice has been added. Transfer the fruit to a preserving pan with an equal weight of sugar and one cupful of water for every 2 lb. of sugar. Boil slowly until the pears are transparent. After removing the scum pour into jam pots. If the syrup is too thin, boil alone until of right thickness.

# Jams and Jellies

## PLUM JAM CONFITURE DE PRUNES

Take clean fruit and remove the stones and stalks. Weigh. Put threequarters of their weight of sugar in a preserving pan, with 1 cupful of water for every 4 lb. of sugar. Boil for 20 minutes, then add the fruit, boiling for a further 20 minutes. Remove the scum as it forms.

## PLUM JAM. ECONOMY RECIPE CONFITURE DE PRUNES

Take clean, dry fruit, removing the stones and stalks. Place in a preserving pan with ¼ lb. of sugar for each lb. of fruit and a cupful of water for every 4 lb. of fruit. Boil for 1 hour, removing the scum. Before bottling stir in a ¼ oz. of salicylic acid for every 15 lb. of fruit.

## RASPBERRY JAM CONFITURE DE FRAMBOISES

Take some moderately ripe raspberries and place in a bowl with threequarters of their weight of sugar. Allow to stand for 12 hours. Pour into a preserving pan and boil for 20 minutes over a moderate heat.

## RED CURRANT JELLY CONFITURE DE GROSEILLES

Press the fruit to extract the juice. Weigh the juice. Take the same weight of sugar and place in a preserving pan with 1 cupful of water for every 4 lb. of sugar. Boil for 20 minutes over a moderate heat, stirring well. Add the red currant juice, bring again to the boil and allow to boil 5 minutes, removing scum.

This jelly may be improved by adding raspberries to the red currants in any proportion up to one-half. The fruits should be pressed together and the juice weighed in the same way.

## RHUBARB JAM CONFITURE DE RHUBARBE

Weigh the rhubarb and cut in pieces. Take four-fifths of its weight of sugar and put in a preserving pan with 1 cupful of water for every 4 lb. of sugar. Boil for 20 minutes, add the rhubarb and again boil for 20 minutes. Remove the scum.

## STRAWBERRY JAM CONFITURE DE FRAISES

Choose clean fruit—as strawberries cannot be washed—and remove the stalks. It is better and more economical to use small fruit. Take threequarters of a lb. of sugar for every lb. of fruit and place in a preserving pan with a cupful of water for every 4 lb. of sugar. Boil for 20 minutes over a moderate heat, stirring all the time. The syrup should then be very thick and white in colour. Add the fruit, bring again to the boil and continue to boil for twenty minutes, removing the scum.

# SWEETMEATS AND CANDY

## CRYSTALLIZED CHESTNUTS MARRONS GLACÉS

Prepare the chestnuts as described in Chestnut Caramel. Instead of placing them in a caramel sauce, dip each in the Glacé Syrup given below.

1 *cup sugar*
½ *cup water*

⅓ *cup golden syrup*

Heat the sugar, syrup, and water, stirring only until the sugar dissolves. Continue the cooking over low heat and without stirring, until the temperature on a sugar thermometer is 300° F., or a little dropped from the spoon into a cup of cold water hardens and cracks. As sugar crystals form on the sides of the pan, they must be wiped away with a wet cloth. When the syrup is done (a delicate straw shade) remove it from the heat and set the pan in boiling water to prevent hardening. Dip the nuts in (on a darning needle) one by one, turning each to coat it thoroughly. Place on a flat glazed surface (heavy waxed paper) and let them cool. If the syrup becomes too thick for dipping, it can be reheated, but do not let it brown. Serves 24 or more.

## CHERRY SWEETMEAT BONBONS AUX CERISES

1 *egg white*
6 *oz. caster sugar*
2 *oz. chopped candied cherries*

1 *oz. ground almonds*
1 *tbs. grated lemon peel*

Whip the egg white until stiff; beat the sugar and other ingredients into it smoothly. Shape the mixture into a thin oblong loaf. Cut in slices with a thin sharp knife. Let mixture dry before serving. Serves 16 to 24.

# Sweetmeats and Candy

## CHESTNUT CARAMEL MARRONS AU CARAMEL

2 cups chestnuts
boiling water

2 cups sugar
½ cup boiling water

Place the chestnuts in boiling water for 10 minutes; drain. Pierce the skin of each nut with a thin sharp knife. Shell and cover with boiling water for 10 minutes. Rub the dark inner skin off. Place on a baking sheet in a slow oven (275° F.) and let dry 30 minutes. Leave the oven door open.

Heat the sugar and a little water in a heavy pan. When it is golden brown, remove from the heat. Immerse the chestnuts in the caramel until thoroughly coated. Remove; drain. Serve as sweetmeats, or serve with a sweet sauce, such as Vanilla Cream. Makes 24 or more marrons, 6 servings.

## CHOCOLATE CROQUETTES CROQUETTES AU CHOCOLAT

4 oz. hazelnuts
4 oz. almonds, blanched
4 oz. sugar

4 oz. grated chocolate (squares)
2 tbs. water
½ cup granulated sugar

Place the nuts on a tin in a slow oven (275° F.) about 20 minutes. Leave the oven door open. Grate the nuts; mix with the sugar and chocolate. Add the water. Heat to boiling, stirring all the time. Boil 2 minutes. Remove from the heat. Let cool enough to handle. Form small balls. Roll them in sugar. Let them cool and dry. Makes about 64 croquettes.

## CHOCOLATE AND ALMOND FONDANTS OLIVES

2 oz. ground almonds
½ tsp. vanilla essence
5 oz. grated chocolate
  (squares)

2 oz. sugar
1 egg white, stiffly beaten
½ cup caster sugar

Mix the almonds, vanilla, and grated chocolate well together. Beat the sugar into the stiffly beaten egg white for 5 minutes. Combine the two mixtures. Beat. Form into small balls the shape of olives. Roll in sugar. Place on waxed paper to dry. Makes 32 or more olives.

## CHOCOLATE FONDANTS LES MARCELINETTES

6 oz. (squares) chocolate
3 oz. butter
1 tsp. coffee essence
⅛ oz. ground almonds

1 egg white, stiffly beaten
granulated sugar
cocoa

Melt the chocolate over hot water; remove from the heat and beat with the butter. Add the coffee essence, almonds, and the stiffly beaten egg white. Mix smoothly. Cover and let stand overnight in a cool place.

Sprinkle the pastry board with sugar. Make balls of the chocolate mixture. Roll them in the sugar, then in cocoa. Let stand for 12 hours in a cool place. Set each in a little paper case or wrap in waxed paper. Makes 28 or more.

## CHOCOLATE CARAMELS CARAMELS AU CHOCOLAT

4 oz. butter
4 oz. grated chocolate
  (squares)

4 oz. sugar
4 oz. honey

Place all the ingredients in a saucepan. Heat slowly. Stir and cook until the mixture reaches 248° F. on a sugar thermometer or a little dropped from the spoon into a cup of cold water forms a firm ball. Remove from the heat; pour into a lightly buttered pan. Let cool a little; cut in squares and continue to cool.

## CHOCOLATE FONDANT SAUCISSON AU CHOCOLAT

8 oz. (squares) chocolate
1 cup almonds, chopped

3 oz. honey

Melt the chocolate over hot water. Mix with the almonds and enough honey to make a thick paste. Shape into a thick sausage roll. Wrap in silver paper. Serves 32 or more.

## COCONUT CARAMEL I CARAMELS À LA NOIX DE COCO

| | |
|---|---|
| ½ *lb. sugar* | 1 *tbs. butter* |
| ⅜ *cup water* | ½ *lb. grated coconut* |
| ½ *cup dark syrup* | 1 *tbs. anisette* |

Put all ingredients except the coconut and anisette in a 1½-quart saucepan. Cook, stirring until the sugar is dissolved. Continue cooking, stirring only enough to prevent burning, until the sugar thermometer registers 245° F., or a little dropped in a cup of cold water forms a soft ball. Remove from the heat; stir in the coconut and flavouring. Mix thoroughly. Pour into a frame or drop by spoonfuls on a greased surface and shape into squares with the hands. Work quickly before the mixture hardens. Makes 14 to 28 pieces.

## COCONUT CARAMEL II AFRICAINS

Let the sugar brown a little in a heavy pan before adding the other ingredients. Use as described. Omit the anisette.

## COFFEE TRUFFLES TRUFFETTES AU CAFÉ

| | |
|---|---|
| 4 *oz. icing sugar* | 4 *oz. butter* |
| 1 *egg yolk* | 2 *tbs. grated or powdered* |
| ½ *tbs. coffee essence* | *chocolate* |

Beat the sugar, yolk, and coffee essence together. Add the butter, just enough to make a thick paste. Form balls; dip or roll in chocolate. Place each in a small paper case. Serve fresh. Makes 24 or more pieces.

## COFFEE CARAMEL CARAMELS AU CAFÉ

| | |
|---|---|
| 8 oz. sugar | a few drops coffee essence |
| 1 cup cream | 2 oz. butter |

Mix all ingredients; heat and stir slowly until boiling. Do not stir after boiling begins. When a drop from the spoon makes a firm ball in a cup of water, remove from the heat. Pour into a buttered pan or 'a frame resting on a greased marble square', as the French candymaker does. When the candy is nearly cold, mark in squares with a sharp knife. Makes 24 or more pieces.

## STUFFED DATES DATTES FARCIES

| | |
|---|---|
| 10 oz. dried or fresh dates | 2 oz. Sugar Syrup |
| 3 oz. ground almonds | Glacé Syrup |

Remove the stones from the dates. Mix almonds and Sugar Syrup together and stuff the dates. Serve plain; or coat with Glacé Syrup, cool, and place in paper cups.

## NEAPOLITAN FONDANT FONDANTS NAPOLITAINS

| | |
|---|---|
| 1 egg white | red food colouring |
| 2 tbs. cream | ½ tsp. rose water |
| 1 lb. icing sugar | green food colouring |
| 2 oz. (squares) chocolate, melted | ½ tsp. orange flower water |
| ½ tsp. vanilla | |

Beat the egg white slightly; add the cream and sugar. Beat smoothly together. Divide into three portions. Mix one portion with the melted chocolate and vanilla until smoothly coloured. Mix one portion with 1 or 2 drops red food colouring and the rose water. Mix the third portion with 1 or 2 drops green food colouring and the orange flower water.

Knead each section smoothly. Shape into a square. Place the coloured portions in a pile, chocolate on the bottom, rose next, and light green on top. Press down gently; cover with waxed paper and let stand with a weight on top for a few hours or overnight. Slice; wrap in waxed paper. Makes about 1 lb.

## TANGERINE FONDANTS MANDARINETTES

6 oz. almonds
boiling water
3 oz. caster sugar
3 tbs. flour

2 tangerines, grated peel only
2 egg whites
red food colouring

Blanch the almonds by plunging them into the boiling water. Let them stand 10 minutes. Drain; wipe off the brown skins. Grate; mix with the sugar, flour, and grated peel. Whip the egg whites until stiff and fold in. Add 1 or 2 drops of red food colouring. Shape into small balls. Place on a greased baking sheet and bake in a moderate oven (350° F.) 10 minutes; increase the heat to 425° F. and bake 10 minutes more, or until the macaroons are browned. Makes 60 or more.

## NOUGAT

1 lb. honey
2 whipped whites of egg
1 lb. dried chopped almonds

some hazel and pistachio nuts
some flavouring and colouring to
taste

Boil the honey, stirring well until a drop allowed to fall on a cold plates solidifies at once. Reduce the heat, add the whipped whites of egg and stir until the honey has the same consistency as before. Add the chopped almonds, nuts, flavouring, and colouring to the mixture and pour into a mould.

## NUT FONDANT NOISETTINES

10 oz. shelled hazelnuts
boiling water

2 oz. sugar (caster)
8 oz. heavy cream

Blanch the nuts by plunging them into the boiling water. Rub the skins off and wipe the nuts dry. Grate them. Mix with the sugar and the cream. Shape in small balls. Place on a baking sheet in a warm oven (275° F.); leave the door open. They should dry in 15 or 20 minutes. Makes 40 to 60 Noisettines.

## CRYSTALLIZED ORANGE QUARTIERS D'ORANGE GLACÉS

*3 oranges*            *Glacé Syrup*

Peel the oranges; carefully separate in sections. Pull off any white pulp or segments. Use 2 forks to coat them. Place a section on one fork (do not pierce with the prongs) and lower the fruit into the hot syrup. Lift up and turn over on the second fork. Lower into the syrup again; lift out. Place on waxed paper to cool. Place in little paper cups. Seedless grapes, strawberries, and sections of pineapple may be used in the same way.

## STUFFED PRUNES PRUNEAUX FARCIS

See Stuffed Dates. Wash the prunes, drain, and remove the stones. If the prunes seem too dry and hard, soak them in water to cover for 1 or 2 hours, then drain, dry, remove stones, and follow the recipe.

## STUFFED WALNUTS NOIX FARCIES

*walnut halves*            *caster sugar*
*ground almonds*          *Glacé Syrup*
*heavy cream*

Select unbroken walnut halves. Mix grated almonds with a very little cream and enough sugar to sweeten. Beat smooth. Spread a generous layer on 1 nut half. Press another half on top. Brush with syrup and let harden, or serve plain.

# BEVERAGES

Most French people drink wine with their meals, but it is advisable to drink appropriate wines with special dishes.

*With oysters*, a dry white wine, Alsacien type. (Alsatian or Rhine wine is suitable.)

*With fish*, white wine, slightly sweeter in type. (Chablis, Muscatel suitable.)

*With meat*, red Bordeaux.

*With game*, red Bourgogne. (Burgundy, some clarets suitable.)

*With sauerkraut*, beer is recommended.

## HOT CHOCOLATE CHOCOLAT

Place 1 square (ounce) of chocolate per serving in a saucepan; add a little hot water and stir until the chocolate is melted and smooth. Add milk slowly, stirring all the while; use 1 cup of milk for each square of chocolate. Beat with a whisk before serving. A tablespoon of fresh cream may be added to each cup before serving. Serve hot.

## COFFEE CAFÉ

After lunch, and sometimes after dinner, a cup of coffee is taken. The coffee used in France is in the form of beans which have been freshly roasted and then ground just before using.

A French coffeepot is composed of two parts: at the top is a strainer in which is placed a tablespoon of ground coffee for each cup of water used. A few grains of chicory may be added. Pour a little boiling water slowly over the coffee to let it swell. Then pour in the rest of the boiling water. Cover the pot. When ready to serve, heat but do not let it boil. When steaming, serve it. Coffee must be served very hot.

*Variation.* Ground coffee may be placed in a small saucepan of boiling water. Allow to boil for a few minutes (5 or less). Remove from the heat; add a few drops of cold water. (This will settle the grounds.)

## TEA THÉ

Warm the teapot by scalding it; drain it. Place in the pot 1 teaspoon of tea for each person and 1 for the pot. Pour boiling water into the pot; cover and let stand 3 to 5 minutes before serving.

# MENUS FOR ALL SEASONS

## (FROM MME CARTER'S HOME)

## SPRING

**SUNDAY**

LUNCH

| Trout with Cream | Truites à la crème |
| Roast Pigeon | Pigeons rôtis |
| Green Peas | Petits pois |
| Chocolate Ice Cream | Glace au chocolat |

DINNER

| Chicken Broth | Bouillon de poule |
| Calf's Brains with White Sauce | Cervelle de veau à la sauce blanche |
| Mashed Potatoes | Purée de pommes de terre |
| Apple Tart | Tarte aux pommes |

**MONDAY**

LUNCH

| Ham and Eggs | Entrée au jambon |
| Mutton Cutlets | Côtelettes de mouton |
| Spinach | Epinards |
| Pancakes | Crêpes |

# *Menus for All Seasons*

DINNER

| | |
|---|---|
| Carrot Soup | Potage julienne |
| Scallops with Grated Cheese | Coquilles St. Jacques gratinées |
| Semolina Mould with Vanilla Cream | Gâteau de semoule |

## TUESDAY

LUNCH

| | |
|---|---|
| Hors-d'oeuvre | Hors-d'oeuvre |
| Calf's Liver with Wine Sauce | Foie de veau sauce bordelaise |
| Fried Potatoes | Pommes de terre frites |
| Lettuce Salad | Salade de laitue |
| Coffee Cream | Crème au café |
| Biscuits | Biscuits |

DINNER

| | |
|---|---|
| Celery Soup | Soupe au céleri |
| Cheese Omelette | Omelette au fromage |
| Carrots Vichy | Carottes à la Vichy |
| Caramel Cream | Crème au Caramel |

## WEDNESDAY

LUNCH

| | |
|---|---|
| Mussels | Moules marinières |
| Boiled Beef | Boeuf bouilli |
| Potatoes | Pommes de terre |
| Apple Fritters | Beignets de pommes |

DINNER

| | |
|---|---|
| Cream Consommé | Consommé velouté |
| Macaroni Timbale | Timbale de macaroni |
| Cream Meringue | Ile flottante |

# Menus for All Seasons

### LUNCH

| | |
|---|---|
| Ham Pancakes | Crêpes au jambon |
| Beef with Piquant Sauce | Boeuf au four |
| Spinach | Epinards |
| Fruit | Fruits |

### DINNER

| | |
|---|---|
| Leek Soup | Soupe aux poireaux |
| Rice with Calf's Liver | Riz au foie de veau |
| Jam Omelette | Omelette à la confiture |

## FRIDAY

### LUNCH

| | |
|---|---|
| Fried Ham Sandwich with Cheese | Croque-monsieur |
| Roast Beef | Rôti de boeuf |
| New Potatoes and Carrots | Pommes de terre et carottes nouvelles |
| Chocoloate Pudding with Cream Sauce | Biscottes au chocolat |

### DINNER

| | |
|---|---|
| Vegetable Soup | Potage printanier |
| Skate with Black Butter | Raie au beurre noir |
| Almond Cream | Gâteau aux amandes |

## SATURDAY

### LUNCH

| | |
|---|---|
| Cheese Tart Lorraine | Quiche Lorraine |
| Cold Meat | Rôti froid |
| Small Onions | Petits oignons |
| Mashed Potatoes | Purée de pommes de terre |
| Fruit | Fruits |

DINNER

| | |
|---|---|
| Sorrel Soup | Soupe à l'oseille |
| Ham Pudding | Pouding au jambon |
| Snow Eggs | Oeufs à la neige |

## SUMMER

**SUNDAY**

LUNCH

| | |
|---|---|
| Stuffed Tomatoes with Meat | Tomates farcies au gras |
| Creamed Rabbit | Lapin à la crème |
| Potatoes | Pommes de terre |
| Fruit Ice | Glace Plombières |

DINNER

| | |
|---|---|
| Lettuce Soup | Soupe à la laitue |
| Baked Fillets of Sole | Sole au gratin |
| Apricot Tart | Tarte aux abricots |

**MONDAY**

LUNCH

| | |
|---|---|
| Hors-d'oeuvre: cucumber, shrimps | Hors-d'oeuvre: concombres, crevettes |
| Roast Veal | Rôti de veau |
| Potato Croquettes | Croquettes de pommes de terre |
| Fruit | Fruits |

DINNER

| | |
|---|---|
| Tomato Soup | Soupe aux tomates |
| Ling à l'Américaine | Lotte à l'américaine |
| Chocolate Surprise | Crème glacée |

# Menus for All Seasons

### LUNCH

| | |
|---|---:|
| Macaroni and Veal Croquettes | Croquettes de veau et macaroni |
| Asparagus | Asperges |
| Sauce Mousseline | Sauce mousseline |
| Cherry Tart | Tarte aux cerises |

### DINNER

| | |
|---|---:|
| Vegetable Soup | Potage printanier |
| Stuffed Artichokes with Meat | Artichauts farcis au gras |
| Rum Omelette | Omelette au rhum |

## WEDNESDAY

### LUNCH

| | |
|---|---:|
| Eggs with Cheese | Oeufs en surprise |
| Grilled Veal Cutlets | Côtelettes de veau grillées |
| French Beans | Haricots verts |
| Potatoes | Pommes de terre |
| Soufflé Fritters | Beignets soufflés |

### DINNER

| | |
|---|---:|
| Sorrel Soup | Potage à l'oseille |
| Cauliflower with Cheese | Choufleur au gratin |
| Liver Pâté | Pâte de foie de porc |
| Lettuce Salad | Salade de laitue |
| Chocolate Sponge Fingers | Biscuits au chocolat |

## THURSDAY

### LUNCH

| | |
|---|---:|
| Hors-d'oeuvre: radishes and cauliflower | Hors-d'oeuvre: radis, choufleur |
| Ox Tongue with Piquant Sauce | Langue de boeuf sauce piquante |
| Potatoes | Pommes de terre |
| Vanilla Cream | Crème à la vanille |

**DINNER**

| | |
|---|---|
| Beef Bouillon | Bouillon de boeuf |
| Cheese Tart Lorraine | Quiche Lorraine |
| Jam Pancakes | Crêpes à la confiture |

**FRIDAY**

**LUNCH**

| | |
|---|---|
| Soufflé Nantua | Bouchées Nantua |
| Stewed Beef with Carrots | Boeuf à la mode |
| Fruit | Fruits |

**DINNER**

| | |
|---|---|
| Vegetable Soup | Potage printanier |
| Cheese Entrée | Coquilles au parmesan |
| Mashed Potatoes | Purée de pommes de terre |
| Raspberry Tart | Tarte aux framboises |

**SATURDAY**

**LUNCH**

| | |
|---|---|
| Hors-d'oeuvre: shrimps and tomatoes | Hors-d'oeuvre: crevettes, tomates |
| Stewed Veal with White Sauce | Blanquette de veau |
| Strawberry Rice | Fraises au riz |

**DINNER**

| | |
|---|---|
| Lettuce Soup | Potage à la laitue |
| Omelette with Mushrooms | Omelette aux champignons |
| Stuffed Eggplant | Aubergines farcies |
| Peaches Condé | Pêches à la Condé meringuées |

# AUTUMN

**SUNDAY**

### LUNCH

| | |
|---|---|
| Ham Soufflé | Soufflé au jambon |
| Roast Partridge | Perdreaux rôtis |
| Fried Potatoes | Pommes de terre frites |
| Chicory Salad | Salade de chicorée |
| Vanilla Ice Cream | Glace à la vanille |

### DINNER

| | |
|---|---|
| Pea Soup | Soupe aux pois cassés |
| Crab mayonnaise | Tourteau à la mayonnaise |
| Custard | Crème renversée |

**MONDAY**

### LUNCH

| | |
|---|---|
| Hors-d'oeuvre: sardines, cucumbers | Hors-d'oeuvre: sardines, concombres |
| Saddle of Mutton with Red Currant Jelly | Filet de mouton à la gelée de groseilles |
| Chestnut Purée | Purée de marrons |
| Cream Pralines | Crème pralinée |

### DINNER

| | |
|---|---|
| Onion Soup | Soupe aux oignons |
| Braised Endives | Endives braisées |
| Hare Pâté | Pâté de lièvre |
| Salad | Salade |
| Rice Tartlets | Tartelettes au riz |

**TUESDAY**

   LUNCH

Creamed Eggs                             Oeufs à la crème
Russian Cabbage                       Chou à la russe
Pears in Wine                          Poires au vin

   DINNER

Leek Soup                         Soupe aux poireaux
Sheep's Trotters            Pieds de mouton poulette
Potatoes                       Pommes de terre
Chocolate Pudding with Cream Sauce     Biscottes au chocolat

**WEDNESDAY**

   LUNCH

Peasant Omelette                      Omelette au lard
Boiled Chicken with Rice                 Poule au riz
Apple Fritters                    Beignets de pommes

   DINNER

Pea Soup                       Soupe aux pois cassés
Noodles with Minced Beef       Nouilles à la bolognaise
Sylvabella                            Sylvabelle

**THURSDAY**

   LUNCH

Stuffed Mushrooms                Champignons farcis
Veal Fillets with Cream    Escalopes de veau à la crème
Mashed Potatoes        Purée de pommes de terre
Fruit                                 Fruits

   DINNER

Pumpkin Soup                   Soupe au potiron
Grilled Herrings                    Harengs grillés
Baked Apples            Pommes cuites au four

# Menus for All Seasons

### LUNCH

Eggs with Anchovies and Butter — Oeufs durs au beurre d'anchois

Shoulder of Mutton with mixed Vegetables — Ragoût de mouton aux légumes
Alsatian Tart — Tarte Alsacienne

### DINNER

Leek Soup — Soupe aux poireaux
Pilaff — Moules en riz
Apple Compote — Compote de pommes

## SATURDAY

### LUNCH

Shrimps in Scallop Shells — Coquilles aux crevettes
Porterhouse Steak with Fried Potatoes — Châteaubriand aux pommes de terre frites

Snapdragon Pears — Poires flambées

### DINNER

Tomato Soup — Soupe aux tomates
Stuffed Fillets of Veal — Les oiseaux sans têtes
Braised Celery — Céleri braisé
Lemon Tart — Tarte au citron

## WINTER

SUNDAY

### LUNCH

Cheese Soufflé — Soufflé au fromage
Chicken with White Wine — Poulet chasseur
Mashed Potatoes — Purée de pommes de terre
Apple Tart — Tarte aux pommes

# Menus for All Seasons

### DINNER

Cress Soup · Soupe au cresson
Chicken Scallops · Coquilles de volaille
Braised Endives · Endives braisées
Chocolate Cake · Gâteau au chocolat

## MONDAY

### LUNCH

Hors-d'oeuvre · Hors-d'oeuvre
Mutton Cutlets · Côtelettes de mouton
French Beans · Haricots verts
Salad · Salade
Pancakes Boulonnais · Crêpes boulonnaises

### DINNER

Leek Soup · Soupe aux poireaux
Eel with Tartare Sauce · Anguille à la Tartare
Potatoes · Pommes de terre
Snow Eggs · Oeufs à la neige

## TUESDAY

### LUNCH

Mussels in Scallop Shells · Coquilles de moules
Roast Veal · Rôti de veau
Brussels Sprouts · Choux de Bruxelles
Potatoes · Pommes de terre
Fruit · Fruits

### DINNER

Onion Soup · Soupe à l'oignon
Omelette Bretonne · Omelette bretonne
Rabbit Pâté · Pâté de lapin
Green Salad with Olives · Salade aux olives
Apple Rice · Pommes au riz

# *Menus for All Seasons*

### LUNCH

| | |
|---|---|
| Soused Herrings | Harengs marinés |
| Stuffed Cabbage | Chou farci |
| Apple Meringues | Pommes meringuées |

### DINNER

| | |
|---|---|
| Carrot Soup | Potage julienne |
| Ham and Eggs | Entrée au jambon |
| Chestnut Cream Auvergnat | Gâteau Auvergnat |

THURSDAY

### LUNCH

| | |
|---|---|
| Hors-d'oeuvre | Hors-d'oeuvre |
| Veal loaf | Pain de veau |
| Braised Endives | Endives braisées |
| Potatoes | Pommes de terre |
| Fruit | Fruits |

### DINNER

| | |
|---|---|
| Vegetable Soup | Potage printanier |
| Veal Kidneys with White Wine | Rognons de veau au vin blanc |
| Potatoes | Pommes de terre |
| Rice Caramel with Vanilla Cream | Gâteau de riz |

FRIDAY

### LUNCH

| | |
|---|---|
| Eggs Bûcheronne | Oeufs bûcheronne |
| Tripe à la mode de Caen | Tripe à la mode de Caen |
| Pears in Wine | Poires au vin |

### DINNER

| | |
|---|---|
| Pea Soup | Soupe aux pois cassés |
| Scallops with Grated Cheese | Coquilles St. Jacques gratinées |
| Chocolate Sponge Fingers | Biscuits au chocolat |

# Menus for All Seasons

**SATURDAY**

**LUNCH**

| | |
|---|---|
| Hors-d'oeuvre | Hors-d'oeuvre |
| Boned Shoulder of Mutton with Turnips | Epaule de mouton aux navets |
| Apple Tart | Tarte aux pommes |

**DINNER**

| | |
|---|---|
| Cabbage Soup | Soupe au chou |
| Noodles Milanaise | Gâteau milanais |
| Apple Soufflé | Soufflé aux pommes |

# DINNERS FOR MORE IMPORTANT OCCASIONS

## SPRING

| | |
|---|---|
| Chicken Broth | Bouillon de poule |
| Duck with Olives | Canard aux olives |
| Roast Veal | Rôti de veau |
| Green Peas | Petits pois |
| Suzette Pancakes | Crêpes Suzette |
| | |
| Tomato Soup | Soupe aux tomates |
| Stewed Chicken | Poulet en cocotte |
| Roast Leg of Mutton | Gigot de mouton rôti |
| Cauliflower | Choufleur |
| Chocolate Surprise | Crème glacée |
| | |
| Madeira Soup | Bouillon au madère |
| Crayfish Belle-Vue | Langouste en belle-vue |
| Chicken Pie | Coq en pâte |
| New Potatoes and Carrots | Pommes de terre et carottes nouvelles |
| Liqueur Soufflé | Soufflé à la liqueur |
| | |
| Cream Soup | Soupe onctueuse |
| Trout Meunière | Truites meunière |

## Dinners for more Important Occasions

Stuffed Chicken                    Poulet farci
Potato Croquettes          Croquettes de pommes de terre
Salad                                    Salade
Pistachio Ice Cream            Glace à la pistache

## SUMMER

Beef Bouillon                    Bouillon de boeuf
Salmon Steaks            Tranches de saumon grillées
Fillet of Beef with Olives      Filet de boeuf aux olives
French Beans                    Haricots verts
Coffee Ice Cream                Glace au café

Cream Consommé                Consommé velouté
Scallops with Port Wine   Coquilles St. Jacques au porto
Duck with Green Peas        Canard aux petits pois
Peach Melba                        Pêche melba

Bisque                            Potage bisque
Chicken with Port Wine        Poulet au porto
Fried Fillets of Beef                Tournedos
Béarnaise Sauce                Sauce béarnaise
Stuffed Mushrooms and Tomatoes    Tomates et champignons
                                       farcis
Praline Ice Cream               Glace au praliné

Madeira Soup                    Bouillon au madère
Lobster à l'Américaine        Homard à l'américaine
Roast Chicken                     Poulet rôti
Potatoes Chamonix       Pommes de terre Chamonix
Chocolate Marquise            Marquise au chocolat

# Dinners for more Important Occasions

## AUTUMN

| | |
|---|---|
| Tomato Soup | Soupe aux tomates |
| Sole Marguery | Sole à la Marguery |
| Roast Partridge | Perdreaux rôtis |
| Salad | Salade |
| Coupe Jacques | Coupe Jacques |

| | |
|---|---|
| Cream Consommé | Consommé velouté |
| Grilled Lobster, Sauce Américaine | Homards grillés à la sauce américaine |
| Roast Venison | Chevreuil rôti |
| Marinade Sauce | Sauce marinade |
| Chestnut Purée | Purée de marrons |
| Liqueur Soufflé | Soufflé à la liqueur |

| | |
|---|---|
| Beef Bouillon | Bouillon de boeuf |
| Ham Pancakes | Crêpes au jambon |
| Stuffed Chicken | Poulet farci |
| French Beans | Haricots verts |
| Salad | Salade |
| Sylvabella | Sylvabelle |

| | |
|---|---|
| Bisque | Potage bisque |
| Vol-au-Vent with Sweetbreads | Vol-au-vent au riz de veau |
| Duckling Rouennais | Caneton Rouennais |
| Fried Potatoes | Pommes de terre frites |
| Fruit Ice Cream | Glace Plombières |

## WINTER

| | |
|---|---|
| Prawn Soup | Potage aux bouquets |
| Cheese Soufflé | Soufflé au fromage |
| Saddle of Mutton with Red Currant Jelly | Filet de mouton à la gelée de groseilles |
| Cauliflower, Potatoes | Choufleur, pommes de terre |
| Chestnut and Chocolate Cream | Gâteau aux marrons au chocolat |
| | |
| Cream Soup | Soupe onctueuse |
| Lobster à la Morlaise | Homard à la Morlaise |
| Roast Stuffed Turkey | Dinde farcie |
| Chestnut Purée | Purée de marrons |
| Coffee Ice Cream | Glace au café |
| | |
| Bisque | Potage bisque |
| Woodcock Salmis | Salmis de bécasse |
| Roast Fillet of Beef | Filet de boeuf rôti |
| Spinach | Epinards |
| Chocolate Sponge Fingers | Biscuits au chocolat |
| | |
| Cream Consommé | Consommé velouté |
| Turbot | Turbot |
| Mousseline Sauce | Sauce mousseline |
| Stuffed Pheasant | Faisan farci |
| Chicory Salad | Salade de chicorée |
| Suzette Pancakes | Crêpes Suzette |

# ENGLISH INDEX

Afternoon cake, 167, 168
Almond
  Cakes, 177
  Cream, 153
  Fondants, Chocolate and, 225
  Turnovers, 177
Almonds, Salted, 215
Alsatian
  Soup, 25
  Tart, 205
Anchovies, 15
  and Butter, Eggs with, 14
  Eggs with, 14
Apple
  Charlotte, 190
  Compote, 191
  Cream, 191
  Crumble, 189
  Custard, 191
  Dumplings, 189
  Fritters I, 185
  Fritters II, 186
  Jam, 220
  Jelly, 190
  Meringues, 191
  Pie, 206
  Rice, 192
  Soufflé, 199
  Tart, 206
  Turnovers, 192
Apples
  Alsacienne, 188
  Baked, 189
  Bordalone, 190
  Stewed, Sausages with, 53
Apricot
  Jam, 221
  Tart, 206

Ardennes Cake, 168
Aromatic Cucumbers, 18
Artichoke Hearts, Stuffed, 55
Artichokes, 16
  Jerusalem, 17, 133
  Poached Eggs with, 45
  Stuffed with Meat, 56
Asparagus, 133
  Served Cold, 133
  Tips, 134

Baba
  Savarin, Rum, 173
  Savoy, Rum, 173
Bacon
  Lettuce with, 59
  Potatoes with, 145
Banana Tart, 206
Beans
  Baked, Mutton with, 106
  Broad, 135
  French, 135
    Bottled, 220
    with Oil, 17
    Roast Leg of Mutton with, 103
    Sheep's Kidneys with, 109
  with Tomatoes, Butter, 136
Béarnaise, 122
Béarn Cake, 168
Beef, 96–102
  Boiled, 98
    Cold, 98
    with Herbs, 15
  Bouillon, 21

Beef—(cont'd)
  Bourguignon, 96
  with Carrots, Stewed, 101
  Croquettes, 38
  Fried Fillets of, 99
  Minced
    with Noodles, 35
    with Potatoes, 97
  with Olives, Fillet of, 99
  with Onions, Braised, 97
  Ox Tongue in Piquant Sauce, 99
  Oxtail Hotpot, 100
  in Piquant Sauce, 97
  Roast, 102
  with Sausage, Rolled, 101
  Steak, Porterhouse, 100
Beets, 17
Beverages
  Coffee, 231
  Hot Chocolate, 231
  Tea, 232
Bilberry Tart, 207
Biscuit Cake
  with Chocolate Cream, 154
  with Coffee Cream, 154
Biscuits
  Cream, 179
  Creamed, 164
  Dollar, 180
  Hazelnut, 180
  Jam, 181
  Salted, 215
  Shortbread, 184
Bisque, 22
Boned Shoulder of Mutton with Turnips, 104
Bouillon, Beef, 21
Brains
  Calf's, 48
  with Cream Sauce, 49
Bramble Jelly, 221
Bread
  Fritters, 186
Brioche, 177
  Sultana, 178

Broad Beans, 135
Broth, Chicken, 23

Cabbage
  à la Bourgeoise, 136
  with Cheese, 136
  Flanders Red, 137
  Partridge with, 78
  Pickled, 17
    Red, 137
  Pigeons, with, 92
  Russian, 56
  Soup, 26
  Stuffed, 57
    Red, 57
Cakes, 167–76
  Afternoon, 167, 168
  Ardennes, 168
  Béarn, 168
  Biscuit, with Chocolate Cream, 154
    with Coffee Cream, 154
  Chocolate, 169, 170
  Coffee Cream, 170
  Four Quarters, 171
  Genoa, 172
  Hasty, 169
  Kougloff, 171
  Polish, 172
  Rum
    Baba Savarin, 173
    Baba Savoy, 173
    Fruit, 173
  Spice
    or Gingerbread, 174
    with Marmalade, 174
  Sponge, 174
    Madeleine, 175
    Mousseline, 175
    Savoy, 175
  Swiss Roll, 176
  Walnut, 176
Cakes, Small, 177–84
  Almond, 177
    Turnovers, 177
  Biscuits

# English Index

Cakes, Small—(cont'd)
 Cream, 179
 Dollar, 180
 Hazelnut, 180
 Jam, 181
 Shortbread, 184
 Brioche, 177
  Sultana, 178
 Buns
  Cream, 180
  Sultana, 185
 Cats' Tongues, 178
 Cream Cakes, 162
 Honey, 181
 Jam Sablés, 182
 Macaroons, 182
  Coconut, 183
  Honey, 183
  Malines, 183
 Madeleines, 183
 Meringues, 179
  Chocolate, 179
 Sultana, 184
 Swiss, 185
 Turnovers
  Almond, 177
  Lemon, 182
Calf's Brains, 48
 with Cream Sauce, 49
Calf's Head, 118
Calf's Liver,
 with Rice, 36
 Sauté, 117
 with Wine Sauce, 117
Caper Sauce, 120
Carrot Soup, 26
Carrots
 with Butter, 138
 Stewed Beef with, 101
 Vichy, 138
Cats' Tongues, 178
Cauliflower, 18
 with Cheese, 138
 with Tomato Sauce, 139

Celery
 Braised, 139
 Soup, 27
Cereal and Cheese Entrées, 31
Cereal Dishes (Entrées)
 Cheese
  Entrée, 36
  Pudding, 37
  Tart Lorraine, 37
 Gnocchi
  Italian Cheese, 31
  Parisienne, 32
 Macaroni
  Cheese, 32
  Timbale, 33
 Noodles
  How to Make, 33
  Milanaise, 34
  with Beef, Minced, 35
  with Cheese, Grated, 34
  with Ham, 35
  with Tomatoes, 35
 Ravioli, Cheese, 37
 Rice
  with Calf's Liver, 35
  Italienne, 35
 Semolina Cheese Fingers, 36
Chantilly Sauce, 122
Chasseur Sauce, 111
Cheese
 Beignets, 212
 Biscuits, 213
 Cabbage with, 136
 Cauliflower with, 138
 Eggplant with, 58
 Eggs, 214
 Eggs with, 42
 Entrée, 36
 Fingers, Semolina, 36
 Gnocchi, Italian, 31
 Macaroni, 32
 Mushrooms with, 141
 Noodles with, 34
 Omelette, 45
 Pasties, 214

Cheese—(*cont'd*)
  Potatoes with, 145
  Pudding, 37
  Ravioli, 37
  Sandwiches, 217
    Cream, 217
    Fried Ham and, 50
    Hot, 212
  Sauce, 120
    Potatoes with, 146
  Scallops with, 74
  Soufflé, 47
  Squares, 215
  Straws, 213, 214
  Tart Lorraine, 37
  Toasties, 215
Cherry
  Sweetmeat, 224
  Tart, 207
Chestnut
  Caramel, 225
  Charlotte, 155
  and Chocolate Cream, 157
  Cream, 156
    Auvergnat, 156
    Chantilly, 157
    Magda, 157
    Mont Blanc, 156
  Jam, 221
  Purée, 139
    Baked, 155
Chestnuts, Crystallized, 224
Chicken
  in Aspic, 87
  Braised, 85
  Broth, 23
  in Casserole, 83
  Pie, 84
  with Port Wine, 82
  with Rice, Boiled, 83
  Roast, 84
  Scallops, 50
  Stuffed, 85
  with White Sauce, 86
  with White Wine, 86

Chicory Salad, 150
Chocolate
  and Almond Fondants, 225
  Cake, 169, 170
  Caramels, 226
  Charlotte, 158
  Cornets, 159
  Cream, 158
    Biscuit Cake with, 154
    Chantilly, 160
    Chestnut and, 157
    Dessert, 158
  Croquettes, 225
  Fondant, 226
  Fondants, 226
  Hot, 231
  Ice Cream, 195
  Marquise, 161
  Meringues, 179
  Mousse, 159
  Pudding with Cream Sauce, 160
  Soufflé, 199
  Sponge Fingers, 160
  Surprise, 159
Coconut
  Caramel, 227
  Cream, 161
  Macaroons, 183
Coffee, 231
  Caramel, 228
  Cream, 162
    Biscuit Cake with, 154
    Cake, 170
    Chantilly, 161
    Filling, 171
  Ice Creám, 195
    Liégeois, 196
  Mousse with Biscuits, 162
  Soufflé, 200
  Truffles, 227
Cold Boiled Beef, 98
Consommé, Cream, 24
Cornflour Custard Tart, 208
Coupe Jacques, 196
Court Bouillon, 63

# English Index

Crab
  Mayonnaise, 70
  Soup, 23
  Thermidor, 71
Crayfish Belle-vue, 73
Cream
  Biscuits, 179
  Buns, 180
  Cakes, 162
  Cheese Sandwiches, 217
  Consommé, 24
  Filling
    Coffee, 171
    Walnut, 171
  Meringue, 163
  Pastry, 165
  Rhubarb, 194
  Sauce, 120
  Soup, 24
Creamed
  Biscuits, 164
  Pralines, 163
Creams
  Almond, 153
  Caramel, 155
  Chantilly, 163
  Chestnut, 156
    Auvergnat, 156
    and Chocolate, 157
    Chantilly, 157
    Magda, 157
    Mont Blanc, 156
  Chocolate, 158
    Biscuit Cake with, 154
  Coconut, 161
  Coffee, 162
    Biscuit Cake with, 154
    Chantilly, 161
  Mocha, 164
  Pastry, 165
  Vanilla, 153
Cress Soup, 27
Croquettes, 38–41
  Beef, 38

Croquettes—(cont'd)
  How to Fry, 38
  Lentil, 39
  Macaroni, 39
    Napolitaine, 40
    and Veal, 39
  Potato, 41
    and Ham, 41
  Semolina, 40
Crystallized
  Chestnuts, 224
  Orange, 230
Cucumber Salad with Cream, 151
Cucumbers, 18
  Aromatic, 18
  with Cream, 18
Curried Leg of Mutton, 102
Curry Sauce, 120
Custard, 163
  Apple, 191

Dates, Stuffed, 228
Desserts, 153–201. See also Cakes,
    Creams, Fruits, Mousses, Soufflés,
    Omelettes, Pancakes, Pies and Tarts
  Chestnut
    Charlotte, 155
    Purée, Baked, 155
  Chocolate
    Charlotte, 158
    Cornets, 159
    Cream, 158
    Marquise, 161
    Mousse, 159
    Pudding with Cream Sauce, 160
    Sponge Fingers, 160
    Surprise, 159
  Coffee
    and Chocolate Mousse, 161
    Mousse with Biscuits, 162
  Cream
    Cakes, 162
    Meringue, 163
  Creamed
    Biscuits, 164
    Pralines, 163

Desserts—(cont'd)
  Custard, 163
  Frangipane, 164
  Rice Caramel with Vanilla Cream, 164
  Semolina Mould with Vanilla Cream, 165
  Snow Eggs, 165
  Sylvabella, 166
  Yule Log with Coffee Cream, 166
Dollar Biscuits, 180
Doughnuts, French, 188
Dried Butter Beans with Tomatoes, 136
Duck
  with Green Peas, 89
  with Olives, 89
  with Onions, 88
  with Orange, 90
  Pâté, 128
    Wild, 132
  Salmis, 88
  with Turnips, 88
Duckling Rouennais, 89

Eel with Tartare Sauce, 69
Egg
  Hors-d'oeuvre, 14
  Sandwiches, 217
  and Tomato, 14
Egg Entrées, 41
Eggplant
  with Cheese, 58
  Fried, 140
  Stuffed, 58
  with Tomatoes, 140
Eggs. See also Hors-d'oeuvre, Omelettes, and Soufflés
  with Anchovies, 14
    and Butter, 14
  with Artichokes, Poached, 45
  Bucheronne, 41
  Cheese, 214
  with Cheese, 42
  Creamed, 42
  and Ham, 49
  in Jelly, 43

Eggs—(cont'd)
  Justine, 42
  Mayonnaise, 14
  with Piquant Sauce, 43
  Rossini, 43
  with Spinach, 148
  Swedish, 44
  with Tomatoes, 44
  with White Sauce, 44
Endive
  Braised, 140
  Salad, 151
Entrées, 31–62
  Cereal and Cheese, 31
  Croquettes, 38
  Egg, 41
  Meat and Poultry, 48
  Vegetable, 55

Fillet of Beef with Olives, 99
Fillet of Pork Marinade, 110
Fillets of Veal with Bacon, 113
Filling
  Coffee Cream, 171
  Walnut Cream, 171
Fish, 63–75
  Court Bouillon, 63
  Crab
    Mayonnaise, 70
    Thermidor, 71
  Crayfish Belle-vue, 73
  Eel with Tartare Sauce, 69
  Fried, 64
  Herrings
    Grilled, 65
    Smoked, 15
    Soused, 65
    in White Wine, 65
  How to Boil, 63
  Ling à l'Américaine, 66
  Lobster
    à l'Américaine, 71
    Grilled, Sauce Américaine, 72
    à la Morlaise, 72

# English Index

Fish—(cont'd)
Mackerel in Brown Sauce, 67
with Mayonnaise, 15
Mussels, 73
with Rice, 74
in Scallop Shells, 74
Pie, 64
Salmon Steaks, 66
Scallops
with Grated Cheese, 74
with Port Wine, 75
Shrimps in Scallop Shells, 75
Skate with Black Butter, 68
Sole
Baked Fillets of, 67
Marguery, 67
Meunière, 68
Trout
with Cream, 69
Meunière, 68
Turbot with White Sauce, 69
Flanders Red Cabbage, 137
Four Quarters, 171
Frangipane, 164
French Beans, 135
with Oil, 17
French Cake Icing, 167
French Doughnuts, 188
Fritters
Apple, 185, 186
Bread, 186
Maize, 187
Soufflé, 188
Viennese, 187
Frog's Legs in Butter, 51
Fruit
Cake, Rum, 173
Ice Cream, 196
Fruit, 188–195. See also Apples, Cherry,
Orange, Peaches, Pears, Rhubarb,
and Strawberry

Garlic Sauce, 123
Game, 76–82. See also Hare, Partridge,
Pheasant, Quail, Rabbit, Snipe,
Venison, and Woodcock

Game—(cont'd)
Marinade Sauce, 77
Pickling Mixture, 76
Genoa Cake, 172
Gingerbread, 174
Gnocchi
Italian Cheese, 31
Parisienne, 32
Goose
Giblets, Stewed, 90
Pâté, 128
Roast, 91
Grape Tart, 208
Gravy, 108
Green
Olives, 18
Peas, 143
Salad with Olives, 151
Sauce, 121
Guinea Fowl with Grapes, 91


Ham
and Cheese Sandwiches, Fried, 50
and Eggs, 49
Boiled, 109
in Pie Crust, 109
Braised, 110
Croquettes, Potato and, 41
Noodles with, 35
Omelette with, 46
Pancakes, 49
Pudding, 49
Soufflé, 47
Tartlets, 50
Veal and
Fillets, 110
Pâté, 132
Hare or Rabbit
Jugged, 80
Roast, 79
Hare Pâté, 129
Hasty Cake, 169
Hazelnut Biscuits, 180
Herb Sauce, 123

Herrings
  Grilled, 65
  Smoked, 15
  Soused, 65
  in White Wine, 65
Hollandaise Sauce, 123
Honey
  Cakes, 181
  Macaroons, 183
Hors-d'oeuvre, 13–19
  Egg, 14
  Meat and Fish, 15
  Vegetable, 16

Ice Creams, 195–7
  Chocolate, 195
  Coffee, 195
    Liégeois, 196
  Coupe Jacques, 196
  Fruit, 196
  with hot chocolate sauce, 196
  Peach Melba, 196
  Pear Melba, 197
  Pistachio, 197
  Praline, 197
  Vanilla, 197
Icing, French Cake, 167
Italian Cheese Gnocchi, 31

Jam
  Apple, 220
  Apricot, 221
  Biscuits, 181
  Chestnut, 221
  Omelette, 197
  Pancakes, 199
  Pear, 221
  Plum, 222
  Raspberry, 222
  Rhubarb, 223
  Sablés, 182
  Strawberry, 223
Jellied Sauce, 121
Jelly
  Apple, 190
  Bramble, 221

Jelly—(cont'd)
  Orange, 193
  Red Currant, 222
Jerusalem Artichokes, 17, 133
Jugged Hare or Rabbit, 80

Kidneys
  with French Beans, 109
  Grilled Sheep's, 108
  Veal, 116
    with White Wine, 116
Kougloff, 171

Lark Pâté, 130
Leek Soup, 27
Leg of Mutton Marinade, 105
Lemon
  Tart, 208
  Turnovers, 182
Lentil
  Croquettes, 39
  Stew, 141
Lettuce
  with Bacon, 59
  and Fruit Salad, 152
  Salad, 152
  Sandwiches, 217
  Soup, 27
Ling à l'Américaine, 66
Liqueur Soufflé, 200
Liver
  Pâté, 130
  with Rice, Calf's, 36
  Sauté, Calf's, 117
  with Wine Sauce, Calf's, 117
Lobster
  à l'Américaine, 71
  à la Morlaise, 72
  Grilled, Sauce Américaine, 72

Macaroni
  Cheese, 32
  Croquettes, 39
    Napolitaine, 40
    and Veal, 39
  Timbale, 33

# *English Index*

Macaroons, 182
  Coconut, 183
  Honey, 183
Mackerel in Brown Sauce, 67
Madeira
  Sauce, 124
  Soup, 24
Madeleine Cakes, 183
Maize Fritters, 187
Malines, 183
Marinade, 105, 110
  Sauce, 77
Marrows, Vegetable, 62
Mayonnaise, 124
Meat, 96–118. *See also* Beef, Mutton,
    Pork, and Veal
Meat and Poultry Entrées, 48–55
Meat and Fish
  Hors-d'oeuvre, 15
  Soups, 21
Menus, 233–48
Meringues, 179
  Apple, 191
  Chocolate, 179
Milk
  Omelette, 46
  Sauce, 120
Mocha Cream, 164
Mousse
  Chocolate, 159
  Coffee, with Biscuits, 162
  Orange, 193
Mousseline Sauce, 125
Mushroom Sauce, 121
Mushrooms
  with Cheese, 141
  Omelette with, 46
  in Sauce, 141
  Stuffed, 59
Mussels, 16, 73
  with Rice, 74
  in Scallop Shells, 74
Mustard Sandwiches, 218
Mutton, 102–9
  with Baked Beans, 106

Mutton—*(cont'd)*
  Cutlets, 105
  Kidneys, Sheep's
    with French Beans, 109
    Grilled, 108
  Leg of
    Curried, 102
    with Haricot Beans, Roast, 103
    Marinade, 105
  Pilaff, with Rice, 106
  Saddle of, 108
  Shoulder of, with Turnips, Boned, 104
    with Mixed Vegetables, 104
    with Sorrel, 104
  Trotters, Sheep's, 107

Neapolitan Fondant, 228
New Potatoes with Butter, 145
Noodles
  with Cheese, Grated, 34
  with Ham, 35
  How to Make, 33
  Milanaise, 34
  with Minced Beef, 35
  with Tomatoes, 35
Normandy Sauce, 125
Nougat, 229
Nursery Soup, 21
Nut Fondant, 229

Olives
  Duck with, 89
  Fillet of Beef with, 99
  Green, 18
  Green Salad with, 151
  Tomatoes with, 19
Omelettes
  Bretonne, 45
  Cheese, 45
  with Fried Bread, 46
  with Ham, 46
  How to Make, 45
  Jam, 197
  Milk, 46
  with Mushrooms, 46

R                                                    257

Omelettes—*(cont'd)*
  Peasant, 46
  Rum, 198
Onion
  Pastry, 60
  Sauce, 121
  Soup, 28
Onions
  Beef with, 97
  Braised, 142
  Duck with, 88
  Potatoes with Tomatoes and, 146
  Small, with Raisins, 142
Orange
  Crystallized, 230
  Duck with, 90
  Jelly, 193
  Mousse, 193
  Pancakes, 199
Ox Tongue in Piquant Sauce, 99
Oxtail Hotpot, 100

Pancakes, 198
  Boulonnais, 198
  Ham, 49
  Jam, 199
  Orange, 199
  Potato, 145
  Suzette, 198
Parsnips, Fried, 142
Partridge
  with Cabbage, 78
  Roast, 77
Pastry
  Cream, 165
  Plain, 202
  Puff or Flaky, 203
  Short, 204
  Tart, 205
Pâtés, 127–32
  Brawn, 127
  Duck, 128
  Goose, 128
  Hare, 129
  Lark, 130

Pâtés—*(cont'd)*
  Liver, 130
  Peasant, 131
  Rabbit, 131
  Rillette, 132
  Veal and Ham, 132
  Wild Duck, 132
  Woodcock, 132
Pea Soup, 29
Peach
  Melba, 196
  Tart, 209
Peaches
  Condé, 193
  Parisienne, 194
Pear
  Flan, 209
  Jam, 221
  Melba, 197
  Tart, 209
Pears
  Snapdragon, 194
  in Wine, 194
Peas
  Green, 143
    Bottled, 219
    Duck with, 89
  Purée of Dried, 143
  Tomatoes Stuffed with, 61
Peasant
  Omelette, 46
  Pâté, 131
Pheasant
  Roast, 77
  Stuffed, 77
Pickled
  Cabbage, 17
  Red, 137
Pies. *See also* Tarts
  Apple, 206
Pigeons
  Braised, 92
  with Cabbage, 92
  or Squabs, Roast, 93

# English Index

Pilaff
  Mussels with Rice, 74
  Mutton with Rice, 106
Piquant Sauce, 125
Pistachio Ice Cream, 197
Plain Pastry, 202
Plum
  Jam, 222
  Tart, 210
Poached Eggs with Artichokes, 45
Polish Cake, 172
Pork, 109–111. See also Ham
  Cutlets or Chops, 111
  Fillet of, Marinade, 110
  Pie, Veal and, 54
  Shoulder of, with Vegetables, 111
Porterhouse Steak, 100
Potato
  Croquettes, 41
  and Ham Croquettes, 41
  Pancakes, 145
  Purée, Sausages with, 53
Potatoes
  with Bacon, 145
  Beef Minced with, 97
  Chamonix, 144
  with Cheese, 145
  with Cheese Sauce, 146
  Fried, 144
  Mashed, 144
  Mayonnaise, 18
  New, with Butter, 145
  in Tomato Sauce, Sliced, 146
  with Tomatoes and Onions, 146
Poultry, 82–95. See also Chicken, Duck,
    Goose, Guinea Fowl, Pigeons,
    Squab, and Turkey
Poultry and Meat Entrées, 48–55
Praline Ice Cream, 197
Pralines, Creamed, 163
Prunes
  Rabbit with, 80
  Stuffed, 230
Pudding
  Cheese, 37

Pudding—(cont'd)
    Chocolate, with Cream Sauce, 160
    Ham, 49
Puff or Flaky Pastry, 203
Pumpkin Soup, 29
Purée of Dried Peas, 143
Purée
    Chestnut, 139
    Tomato, Bottled, 219
    Turnip, 148
Quail on Toast, 78, 79
Quenelles, 52

Rabbit
    Creamed, 81
    Pâté, 131
    with Prunes, 80
    Stewed, 80
Rabbit or Hare
    Jugged, 80
    Roast, 79
Raspberry
    Jam, 222
    Tart, 210
Ravioli, Cheese, 37
Red Currant Jelly, 222
Rhubarb
    Cream, 194
    Jam, 223
    Soufflé, 200
Rice, 103
    Apple, 192
    Boiled Chicken with, 83
    with Calf's Liver, 36
    Caramel with Vanilla Cream, 164
    Italienne, 35
    Mutton with, 106
    Strawberry, 195
    Tartlets, 210
Rillette Pâté, 132
Roast
    Beef, 102
    Chicken, 84
    Goose, 91
    Hare, 79

Roast—(*cont'd*)
  Mutton, Leg of, with Beans, 103
  Partridge, 77
  Pheasant, 77
  Pigeons, 93
  Rabbit, 79
  Snipe, 81
  Squabs, 93
  Turkey, Stuffed, 93
  Veal, 112
  Venison, 81
  Woodcock, 81
Rolled Beef with Sausage, 101
Rum
  Baba
    Savarin, 173
    Savoy, 173
  Fruit Cake, 173
  Omelette, 198
Russian
  Cabbage, 56
  Salad, 152

Saddle of Mutton, 108
Salads, 150–152
  Chicory, 150
  Cucumber, with Cream, 151
  Endive, 151
  Green, with Olives, 151
  Lettuce, 152
    and Fruit, 152
  Russian, 152
Salmon
  Steaks, 66
  Tomatoes with, 19
Salsify, Fried, 147
Sandwiches
  Cheese, 217
    Cream, 217
    Hot, 212
  Egg, 217
  Fried Ham and Cheese, 50
  Lettuce, 217
  Mustard, 218
  Shrimp, 218

Sandwiches—(*cont'd*)
  Tomato, 218
  Tuna Fish, 218
  Walnut, 218
Sauces, 119–26
  Américaine, 72
  Béarnaise, 122
  Caper, 120
  Chantilly, 122
  Chasseur, 111
  Cheese, 120
  Cream, 120
  Curry, 120
  Garlic, 123
  Green, 121
  Herb, 123
  Hollandaise, 123
  Jellied, 121
  Madeira, 124
  Marinade, 77
  Mayonnaise, 124
  Milk, 120
  Mousseline, 125
  Mushroom, 121
  Normandy, 125
  Onion, 121
  Piquant, 125
  Shrimp, 121
  Tartare, 126
  Thermidor, 122
  Tomato, 126
  Truffle, 122
Sausage, Rolled Beef with, 101
Sausages
  and Cold Cuts, 16
  with Potato Purée, 53
  with Stewed Apples, 53
Savarin, 173
Savories, Cheese
  Beignets, 212
  Biscuits, 213
    Filling for, 213
  Eggs, 214
  Pasties, 214
  Squares, 215

# English Index

Savories, Cheese—*(cont'd)*
　Straws, 213, 214
　Toasties, 215
Scallops
　with Grated Cheese, 74
　with Port Wine, 75
Semolina
　Cheese Fingers, 36
　Croquettes, 40
　Mould with Vanilla Cream, 165
Sheep's Kidneys
　with French Beans, 109
　Grilled, 108
Sheep's Trotters, 107
Short Pastry, 204
Shortbread Biscuits, 184
Shoulder of Mutton
　with Mixed Vegetables, 104
　with Sorrel, 104
Shoulder of Pork with Vegetables, 111
Shrimp
　Sauce, 121
　Sandwiches, 218
　Soup, 25
Shrimps
　in Scallop Shells, 75
　Tomatoes Stuffed with, 62
Skate with Black Butter, 68
Smoked Herrings, 15
Snails Bourgogne, 51
Snipe or Woodcock, Roast, 81
Snow Eggs, 165
Sole
　Baked Fillets of, 67
　Marguery, 67
　Meunière, 68
Sorrel
　Shoulder of Mutton, with, 104
　Soup, 29
Soufflé Fritters, 188
Soufflés
　Apple, 199
　Auvergnat, 48
　Cheese, 47
　Chocolate, 199
　Coffee, 200

Soufflés—*(cont'd)*
　Ham, 47
　How to Make, 46
　Liqueur, 200
　Nantua, 47
　Rhubarb, 200
　Vanilla, 201
Soups, 20–30
　Alsatian, 25
　Beef Bouillon, 21
　Bisque, 22
　Cabbage, 26
　Carrot, 26
　Celery, 27
　Chicken Broth, 23
　Consommé, Cream, 24
　Crab, 23
　Cream, 24
　Cress, 27
　Leek, 27
　Lettuce, 27
　Madeira, 24
　Nursery, 21
　Onion, 28
　Pea, 29
　Pumpkin, 29
　Shrimp, 25
　Sorrel, 29
　Tomato, 30
　Vegetable, 30
Soused Herrings, 65
Spice Cake
　or Gingerbread, 174
　with Marmalade, 174
Spinach, 147
　Baked, 148
　Creamed, 148
　with Eggs, 148
Spongecake, 174
　Madeleine, 175
　Mousseline, 175
　Savoy, 175
Squabs or Pigeons, Roast, 93
Steak, Porterhouse, 100
Stew, Vegetable, 149

# English Index

Stewed
  Beef with Carrots, 101
  Rabbit, 80
  Veal with White Sauce, 114
Strawberry
  Jam, 223
  Rice, 195
Stuffings, 94
Sultana
  Buns, 185
  Cakes, 184
Suzette Pancakes, 198
Swedish Eggs, 44
Sweetbreads, Vol-au-Vent with, 54
Sweetmeats and Candy
  Cherry Sweetmeat, 224
  Chestnut Caramel, 225
  Chestnuts, Crystallized, 224
  Chocolate
    and Almond Fondants, 225
    Caramels, 226
    Croquettes, 225
    Fondant, 226
    Fondants, 226
  Coconut Caramel, 227
  Coffee
    Caramel, 228
    Truffles, 227
  Dates, Stuffed, 228
  Neapolitan Fondant, 228
  Nougat, 229
  Nut Fondant, 229
  Orange, Crystallized, 230
  Prunes, Stuffed, 230
  Tangerine Fondants, 229
  Walnuts, Stuffed, 230
Swiss
  Cakes, 185
  Roll, 176
Sylvabella, 166

Tangerine Fondants, 229
Tart Pastry, 205
Tartare Sauce, 126
Tartlets, 207
  Rice, 210

Tarts
  Alsatian, 205
  Apple, 206
  Apricot, 206
  Banana, 206
  Bilberry, 207
  Cherry, 207
  Cornflour Custard, 208
  Grape, 208
  Lemon, 208
  Lorraine, 37
  Peach, 209
  Pear, 209
  Plum, 210
  Raspberry, 210
Tea, 232
Thermidor Sauce, 122
Tomato
  and Egg, 14
  Purée, Bottled, 219
  Sandwiches, 218
  Sauce, 126
    Cauliflower with, 139
    Sliced Potatoes in, 146
  Soup, 30
Tomatoes
  Bottled, 219
  Dried Butter Beans with, 136
  Eggplant with, 140
  Eggs with, 44
  Mayonnaise, 19
  Noodles with, 35
  with Olives, 19
  and Onions, Potatoes with, 146
  Stuffed, 60
    with Meat, 61
    with Peas, 61
    with Salmon, 19
    with Shrimps, 62
Tripe à la Mode de Caen, 52
Trout
  with Cream, 69
  Meunière, 68
Truffle Sauce, 122
Tuna Fish, 16
  Sandwiches, 218

Turbot with White Sauce, 69
Turkey
  Giblets, 95
  Roast Stuffed, 93
Turnip Purée, 148
Turnips
  Boned Shoulder of Mutton with, 104
  Duck with, 88

Vanilla
  Cream, 153
  Ice Cream, 197
  Soufflé, 201
Veal, 112–18. *See also* Calf's Brains,
    Calf's Liver and Calf's Head
  Braised or Stewed, 114
  Breast of, Stuffed, 112
  Croquettes, Macaroni and, 39
  Cutlets
    Grilled, 115
    Viennese, 115
    with White Wine, 115
  Fillets of
    with Bacon, 113
    with Cream, 113
    Stuffed, 113
  and Ham Fillets, 110
  and Ham Pâté, 132
  in Jelly, 116
  Kidneys, 116
    with White Wine, 116
  Loaf, 116
  Mayonnaise, 16
  Medallions, 53
  and Pork Pie, 54

Veal—(*cont'd*)
  Roast, 112
  Stewed with White Sauce, 114
Vegetable
  Entrées, 55
  Hors-d'oeuvre, 16
  Marrows, 62
  Soup, 30
  Soups, 25
  Stew, 149
Vegetables, 133–49. *See also* names of
    vegetables
  with Mayonnaise, 19
  Shoulder of Mutton with Mixed, 104
  Shoulder of Pork with, 111
Venison, Roast, 81
Viennese
  Fritters, 187
  Veal Cutlets, 115
Vol-au-Vent with Sweetbreads, 54

Walnut
  Cake, 176
  Cream Filling, 171
  Sandwiches, 218
Walnuts, Stuffed, 230
Wild Duck Pâté, 132
Woodcock
  Pâté, 132
  Salmis, 82
  or Snipe, Roast, 81

Yule Log with Coffee Cream, 166

# FRENCH INDEX

Africains, 227
Agneau au Curry, Gigot d', 102
Ailloli, 123
Allumettes au Fromage, 214
Alouettes, Pâté d', 130
Amandes Salées, 215
Anchois, 15
  Beurre d', Oeufs Durs au, 14
  Oeufs Durs aux, 14
Anguille à la Tartare, 69
Artichauts, 16
  Farcis au
    Gras, 56
    Maigre, 55
  Oeufs Pochés aux Fonds d', 45
Asperges, 133
  Froides, 133
  Pointes d', 134
Aubergines
  Farcies, 58
  Frites, 140
  au Fromage, 58
  à la Tomate, 140

Baba Savoie au Rhum, 173
Bâtonnets à la Moutarde, 214
Bâtons
  au Fromage, 214
    Petits, 213
Bécasse
  Pâté de, 132
  Salmis de, 82
Bécasses, Bécassines Rôties, 81
Beignets
  à la Levure, 188

Beignets—(cont'd)
  de Maïs, 187
  de Pommes, 185, 186
  Soufflés, 188, 212
  Viennois ou Krapfen, 187
Betteraves, 17
Biscottes au Chocolat, 160
Biscuit au Chocolat, 170
Biscuits
  à la Crème, 164, 179
  au Chocolat, 160
  aux Raisins, 185
  Salés, 215
Bisque
  de Crabes, 23
  Potage, 22
Blanquette de Veau, 114
Boeuf, 96–102
  Bourguignon, 96
  Bouilli, 98
  Bouillon de, 21
  Châteaubriand, 100
  Croquettes de, 38
  au Four, 97
  Haché aux Pommes de Terre, 97
  Langue de, 99
  à la Mode, 101
  aux Oignons, 97
  aux Olives, Filet de, 99
  en Persillade, 15
  Queue de, Bouilli, 100
  Rôti de, 102
  Roulés de, 101
  Tournedos, 99
  Vinaigrette, 98

# French Index

Bonbons aux Cerises, 224
Bouchées Nantua, 47
Bouillon
    de Boeuf, 21
    au Madère, 24
    de Poule, 23
Boules Soufflées, 214
Bouquets, Potage aux, 25
Brioche, 177
    aux Raisins, 178
Bûche de Noël, 166

Café, 231
Café Liégeois, 196
Cailles sur Canapé, 78, 79
Cakes au Chester, 213
Canard
    aux Navets, 88
    aux Oignons, 88
    aux Olives, 89
    à l'Orange, 90
    Pâté de, 128
    aux Petits Pois, 89
    Salmis de, 88
Caneton Rouennais, 89
Caramels
    au Café, 228
    au Chocolat, 226
    à la Noix de Coco, 227
Carottes
    Nouvelles, 138
    à la Vichy, 138
Cassoulet, 106
Céleri
    Braisé, 139
    Soupe au, 27
Cerises
    Bonbons aux, 224
    Tarte aux, 207
Cervelles de Veau, 48
    à la Sauce Blanche, 49
Champignons
    Farcis, 59
    au Fromage, 141
    Omelette aux, 46
    la Sauce, 141

Charcuterie, 16
Charlotte
    au Chocolat, 158
    aux Marrons, 155
    au Pain, 190
Chasseur Sauce, 111
Châteaubriand, 100
Chaussons de Pommes, 192
Chevreuil, Rôti, 81
Chipolatas
    à la Compote de Pommes, 53
    à la Purée de Pommes de Terre, 53
Chocolat, 231
    Biscottes au, 160
    Biscuit au, 160, 170
    Caramels au, 226
    Charlotte au, 158
    Cornets au, 159
    Crème au, 158
    Crème au Beurre au, 154
    Crème Chantilly au, 160
    Croquettes au, 225
    Gâteau aux Marrons au, 157
    Glace au, 195
    Marquise au, 161
    Meringues au, 179
    Mousse au, 159
        de Café, 161
    Saucisson au, 226
    Soufflé au, 199
Chou
    à la Bourgeoise, 136
    Farci, 57
    au Fromage, 136
    Mariné, 17
    Perdrix au, 78
    Pigeons aux, 92
    Rouge
        Farci, 57
        à la Flamande, 137
        Mariné, 137
    à la Russe, 56
    Soupe au, 26
Choufleur, 18
    au Gratin, 138
    Pain de, 139

265

# French Index

Choux à la Crème, 162
Civet de Lièvre ou de Lapin, 80
Compote de Pommes, 191
Concombres, 18
  aux Aromates, 18
  à la Crème, 18
Confit d'Oie, 128
Confiture
  d'abricots, 221
  de Fraises, 223
  de Framboise, 222
  de Groseille, 222
  de Marrons, 221
  de Mures, 221
  de Poires entières, 221
  de Pommes, 220
  de Prunes, 222
  de Rhubarbe, 223
Conserves
  de Pois, 219
  de Tomates, 219
  de Tomates en Purée, 219
Consommé Velouté, 24
Coq en Pâte, 84
Coquilles
  de Crevettes, 75
  de Moules, 74
  au Parmesan, 36
  St. Jacques
    Gratinées, 74
    au Porto, 75
  de Volaille, 50
Cornets au Chocolat, 159
Côtelettes
  de Mouton, 105
  de Porc, 111
  de Veau
    Grillées, 115
    Pannées, 115
    au Vin Blanc, 115
Coupe Jacques, 196
Courgettes Farcies, 62
Court Bouillon, 63
Crabes, Bisque de, 23

Crème
  aux Amandes, 153
  au Beurre
    au Café, 154
    au Chocolat, 154
  au Café, 162
  au Caramel, 155
  Chantilly, 163
    au Café, 161
    au Chocolat, 160
  au Chocolat, 158
  Glacée, 159
  Moka, 164
  à la Noix de Coco, 161
  Pâtissière, 165
  Pralinée, 163
  Renversée, 163
  de Rhubarbe, 194
  à la Vanille, 153
Crêpes, 198
  Boulonnaises, 198
  à la Confiture, 199
  au Jambon, 49
  à l'Orange, 199
  Parmentier, 145
  Suzette, 198
Cresson, Soupe au, 27
Crevette à la Mayonnaise, 218
Crevettes
  Coquilles de, 75
  Tomates Farcies aux, 62
Croque-Monsieur, 50
Croquets aux Noisettes, 180
Croquettes, 38
  de Boeuf, 38
  au Chocolat, 225
  de Lentilles, 39
  de Macaroni, 39
  Milanaises, 41
  Napolitaines, 40
  de Pommes de Terre, 41
  de Semoule, 40
  de Veau et Macaroni, 39

# French Index

Dattes Farcies, 228
Dinde
  Farcie, 93
  Ragoût de, 95
Dollars, 180

Endives Braisées, 140
Entrées, 31–62
  au Jambon, 49
Epaule de Mouton
  aux Navets, 104
  à l'Oseille, 104
Epinards, 147
  à la Crème, 148
  au Gratin, 148
  Pain d', 148
Escalopes
  au Jambon, 110
  de Veau à la Crème, 113
Escargots de Bourgogne, 51

Faisan
  Farci, 77
  Rôti, 77
Fèves, 135
Filet
  de Boeuf aux Olives, 99
  de Mouton à la Gelée, 108
  de Porc Mariné, 110
Flan
  aux Poires, 209
  aux Pommes, 191
Foie
  de Porc, Pâté de, 130
  de Veau, 117
    au Riz, 36
    Sauce Bordelaise, 117
Fondants Napolitains, 228
Fraises au Riz, 195
Frangipane, 164
Friture de Poisson, 64
Fromage
  Allumettes au, 214
  Aubergines au, 58
  Bâtons au, 214
    Petits, 213

Fromage—(cont'd)
  Champignons au, 141
  Chou au, 136
  Omelette au, 45
  Pâté Feuilletée au, 215
  Pâtés au, 37
  Pommes de Terre au, 145
  Ravioli au, 37
  Sauce au, 120
  Soufflé au, 47
  Toast au, 215

Galettes
  au Chester, 212
  Fondantes, 184
Gâteau
  aux Amandes, 153
  des Ardennes, 168
  Auvergnat, 156
  Béarnais, 168
  au Beurre, 168
  au Café, 162
  au Chocolat, 169
  Diabolo, 170
  aux Fruits, 173
  Madeleine, 175
  Magda, 157
  aux Marrons
    Chantilly, 157
    au Chocolat, 157
  Milanais (Nouilles), 34
  Moka, 170
  Mousse, 174
  Mousseline, 175
  aux Noix, 171, 176
  Polonais, 172
  Pour le Thé, 167
  de Riz, 164
  de Savoie, 175
    Roulé, 176
  de Semoule, 165
Gâteaux, Petits
  à la Crème de Lait, 180
  Suisses, 185
Gelèe d'Orange dans les Peaux, 193

267

Gibier, 76–82
Gigot
  d'Agneau au Curry, 102
  de Mouton
    Mariné, 105
    Rôti aux Haricots, 103
Glaces
  au Café, 195
  Chaud-Froid, 196
  au Chocolat, 195
  Coupe Jacques, 196
  Pêche Melba, 196
  à la Pistache, 197
  Plombières, 196
  Poire Melba, 197
  au Praliné, 197
  à la Vanille, 197
Gnocchi
  à la Parisienne, 32
  à la Romaine, 31
Grenouilles Sautées, 51
Grives, Pâté de, 132

Harengs
  Fumés, 15
  Grillés, 65
  Marinés, 65
  au Vin Blanc, 65
Haricots
  Blanc à la Purée de Tomates, 136
  Verts, 135
    en Conserve, 220
    en Salade, 17
Homard
  à l'Américaine, 71
  à la Morlaise, 72
Homards Grillés à la Sauce Américaine, 72
Hors-d'oeuvre, 13–19

Ile Flottante, 163

Jambette aux Légumes, 111
Jambon, 109
  Braisé, 110
  Crêpes au, 49
  en Croûte, 109
  Entrée au, 49

Jambon—(cont'd)
  Escalopes au, 110
  Mousselines au, 50
  Nouilles au, 35
  Omelette au, 46
  Pouding au, 49
  Soufflé au, 47
  et Veau, Pâté, 132

Kougloff, 171

Laitue
  à l'Etouffée, 59
  Soupe à la, 27
Lampions, 181
Langouste en Belle-vue, 73
Langue de Boeuf, 99
Langues de Chats, 178
Lapin
  à la Crème, 81
  Pâté de, 131
  aux Pruneaux, 80
  Ragoût de, 80
Lapin ou de Lièvre
  Civet de, 80
  Râble de, 79
Légumes
  Jambette aux, 111
  à la Mayonnaise, 19
  Ragoût
    de Mouton aux, 104
    de Légumes, 149
Lentilles, 141
  Croquettes de, 39
Lièvre, Pâté de, 129
Lièvre ou Lapin
  Civet de, 80
  Râble de, 79
Lotte à l'Américaine, 66

Macaroni
  Croquettes de, 39
    Veau et, 39
  Croquettes Napolitaines, 40

Macaroni—(cont'd)
  au Gratin, 32
  Timbale de, 33
Macarons
  de Malines, 183
  au Miel, 183
  à la Noix de Coco, 183
Madeleines, 183
Mandarinettes, 229
Maquereaux, 67
Marcelinettes, 226
Marinade, 76
  Sauce, 77
Marquise au Chocolat, 161
Marrons
  au Caramel, 225
  Chantilly, Gâteaux aux, 157
  Charlotte aux, 155
  au Chocolat, Gâteau aux, 157
  Glacés, 224
  Mont Blanc, 156
  Mousse aux, 156
  Purée de, 139, 155
Massepains, 182
Médaillons de Veau, 53
Menus, 233
Meringuées, Pommes, 191
Meringues, 179
  au Chocolat, 179
Morue en Turban, 64
Moules, 16, 73
  Coquilles de, 74
  en Riz, 74
Mousse
  de Café au Chocolat, 161
  au Chocolat, 159
  aux Marrons, 156
  à l'Orange, 193
Mousselines au Jambon, 50
Mouton
  Cassoulet, 106
  Côtelettes de, 105
  Epaule de
    aux Navets, 104
    à l'Oseille, 104

Mouton—(cont'd)
  Filet de, à la Gelée, avec sauce, 108
  Gigot d'Agneau au Curry, 102
  Gigot de Mouton
    Mariné, 105
    Rôti aux Haricots, 103
  Pieds de, Poulette, 107
  Ragoût de, aux Légumes, 104
  au Riz, 106
  Rognons de
    Grillés, 108
    Haricots Verts, 109

Navets
  Canard aux, 88
  Epaule de Mouton aux, 104
  en Purée, 148
Noisettines, 229
Noix Farcies, 230
Nonnettes, 181
Nougat, 229
Nouilles, 33
  à la Bolognaise, 35
  au Gratin, 34
  à l'Italienne, 35
  au Jambon, 35

Oeufs, Voyez aussi Omelettes et Soufflés
  Bûcheronne, 41
  à la Crème, 42
  Durs
    aux Anchois, 14
    au Beurre d'Anchois, 14
  Farcis à la Suédoise, 44
  à la Gelée, 43
  Justine, 42
  à la Martiniquaise, 43
  Mimosa, 14
  à la Neige, 165
  Pochés, aux Fonds d'Artichauts, 45
  sur le Plat aux Tomates, 44
  à la Rossini, 43
  en Surprise, 42
  à la Tripe, 44

# French Index

Oie
Confit d', 128
Ragoût d', 90
Rôti d', 91
Oignons
Boeuf aux, 97
Canard aux, 88
Petits, 142
Purée d', 142
Soupe à l'oignon, 28
aux, 28
Tarte aux, 60
Oiseaux sans Têtes, les, 113
Olives, 225
Canard aux, 89
Filet de Boeuf aux, 99
Salade aux, 151
Tomates aux, 19
Vertes au Foie Gras, 18
Omelette, 45
Bretonne, 45
aux Champignons, 46
à la Confiture, 197
aux Croûtons, 46
au Fromage, 45
au Jambon, 46
au Lait, 46
au Lard, 46
au Rhum, 198
Orange
Crêpes à, 199
Gelée de, 193
Mousse à, 193
Oseille
Epaule de Mouton à l', 104
Soupe à l', 29

Pain
d'Amandes, 177
de Choufleur, 139
d'Epice, 174
Fourré, 174
d'Epinards, 148
de Gènes, 172
Perdu, 186
de Veau, 116

Palais de Dames, 184
Panade, 21
Panais, 142
Parmesan, Coquilles au, 36
Pâte
Brisée, 204
Feuilletée, 203
au Fromage, 215
Poussée, 202
Sablée, 204
à Tarte, 205
Pâté
d'Alouettes, 130
de Bécasse, 132
de Canard, 128
de Foie de Porc, 130
de Grives, 132
de Lapin, 131
de Lièvre, 129
Paysanne ou de Campagne, 131
de Tête, 127
de Veau et Jambon, 132
Pâtés au Fromage, 37
Pêche Melba, 196
Pêches
à la Condé Meringuées, 193
à la Parisienne, 194
Perdreaux Rôtis, 77
Perdrix au Chou, 78
Petites Sèches, 179
Petits
Bâtons au Fromage, 213
Gâteaux
à la Crème de Lait, 180
Suisses, 185
Oignons, 142
Pieds de Mouton Poulette, 107
Pigeons
aux Choux, 92
en Cocotte, 92
Rôtis, 93
Pintade aux Raisins, 91
Plâtrée de Pommes, 206
Pointes d'Asperges, 134
Poire Melba, 197

# French Index

Poireaux, Soupe aux, 27
Poires
   Flambées, 194
   Flan aux, 209
   au Vin, 194
Pois
   Cassés
      Purée de, 143
      Soupe aux, 29
   Conserve de, 219
   Petits, 143
      Canard aux, 89
   Tomates Farcies aux, 61
Poisson, Coquillages, et Crustacés, 63–75
Poisson à la Mayonnaise, 15
Poitrine de Veau Farcie, 112
Pommes
   à l'Alsacienne, 188
   Beignets de, 185, 186
   à la Bourdaloue, 190
   à la Cassonade, 189
   Chaussons de, 192
   Chez-Soi, 191
   Chipolatas à la Compote de, 53
   Compote de, 191
   Cuites au Four, 189
   Flan aux, 191
   Meringuées, 191
   en Pâte, 189
   Plâtrée de, 206
   au Riz, 192
   au Sucre, 190
Pommes de Terre
   Boeuf Haché aux, 97
   Chamonix, 144
   Chipolatas à la Purée de, 53
   à la Crème, 146
   Croquettes de, 41
   Frites, 144
   au Fromage, 145
   au Lard, 145
   à la Mayonnaise, 18
   Nouvelles au Beurre, 145
   en Purée, 144
   en Rondelles, 146
   aux Tomates, 146

Porc
   Côtelettes de, 111
   Filet de, Mariné, 110
   Jambette aux Légumes, 111
   Jambon, 109
      Braisé, 110
      en Croûte, 109
      Escalopes au, 110
Potages *Voyez aussi* Soupes
   Alsacien, 25
   Bisque, 22
   aux Bouquets, 25
   Julienne, 26
   Printanier, 30
Potiron, Soupe au, 29
Pouding au Jambon, 49
Poule
   Bouillon de, 23
   au Riz, 83
Poulet
   au Blanc, 86
   Chasseur, 86
   en Cocotte, 83
   Farci, 85
   en Gelée, 87
   au Porto, 82
   Rôti, 84
   Sauté, 85
Printanier, Potage, 30
Pruneaux Farcis, 230
Purée
   de Marrons, 139, 155
   d'Oignons, 142
   de Pois Cassés, 143

Quartiers d'Orange Glacés, 230
Quatre-Quarts, 171
Quenelles, 52
   de Semoule, 36
Queue de Boeuf, Bouilli, 100
Quiche Lorraine, 37

Râble de Lièvre ou de Lapin, 79
Ragoût
   de Dinde, 95

Ragoût—(cont'd)
  de Lapin, 80
  des Légumes, 149
  de Mouton aux Légumes, 104
  d'Oie, 90
  de Veau, 114
Raie au Beurre Noir, 68
Ramequins, 214
Ravioli au Fromage, 37
Rillettes, 132
Riz
  au Foie de Veau, 36
  Fraises au, 195
  à l'Italienne, 35
  Moules au, 74
  Mouton au, 106
  Pommes au, 192
  Tartelettes au, 210
Riz de Veau, Vol-au-Vent au, 54
Rognons
  de Mouton Grillés, 108
    Haricots Verts, 109
  de Veau, 116
    au Vin Blanc, 116
Rôti
  de Boeuf, 102
  d'Oie, 91
  de Veau, 112
Roulés
  de Boeuf, 101
  de Veau, 113

Sablés à la Confiture, 182
Salade
  de Chicorée, 150
  de Concombres à la Crème, 151
  d'Endives, 151
  de Laitue, 152
  aux Olives, 151
  aux Pommes, 152
  Russe, 152
Salmis
  de Bécasse, 82
  de Canard, 88

Salsifis Frits, 147
Sandwiches
  au Chester, 217
  Crevettes à la Mayonnaise, 218
  à la Moutarde, 218
  aux Noix, 218
  aux Oeufs, 217
  au Pain Complet, 217
  à la Salade, 217
  au Thon, 218
  aux Tomates, 218
Sauce
  Ailloli, 123
  Américaine, 72
  Béarnaise, 122
  aux Câpres, 120
  aux Champignons, 121
  Chantilly, 122
  Chasseur, 111
  Chaud-Froid, 121
  à la Crème, 120
  au Curry, 120
  au Fromage, 120
  Hollandaise, 123
  au Lait, 120
  Madère, 124
  Marinade, 124
  Mayonnaise, 124
  Mousseline, 125
  Normande, 125
  aux Oignons, 121
  Piquante, 125
  Rose aux Queues de Crevettes, 121
  Tartare, 126
  Thermidor, 122
  Tomate, 126
  aux Truffes, 122
  Verte, 123
    aux Fines Herbes, 121
Saucisson au Chocolat, 226
Saumon
  Grillées, Tranches de, 66
  Tomates au, 19
Savarin, 173

# French Index

Semoule
  Croquettes de, 40
  Gâteau de, 165
  Quenelles de, 36
Sole
  au Gratin, 67
  à la Marguery, 67
  Meunière, 68
Soufflé, 46
  Bouchées Nantua, 47
  au Café, 200
  au Chocolat, 199
  au Fromage, 47
  au Jambon, 47
  à la Liqueur, 200
  aux Pommes, 199
  Pontis Auvergnat, 48
  à la Rhubarbe, 200
  à la Vanille, 201
Soupe
  au Céleri, 27
  au Chou, 26
  au Cresson, 27
  à la Laitue, 27
  à l'Oignon, 28
  aux Oignons, 28
  Onctueuse, 24
  à l'Oseille, 29
  aux Poireaux, 27
  aux Pois Cassés, 29
  au Potiron, 29
  aux Tomates, 30
Sylvabella, 166

Tarte
  aux Abricots, 206
  Alsacienne, 205
  aux Bananes, 206
  aux Cerises, 207
  au Citron, 208
  aux Framboises, 210
  au Maïs, 208
  aux Myrtilles, 207
  aux Oignons, 60
  aux Pêches, 209

Tarte—(cont'd)
  aux Poires, 209
  aux Pommes, 206
  aux Prunes, 210
  aux Quetsches, 210
  aux Raisins, 208
Tartelettes, 207
  au Riz, 210
  Roses, 14
Tête de Veau, 118
Thé, 232
Thon, 16
Timbale de Macaroni, 33
Toast au Fromage, 215
Tomates
  Conserve de, 219
    en Purée, 219
  Farcies
    aux Crevettes, 62
    au Gras, 61
    au Maigre, 60
    aux Petits Pois, 61
  Haricots Blancs à la Purée de, 136
  à la Mayonnaise, 19
  Oeufs sur le Plat aux, 44
  aux Olives, 19
  au Saumon, 19
  Soupe aux, 30
Topinambours, 17, 133
Tôt Fait, 169
Tournedos, 99
Tourte Lorraine, 54
Tourteau
  à la Mayonnaise, 70
  Thermidor, 71
Tranches de Saumon Grillées, 66
Tripe à la Mode de Caen, 52
Truffettes au Café, 227
Truites
  à la Crème, 69
  Meunière, 68
Tuiles
  aux Amandes, 177
  au Citron, 182
Turbot à la Sauce Blanche, 69

S

273

# French Index

Veau
    Blanquette de, 114
    Côtelettes de
        Grillées, 115
        Pannées, 115
        au Vin Blanc, 115
    Croquettes de, et Macaroni, 39
    Escalopes de, à la Crème, 113
    Foie de Veau, 117
        au Riz, 36
        Sauce Bordelaise, 117
    en Gelée, 116
    et Jambon, Pâté de, 132
    à la Mayonnaise, 16

Veau—(cont'd)
    Medaillons de, 53
    Oiseaux sans Têtes, 113
    Pain de, 116
    Poitrine de, Farcie, 112
    Ragoût de, 114
    Rognons de, 116
        au Vin Blanc, 116
    Rôti de, 112
    Roulés de, 113
    Tête de Veau, 118
Viandes, 96–118
Vol-au-Vent au Riz de Veau, 54
Volailles, 82–95

# Notes

# Notes

# Notes

# Notes

# Notes

# Notes

# Notes

# Notes

# Notes

# Notes

# Notes

# Notes

# Notes

# Notes